W9-AQT-205

PROSCENIUM AND SIGHT-LINES

by the same author

*

STAGE SETTING
For Amateurs and Professionals

CHANGEABLE SCENERY:
Its Origin and Development in the British Theatre

THE MEDIEVAL THEATRE IN THE ROUND

THE SEVEN AGES OF THE THEATRE

THE OPEN STAGE

ETC.

PROSCENIUM AND SIGHT-LINES

A Complete System of Scenery Planning and a Guide to the Laying Out of Stages for Scene-Designers, Stage-Managers, Theatre Architects and Engineers, Theatrical History and Research Workers and those concerned with the planning of stages for small halls

by
RICHARD SOUTHERN

THEATRE ARTS BOOKS
NEW YORK

Revised Edition, first published in 1964 by
Theatre Arts Books
333 Sixth Avenue New York 10014

Printed in Great Britain

Library of Congress Catalog Card Number: 64-24583

CONTENTS

CHAPTER TWO
PRELIMINARY POINTS CONCERNING SIGHT-LINES

CHAPTER THREE
SIGHT-LINES AND SMALL STAGES

CHAPTER FOUR
SIGHT-LINES AND FULL STAGES

APPENDICES

FOREWORD TO SECOND EDITION

In the period of time since this book was first published I have both used the method described in it consistently in all the planning I have done for the theatre, and repeatedly demonstrated it in detail to classes of students. This means that it has had some twenty-five years of testing by practical application. To me it has proved the most valuable aid to my work in theatre design that I have ever discovered; and now that an opportunity has come for a second edition of the book, there is nothing in the method itself nor in the application of it in practice that I would wish to alter.

On the other hand there is admittedly much in the tone of the book that appears old-fashioned now. For instance, there may seem to modern eyes an exclusive preoccupation with the form of the picture-frame type of stage. I see no cause, however, to alter this, for the simple reason that one of the best preparations for any innovation in theatre technique is a thorough grounding in the tradition obtaining previously. I am perhaps the more inclined to leave this characteristic of the book untouched in view of the reputation I have been given for showing too great an interest in what I call the 'open' stage—notwithstanding (as Thomas Hardy observed in the Introductory Note to his last book) the surprises to which I could treat my critics by uncovering a place here and there to them in the volume. . .

In general, then, the reader will find much traditional stuff in Sections 15 and 16, and he will find the quotations of dimensions of London theatres, quoted from *Who's Who in the Theatre*, to contain references to buildings now pulled down. But the matter is not invalidated. Again, the little Appendix on lighting has an old-fashioned air now; but there is, I believe, little in it that is actually misleading. In this respect Frederick Bentham's *Stage Lighting*, for instance, is by no means an 'up-to-date' book any longer, nor is Peter

Bax's *Stage Management*, but for all that they are both well worth the reading by any serious workman in the theatre.

In particular, I might revise the use of the word 'slips' in connection with grooves on p. 17, since it could be confused with the old term 'slips' as used of the side-ends of a gallery near the stage. The opening words on pp. 21 to 23 may be today a little harsh of some new theatres but they are, alas, still too true of others. To p. 33 might be added some account of the highly elaborate moving stages (sinking, sliding and/or revolving) that have in the last decades been built on the Continent, particularly in Germany; but this would not alter any item of the system of sight-lines. There are some references to the idea of a *raked* stage—for instance, on pp. 106 and 114—which still have their force, though some people have recently stated advantages in a raked stage for certain purposes. The references on p. 43 to using the understage space as a store must be read with recognition of the possible prohibitions of the local licensing authority in mind.

One or two errors in text have been corrected and a diagram or two clarified.

There is a single addition to the Supplementary Measurements that could well be made in practice, and this is the subject of a short footnote on p. 115.

And lastly, an appeal to architects. In designing a theatre you should plan the stage first, and then the auditorium to fit it. You should plan the stage around the figure of the performing actor, who is the centre and kernel of the show. If the actor is to have scenery on that stage *you must include the indication of a specimen set of that scenery upon the plans of your stage* before you can properly perfect the design of that stage. To design a stage irrespective of the scenery to be used upon it, or in ignorance of the nature of that scenery and of the system by which it will be masked and shifted, is a simply heartbreaking cause of inadequacy in modern theatre design.

I have told this fact to every architect with whom I have collaborated in a theatre design, yet I have not found one who has taken notice of what I said. R.S. 1964

A NOTE BY AN EIGHTEENTH-CENTURY SCENIC ARTIST

It was in speaking of the craft of 'feigning relief' in scene painting that Baldassare Orsini used the following words, but they are so closely applicable to this other scenic subject of sight-lines that I take leave to extend their meaning to it. They are from his *Scene del Nuovo Teatro del Verzaro.*

'One must realise that the artist ought to be furnished with sound theory and that without this he can do no more than colour mechanically the canvases of the scene. . . . Here I place theory before practice. This preference cannot but be received with a black visage by some who are called practitioners of the craft and who, every day, go fouling theatrical canvases persuading themselves that the painting of scenes cannot be placed among those things which are reduceable to a rigorous plan, and that one cannot combine chiaroscuro and accuracy so that they are not at strife with one another. The undertaking indeed is difficult but it is possible.'[1] (1785)

[1] Comprendasi da ciò, che l'artefice debba essere munito di buona teorica, e che senza di questa non potrà far altro che tingere meccanicamente coi colori le tele della scena. . . . In questo caso io antepongo la teorica alla pratica. Questa proposizione non potrà essere accolta che con viso brusco da certi che si dicono praticoni del mestiere, che tutto dì vanno sporcando tele teatrali, persuadendosi, che il pittoresco della scena non possa stare con ciò che è riducibile a rigorosa pianta, e che non si possa maritare insieme il chiaroscuro, e l'esattezza, così che non abbian lite tra loro. L'impresa per verità è difficile, ma è possibile.

ADDRESS

'And so, if the Painter or Architect wishes to paint or plan the Scenes for a Theatre, whether already built or only in project, he must draw on paper the plan and the section. . . .'

(*Volendo dunque un Pittore, ò Architetto dipingere, ò disegnare le Scene di un Teatro fatto, ò da farsi, è necessario farne in carta la pianta, ed il profilo. . . .*)

ANDREA POZZO, *Prospettiva de pittori et architetti* (2nd part) Roma, 1700

SECTION I

ADDRESS

The system of sight-lines—its use to architects—its use to those concerned with small halls—its use to research-workers on theatrical history—its use to scene-designers

---

Sight-lines afford a method of thinking about a stage. The method was first evolved to help to think out and fit scenery to a stage, but it became clear that it enabled one equally well to fit the parts of a stage themselves together and to plan them in as just a relation and proportion as it had helped one to plan scenery. Furthermore, as the gear and equipment of a stage are in a sense part of the stage itself in that their nature and positions and good-working are entirely interdependent with the nature, shape, and dimensions of the stage, the system of sight-lines is a valuable help to the planning of equipment.

It enables one to think about a stage in two directions: starting from the means present in any instance, it helps the *scene-designer* to go forward and use them to the best advantage to achieve a given effect or scheme, and it also helps the *architect* and the *machinist* (to use an old word) to go backward, as it were, from those means and reconsider them so that they can arrive at the point of altering or bettering the means themselves, apart from a specific effect and for the purposes of general use.

As a system it will not of course introduce one to new pieces of equipment, but once given the pieces it can very materially help one to place and employ them to best advantage, and conversely it may often suggest in a given difficulty what new piece of equipment needs designing to meet that difficulty, and in this way does, in fact, lead to the discovery and perfecting of mechanisms and forms that would else have been untried.

The science of sight-lines, then, affords a system to help the study of the practical features of any stage, whether already existing, or only in project, in such a way as to aid one in:

(1) Testing a project for a stage, or adapting an existing building to a stage, or improving an existing stage;

(2) Planning and placing the working equipment and the elements of general stage-setting on a given virgin stage so as to be most useful for their purposes;

(3) Planning, testing, and inventing arrangements, shapes, and uses of scenery for specific scenes in shows upon any given stage.

The system of sight-lines was evolved to help the scene-designer, and it is from his angle that it is discussed in the light of practice in Sections 11 to 14 of this book, but it is made public now in the knowledge that, in the form given, it can be of use not only to a scene-designer but to any one concerned in any way with studying the practical, specific features of a theatre stage.

It would be presumptuous of me to attempt to make any special adaptation of the system for the architect. It is far better for me to offer him the system as it is, for him to make his best use of it. But it is partly the encouraging assurance of Mr. Carter, once librarian of the Royal Institute of British Architects, that certain of the points would be of use to his profession that has led me to make such suggestions as I have in the architect's sphere and to cast the sections on sight-lines in so careful a form in the hope of supporting scientific scrutiny.

In exactly the same way another group of people, those connected with the drafting of schemes for social centres and especially village halls, will find the system a guide to their study of that part of the building concerned with the stage and its specific use, but I have not for that reason made any special application of it to their subject—they know more of village halls than I do. The National Council of Social Service especially has studied the village hall and community centre. Here again, had I not had the Council's very kind interest and most courteous discussion over their pamphlet, 'Village Halls, their construction and maintenance,'[1] I should not have extended the system so far as I have to the little stage, that specialized side of the theatre with its special needs, requiring as careful thought and as scientific a method as the full-size professional theatre.

For those again who are researching into the history of theatrical machinery, architecture, or scenery, the system of sight-lines may offer instant criticism or confirmation of a tentative theory. If, for instance, the sight-lines can be established for a given eighteenth-century theatre in which, theory holds, backcloths were used, they may instantly proclaim on a section that that theatre had no headroom for flying such cloths, then the research-worker is turned to examine other possibilities, or perhaps to the discovery that it was not a backcloth at all but a 'pair of flats', or a deep border with a couple of framed 'leg-wings'. Similarly, no theory of the method of using the sets of slips, or the grooves, can be entertained unless it can be shown to be reasonably consistent with the demands of sight-lines. And though it may be proved that the view from the nearer corner seats was far more lightly dismissed in the eighteenth century, yet the sight-line system must contribute a theory as to the extent of that dismissal. Indeed, an essay on 'The History of the Regard in which Consistent Masking was Held' might form interesting reading.

Finally and chiefly, to all my fellow scene-designers I tender a system which I know they all use in part but which the hurly-burly of the theatre has, it seems, prevented any from elaborating to a self-contained practice of general application. Especially important is it to have the system recorded now that scene design is being practised by outside artists who naturally have little initiation into the traditional technicalities of a specialized craft, nor (most of them) the time to conduct research into it for themselves. These will offer a most welcome boon to the theatre of their century if they will

[1] Published in 1935, revised in 1938.

include in their designs certain practical considerations such as will readily arise out of the system I shall outline, and their designs will, when handed over to the traditional theatre craftsmen to embody in the material of scenery, be both easier to achieve, and the more likely to avoid finished constructions that shock their artist with modifications, additions, or omissions that he himself might have seen inevitable.

To that best designer of all, the man attached to his own theatre and responsible for both his design and its realization, this system in some form is indispensable.

CHAPTER ONE

General Remarks on the Planning of a Useful Stage

SECTION 2

THE GENERAL INADEQUACY OF STAGE PLANS

The stage designed without theatrical advice—a stage must be fit for its scenery as scenery must be fit for its stage

It is difficult to realize that a theatre to-day may be designed without the assistance or advice of the theatrical profession. But so it is.

Thus we find much dissatisfaction with the present form of the stage, and rarely do we see a theatre whose stage is designed as a proper instrument to aid and contribute towards the presentation of a theatrical show.

A stage to-day is the result of the combination of the ideas of a business-man with those of an architect, sometimes with contributions from an engineer and, more rarely, an electrician. And the result may be an admirable example of the best in those departments. *But the theatrical profession has not been represented.*

The building of an efficient stage, whether in village hall or national theatre, can only come from recognition of the claims of many specialist technicians, including theatrical technicians. There must be examined, and correlated with the rest, the technique of the producer, of the specialist scene-designer—not merely of a painter of this or that famous picture—of the stage-manager, and of the master carpenter. It is incredible that building should proceed without the voice of any of these.

Theatrical machinery is a very fine servant, but it must have good quarters. To-day its quarters have become so ill designed that the servant is degraded to a drab and the service curtailed to a humdrum dullness, with no outlet for stimulation or invention.

I would emphasize that I do not lay this at the architect's door, though he would be in a better position to help had he studied the traditional science of stage-machinery in the eighteenth and nineteenth centuries. It is rather the fault of a phase of fashion which saw the temporary rise of naturalistic drama and the decay of theatrically fascinating spectacle. The 'play of ideas' so occupied the attention that it was forgotten how the appearance of a show could contribute to its theatricality and its stimulus; forgotten, too, were the possibilities latent in finely planned tools. In the theatre the simple hand-worked flying system, for instance, is considered to be brought sufficiently up to date if you install counterweights. But not only were counterweights used in the eighteenth-century theatre, they were used to far more ingenious ends and to operate a system of vastly more intricate and amusing mechanism—a system designed to be theatrical in its working, and a part of the show.

Then the theatre architect and the machinist—if indeed they were not one and the same—worked together.

In my own time I have often heard carpenters and stage-managers pick with indisputable precision on points in the planning of a stage where the day-to-day work, to say nothing of future development, is hindered by inadequate design. I stress this point: a stage should 'work' easily. In smaller stages and halls it seems to be held that a trifle extra difficulty in the work here or there, an inadequacy of space or a very limited range of flexibility in set shapes and rearrangements, means so very little that it is not worth thinking about (and indeed no method has till now been formulated by which these problems could be thought about). That is vitally wrong. The 'small obstacle' or the lack of three feet of space at a vital spot may hinder the development of a healthy school of setting. We must remember that, even if it seem a slight point, to the company, the inconvenience is ever present. For an experienced stage-carpenter it may mean a job of extra work that is as long as his days in the theatre. It may shackle the work of a less-experienced carpenter till it becomes a monotony and any progress a dream.

With professional stages the trouble is not obvious because the line of master carpenters are amazing for their knowledge of their job, and their ability to fit in to awkward conditions. Though maybe none but the carpenter knows how difficult the problem really is.

But in a small stage there is no margin for inadequacies.

To put the thing in a nutshell, we have theatres designed that won't take their machinery. Not only that—*we have theatres designed that won't even take any scenery comfortably*. It is not my intention here to plead for the return of elaborate machinery, nor to magnify any one type of scenery, advanced or traditional, but it is my intention to plead very strongly for theatres that will at least allow the stage to be decently set for the presentation of a show, *whatever its style*, and will answer to the more obvious demands of the 'movement of scenery' of at least a straightforward sort.

My plea will not be merely rhetorical, it will take the form of submitting a system by which the reciprocal relations of a stage plan with the forms of scenery placed upon it can be tested.

It is a simple system, but without it the study of machinery and the complications of developed sets is of little use. Therefore I confine myself in this book to the system and postpone consideration of scenery and machinery.

I shall be content if I mark in my introductory chapter those points in stage-planning which most need the correction of sight-lines, so as to advise my reader where the system may first be applied.

We cannot have a live and developing theatre if we fail to lay a masterful hand on the shape of the stage and apply a reasonably experienced and inventive mind to the nature of its machinery. We must turn the stage into a place where shows can be put on, and put on amusingly, interestingly, inventively, theatrically, efficiently, without a chaos of argument between effects and means. We must in all practical wisdom go 'towards a New Theatre'. If Craig give us the banner, herein is offered one of the spades.

SECTION 3

THE FIVE TYPES OF SET IN COMMONEST USE

The Pure Curtain Set—the Detail Set—the Wing-and-Cloth Set—the Box Set—the Cyclorama Set

---

The use of a stage is to present shows upon, and nearly all its features, saving the doors, the ventilation, and the acoustics, are connected with stage-setting or scenery.[1] A stage to-day is not merely a platform, it is a room. So much is the shape of a stage connected with scenic apparatus that all the sides of the room depend for their principal design upon scenery. And a stage is a six-sided room, for top and bottom are pressed into service and need even more specific designing than the walls.

There is a reciprocity about the fitting of scenery to a stage —not only must the scenery fit the stage but the stage must be fit to receive the scenery. The working of the scenery depends on the equipment of the stage, and the equipment of the stage is dependent on the working involved by the scenery.

It is then important to decide what styles of scenery are likely to be worked on the stage and what each style consists of. A certain stage may be required that is to take only certain styles of scenery. Its design, then, may be very different from that of another stage planned to take other styles of scenery. But it must be remembered that an arbitrary limitation of a stage's possibilities regarding types of set should only be made after the most careful consideration of the future

[1] *Stage-setting* embraces scenic generalities, mostly fixed, and suitable to any play, such as sets of curtains, a cyclorama, proscenium wings, and so forth; *scenery* is more sharply particularized and embraces pieces or sets of pieces specifically designed and painted for a particular scene, and having to be removed before another scene can be set.

work probable on that stage. A thoughtless restriction to a single type of scenery will place future companies in a most unhealthy position for the development of their work. They can get nowhere beyond their original field without expensive modification. Lack of foresight and blindness to the possible lines of theatrical progress are fatal limitations in any one connected with the planning of a stage.

On the other hand the application of this very foresight may show that certain types of set will be rarely used on a given stage. For instance, a village hall may well be designed with no regard—and even with an express intention of hindering—styles based on sham or merely imitative realism, which are liable to be expensive and inartistic in the circumstances. Such styles are certain to include the full 'box set' style, and a village stage not designed to accommodate easily that style may still be excellent for its purpose, involving the use of the 'detail' or other more suggestive style of scenery.

It may even be said that no village hall will ever want to use either full wing-and-cloth sets or box sets, and a design of stage that does not provide for these may remain adequate throughout the company's history, and limit them not at all, but it must not for that reason be supposed that no provision for any use of *flats* is necessary on a village stage—there are many vastly important uses for flats beside the realistic uses in the above two styles. And thoughtless design may entirely forbid the use of these supremely valuable elements of setting, as we shall go on to show.

On the other hand, a very different outlook should govern the plan of a larger stage. It is of cardinal importance that we should remove from our minds the common fallacy that a well-designed stage is one that allows the exploitation to the full of one pet type of scenery, but need provide no facilities for other types. Such a view is leading to the deadening sameness about the policies of certain of our theatres. Especially in the so-called advanced theatre must we beware of a plan that arrogantly disregards all styles but its own speciality of the moment—a plan that leads us to endless labour and compromise, or even complete breakdown, when we seek to stage any of the other styles. A well-designed stage is one that permits us to use to the fullest the widest range of styles. Restriction on styles of set leads inevitably to failure through a growing boredom in the audience. That is partly why so many 'advanced' theatres of a few years ago are now cinemas. They could use an immense number of 'architectural units' but they could not hang a ceiling or fly a border.

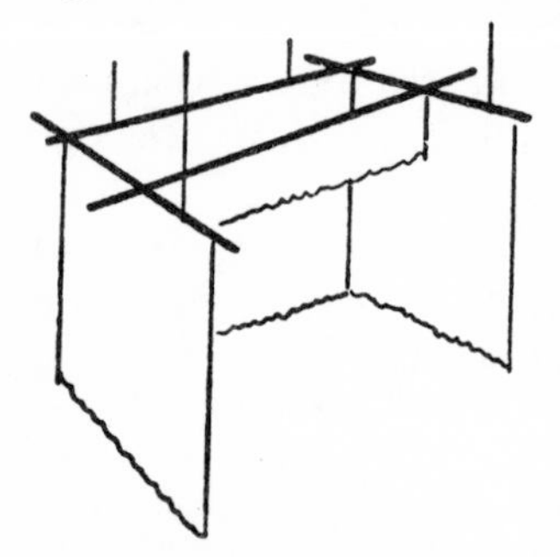

Fig. 1. The Pure Curtain Set.

There are not many styles we need study; in discussing them I shall limit myself to traditional forms. Many — too many — confusing sub-divisions of style are observable. At the risk of seeming to ignore these I shall confine myself to the straightforward, more or less traditional key-shapes of set, for I know that within these lies all the necessary ground for individual experiment.

I have elsewhere divided theatrical setting into eight main heads,[1] of these we here ignore the first three—Costume Setting, Symbol Setting, and Background Setting—they are more a matter for the setting-designer than the architect, and in them the designer's problem is to adapt himself to his conditions, whatever those may be, calling in no respect upon them to help him. But to distinguish the other five is of importance to any one who plans a stage, for each demands special conditions. They are the Pure Curtain Set, the Detail Set, the Wing-and-Cloth Set, the Box Set, and the Cyclorama Set. These five varieties may be briefly diagrammatized as in Figs. 1 to 5.

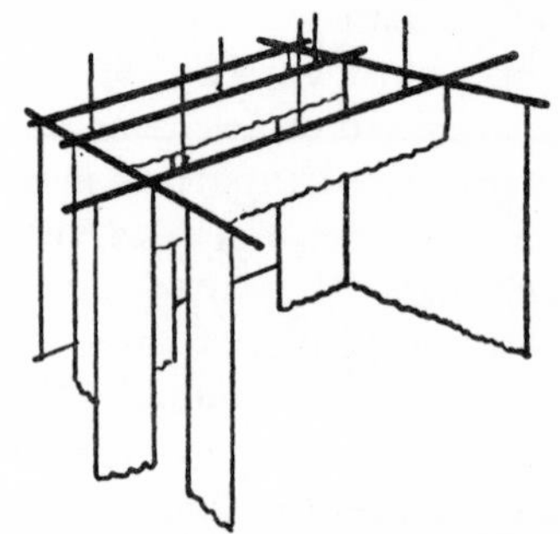

Fig. 2. The Detail Set: only the stage-setting, or surround of curtains, is shown here—in, or against, this setting many varieties of details of scenery may be placed.

They have three points common to each, and the indivi-

[1] Cf. *Drama*, January 1935.

dual variations of these common points are of considerable importance in stage design: each has a back, sides, and a top. The first common element, the back, is in the first four types, a simple upright plane, either a hanging curtain (Figs. 1 and 2), a hanging canvas (Fig. 3), or a standing, framed-out canvas, probably in separate sections, called *flats* (Fig. 4). The back of the fifth type is curved and possibly built permanently and plastered.

The second common element is the sides. The sides of Figs. 1, 2, and 4 are similarly plain walls, in the first two examples

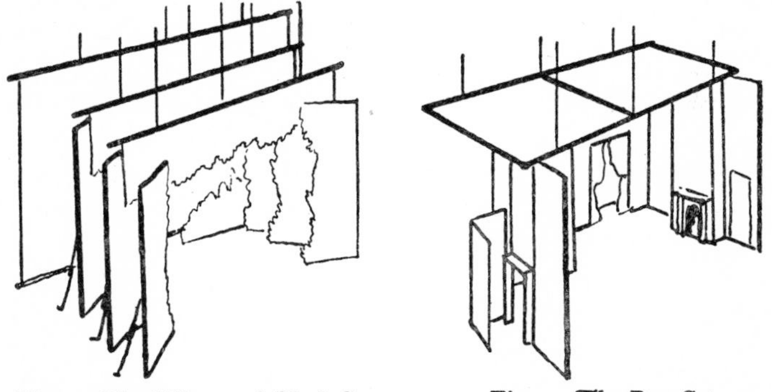

Fig. 3. The Wing-and-Cloth Set. *Fig. 4. The Box Set.*

they are walls of curtain, in the other of canvassed flats joined edge to edge. For Fig. 3 the sides are made by setting the flats each at a similar angle, forming rows of 'wings'. In Fig. 5 the sides are different in a rather important respect; they are partly supplied by the sides of a 'false proscenium arch' which stands behind the real one, and partly by the curved-forward 'horns' of the back wall or cyclorama.

The third and last common element is some means of 'masking-in' the top. In Figs. 1, 2, and 3 one or more 'borders' are used. Above the walls of Fig. 4 a framed-up canvas ceiling is hung. The top of Fig. 5 is masked partly by the top of the false proscenium and partly by the great height and coved top of the cyclorama.

These five types of set each make special demands on the stage on which they are put up. To them we should add for completeness one sub-division in which are made, perhaps, the greatest demands of all on stage structure. This extension includes all types of elaborately built or trick sets. Generally these fall into the main group of the wing-and-cloth style; more rarely do they occur in the box style. So far as the elementary masking of sides and top and back are concerned they have perforce to follow orthodox lines, but they make especial demands on the stage in respect of the large movable trucks on which the built units of the sets are constructed, or

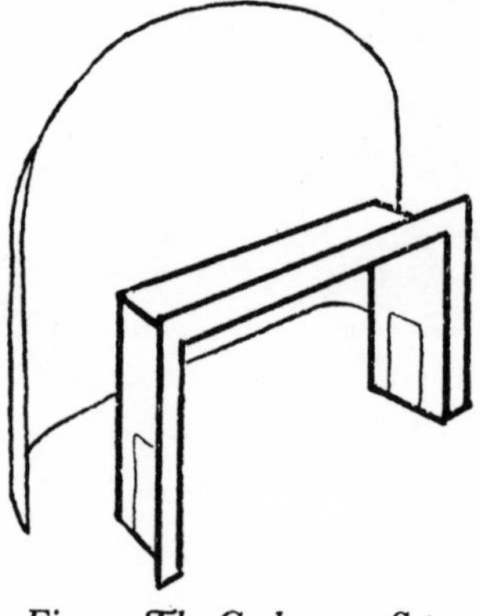

Fig. 5. The Cyclorama Set.

in respect of the rising and sinking bridges in the stage floor from the nature of which the sets take their shape, or of the revolving parts of the stage upon which the system of the scene-change may depend.

This sub-division of built- and trick-scenery is especially important when we come to consider the movement of scenery.

There are resumed all the main methods of making an orthodox stage set.

Now in fitting any of these types of set to a stage, the setting has to be put up behind a *proscenium opening*, which conditions every one of the set's dimensions in a way that will be explained, and one especial requirement must be observed: *the set must mask.*

SECTION 4

THE FIRST TWO ESSENTIAL PRINCIPLES OF STAGE PLANNING

Suitability for settings—suitability for working

Masking means that a set must be of a size to suit certain conditions imposed by the proscenium and its relation to the spectators' seats, and must be arranged so that no spectator can see over or round or through the scenery at any undesired point.

Now the first essential principle in stage-planning emerges from this, for certain proscenium conditions may demand from the setting an arrangement and dimension of parts that will not fit the stage behind, because the stage has been planned without taking into account the proscenium conditions. So:

A stage must be planned to accommodate settings of such size and arrangement as are imposed by the characteristics of its own proscenium opening. The designs of these three, setting, stage, and proscenium opening, are interdependent. None can be planned without relation to the others.

The means for examining this relation is the system of sight-lines. The dimensions of all pieces of scenery are conditioned by the relation of the edges of the proscenium opening with the two virtually outermost seats in the auditorium of the theatre. If the back-stage space is not adequately planned with regard to this relation no scene design can ever be straightforward, and indeed some forms of scenery may be completely prohibited. It is true that an understanding scene-designer can and will design a set that will get round obstacles of this nature, but his only method will be found to be the diminishing and duplicating of certain pieces, which increases his expenditure, not only on scenery but on lighting, and complicates and lengthens his scene-changes.

It is from these scene-changes that the second essential principle of stage-planning emerges in this way:

Not only must a stage-plan allow for the adequate setting of static scenery, but also for the movement of scenery—it must be favourable to 'packing' and to 'working'.

The nature of packing and working we must now consider.

SECTION 5

THE MOVEMENT OF SCENERY

How scene-changes affect the plan of a stage—the effect of the five styles

When a theatrical show takes place from beginning to end in the same scene, that scene is said to be a standing scene.

But when the show contains two or more different scenes, a new situation is created, for scenery must now be changed and that means, in effect, that a different stage is now required. There must now be space in the wings to pack the scenery and furniture of past or forthcoming scenes. There must be a staff of stage-hands, there must be equipment with which to move the scenery. Work, space, and machinery are essential, and even the atmosphere behind the scenes is vastly different; gone is that long, waiting feeling in a sense of sleepy space in which a visitor behind the scenes hears and feels no more than the oddly muffled voices of the actors out on the stage and hidden by the set walls. The stage seems almost to echo to their murmurings like an empty house and the only distraction is a slow tip-toeing player, now and then, seeming very solitary as he creeps to a door to await a cue, or strides away a little more quickly to his dressing-room, down the strip of fibre matting laid to deaden footsteps. All goes on quietly and serenely in an ample space.

But in a show with many scenes, the very air has a different breath behind. Not a touch of the cathedral now. Now every sense must be alert, every step picked with a lively eye, watching for cables, avoiding piles of furniture, threading in and out the congestion of great packs of scenery. Many more people are there, very softly putting all ready for a change, but, soft as they are, they, and that occasionally rippling complex of lines and battens in the dimness above and around, kill for ever any sense of stillness. In a show with a standing scene, the atmosphere behind may be—to a visitor—strikingly peaceful, almost dreamy, one of the most restful in the world.

But when scenery moves no rest ever settles. And it is to the expediting of that movement and to its smooth efficiency that an understandingly planned stage contributes so much.

The nature of the movement of the five main set-types above described is as follows:

The Pure Curtain Set, a more or less infertile field is, properly speaking, static.

With the Detail Set, the curtains themselves can rarely be changed expeditiously during a show, save that traverse curtains may be drawn on and off, and perhaps straight sides be turned into wing sides, but the details of scenery are all movable and are generally slid or carried to the side and packed in the wing-spaces. Once in a while a small roller-cloth is used in a centre-back opening.

In Wing-and-Cloth Sets, whose nature generally tends to suit them to-day less to straight drama shows and more to spectacular shows, in many scenes, there are made possibly the heaviest demands of all on packing and working space. Generally every element must move. Wings and groundrows are slid or *run* off sideways, borders must go up, and backcloths and cutcloths can rarely be got rid of satisfactorily save by full flying, or going aloft a distance exceeding their own height.

In Box Sets the ceiling goes up, the flats are run to packs at the side, and, if the next set does not require the ceiling, that must be either 'booked', or else dropped vertical and flown entire. The box-chamber is the type of set most demanded to-day by straight plays, and such plays are generally in one or only a few scenes. Setting here is generally realistic, and furniture and property packs may become a very considerable item.

In Cyclorama Sets there is less movement; most of the scenery is in the form of set-pieces or rostrums and so forth and tends to belong to the Detail class and is similarly moved by simple hand-lifting or by running. Ideally, full-cyclorama sets of any elaboration demand a moving stage.

The system of movement in the additional sub-division of built and trick stuff (mentioned in Section 3) is highly elaborate and specialized. It is governed by no fixed procedure but the thoroughly understood tradition of the normal, and to discuss its possibilities fully would entail an analysis of scores of special cases where the system was specially evolved for the occasion and will probably never be used again in exactly the same way. Generally speaking, elaborately built stuff is constructed on special tables or trucks—the term *boat-truck* is often used—which may on occasion be big enough to carry the whole of one side of a set. In the change, the whole unit is pushed from its place and wheeled to the wings or (more likely, because of its size) to a special scene-dock off-stage. Trucks are particularly suitable for vast units of setting that lie up-and-down stage or diagonally. For those which lie parallel to the footlights another system may be used (often seen on the Continent) where the scenery is built on that part of the stage floor called a *bridge*, which is really a lift. There may be three or more of these bridges on a large stage, each three to six feet wide and reaching right across the stage. Usually these bridges are capable of rising or sinking; very occasionally they may be found so elaborately built that, after sinking, they travel to the side to give place to another bridge which rises and takes the place of the first with another set of scenery. The system may be so extended that the complete stage floor moves and is replaced by another.

And, finally, there is the system in which a part or parts of the stage revolve like a turn-table, taking with them a greater or smaller part of the set or, sometimes, the whole of several sets built back to back in sectors of the circle.

There are to be added those systems in which the trick movement is in the scenery itself and is independent of any stage mechanism, such as in the quick changes of double-sided, dropping flaps, or the turning of a pivoted built unit, or the alteration of some part of that unit as by sliding the front away. But these (very generally speaking) are the affair of the machinist not the stage-architect, and may be held to accept and follow, rather than make demands upon, the existing stage lay-out.

These movements of scenery are among many factors governing the planning of the six walls of a stage. Let us now turn to those six walls.

SECTION 6

THE SIX SIDES OF A STAGE, AND RECOMMENDATIONS FOR THEIR PLANNING

(1) The floor—(2) the top—(3) the back—(4) the front—(5) and (6) the two sides

Detailed points about the planning of large stages are manifold and complicated. They would form a specialist discussion of great length—but even then, in practice and coming down to special cases, each problem will probably have to be solved in the special terms of its own case, and not by a formula of general principles. Moreover, the system of sight-lines alone will offer a better aid to the individual examination of these special cases as they arise than would a long account of imaginary instances or of examples from already built theatres.

So in the following brief discussion of the requirements of stages I shall confine myself to the broader points and, rather than analyse the finer requirements of large stages, concern myself chiefly with the more pressing needs, and in especial those of small stages, where the margin for error is so much narrower.

There is none of the following principles that is not applicable to big stage work, and if we can make precise these more elementary points we shall be in a far better position to advance into the highly specialized details of a larger scale.

It may be that the designer upon a large stage, if it is well planned, has so much space and has at his call so many aids for fitting his scenery that he is rarely confined to a margin of inches—or even feet—for the dimensions of his pieces. After a little experience he will learn how broadly to size his scenery so that he is always on the safe side and the amount of waste he thus incurs will often be a negligible item. But here and there, even in his broadest work, he will be faced with a position where the nicest economy is necessary to fit exactly the right-sized piece into the exact minimum space. There is no surer means of handling such problems than the system of sight-lines.

But if, on ample stages, work may so frequently pass with a mere half-dozen major measurements and a skilled knowledge of the job, there is by no means that freedom permissible on a small stage. On a small stage the most exact application of sight-lines is needed. It is more necessary to small scenery than to large. This is one of the very few points on which the amateur ought to be more precise than the professional needs to be.

By far the finest training for large scenery work is a period of designing for tiny, ill-spread stages where the importance of sight-lines can be fully learned by exacting experience. Then the wholesome habit of checking every size and space will be inculcated early and it will be a designer with valuable practical qualifications that emerges from confinement to the sometimes embarrassing freedom of great space—a designer who in nice quandaries will solve with comparative ease what a man without his apprenticeship would strain over or dismiss with a compromise.

Because, then, the value of the sight-line system is more forcibly apparent upon a stage with limitations we shall confine most of our study to these smaller, trickier stages.

Concerning the drawing up of plans for normal smallish stages we can now make the following observations.

The floor of a stage, perhaps because it is the aspect most considered in a ground plan, is thought about a good deal, but the second side, the top, is far too frequently forgotten and it is almost of the first importance to the staging of a show. The third side is the back, which has a possible function for setting far too often ignored. The 'fourth wall' has had much theory built on its name, but little devoted to its function or to the proscenium opening within it—occupying so much of its space with a vacancy that thoughtless people talk of the fourth wall as an imaginary one. Finally, that the fifth and sixth walls—the two sides—are more than mere boundaries and should be in fact repositories is so rarely acknowledged that many a company's whole life is stunted like the roots of a pot-bound plant by its own stage side-walls.

The following discussion of the six sides of a stage is framed to emphasize the points where inadequacies in planning are commonest. The six 'sides' will be taken one by one and the danger points of each summarized at the head of the description. Next will follow an elaboration of the points in the summary. This elaboration will deal directly with certain points, but about those for the proper understanding of which an application of the sight-line system is necessary, details will be deferred till the convenient place in the book.

Finally, the notes on each 'side' will conclude with the various demands made upon it by each of the five types of scenery.

Especially is this list of danger points addressed to those responsible for the planning of the many stages that are coming into being, in so astonishing a number, in schools, in town and village halls, in occupational centres and club huts; stages upon which, if they are ignorantly built, an inexperienced company of players can never progress beyond a delusion that theatres in huts are poor fun and can never hold that glamour and allure of presentation that a 'real stage' can or be equal—and better—homes for advanced work and experiment.

THE FIRST SIDE—THE FLOOR

Summary

Concerning the floor of the stage,
(*a*) it should be flat;
(*b*) it should be the right height;
(*c*) it should be continuous to the side walls of the stage;
(*d*) it should have very wide wing spaces;
(*e*) it may usefully contain traps;
(*f*) it should be capable of receiving screws.
Concerning the floor of the auditorium,
(*a*) the seating should have side gangways;
(*b*) the floor should be either raked or else stepped at the back.

Notes

(*a*) A stage floor should be flat. Stage rake is a tradition connected with perspective scenery. Kranich[1] gives so complete a review of this question of stage rake that I cannot do better than summarize his points. He says:

'The popular idea of the oldest arrangement of the whole stage machinery, the "absolutely essential stage rake", must be completely removed . . . the stage rake is the basic defect of a House that brings all the other technical deficiencies in its train.' And he adds that the only reasons ever advanced for a raked stage in modern years are:

(1) That the players (especially dancers) can move (and leap) towards the audience more easily and spectacularly.

(2) That in crowd scenes the back players are better seen.

(3) That front-seat spectators have a more favourable line of sight.

These excuses for the rake he dismisses on the grounds: (1) that the modern actor (and dancer) moves (and leaps) in all directions; (2) that if the purpose of stage rake be to show the actors at the back, then a rake, not of the usual 3·2 per cent., but of 20 per cent. is necessary; and as that is impossible, proper grouping always entails rostrums for the back rows, so the rake is not necessary anyway; (3) if the pit seats are on a sloping floor, it is all one whether the stage is raked or not.

Against the claimed advantages of a rake must be set the actual disadvantages:

The side flats of all chamber sets must be shaped at the bottom to suit the rake, hence those built for one side of the stage will not suit the other, nor can they be used at the back of any set.

If you stand furniture against such a specially shaped side-flat, then it stands aslant with regard to the flat, or leans forward if it is against the back wall.

If, however, you use rectangular, normal flats on a raked stage, the down-stage flat cannot be fitted cleanly against the inner proscenium but will leave a wedge-shaped gap; further,

[1] Fr. Kranich, in *Bühnentechnik der Gegenwart*, vol. i, p. 117 and following. (R. Oldenbourg, Munich, 1929.)

all pictures and chandeliers, etc., will hang vertically, and not, therefore, following the tilt of the walls; and no side door whose hinges are up-stage will open and shut without jamming, nor, if they are down-stage will the door stay shut unless latched.

Further, on a raked stage scene handling by means of trucks is far more difficult, and indeed unsafe, for a truck may start down the slope of its own accord.

When finally we read in Stieglitz (*Enzyklopädie der bürgerlichen Baukunst*, 1797) that 'This Falling of the Stage is necessary on account of the perspective of the decorations, for the level of the stage must run to the Vanishing Point, else, were it laid flat it would appear to the spectators, especially those in the Pit, shorter than it really is, and not its rightful depth,' we may, I think, agree that the rake has outstayed its purpose and has to-day no single virtue to recommend it at all.

(*b*) The height of the stage floor above that of the auditorium is governed by two factors, the distance of the nearest row of spectators and that of the farthest. It must be higher as the farther seats are more distant. But it must not be so high as to cause uncomfortable craning upwards from the nearest seats; the nearer these are, the lower the maximum stage height possible.

(*c*) The stage itself should carry unbroken to the side walls or at least be capable of extension to these when it is used for a show. A drop at the sides is a physical danger, an artistic limitation, and a practical curse. In small halls where temporary extensions are needed to fill up, these must not creak under footsteps.

But I should like to extend this point. I would beg that no architect should plan the stage nor its directly-adjoining wing- and packing-spaces, nor its corridors of approach, so that differences of floor-level are incurred. I know there are circumstances in which what I ask will be regarded as excessive, and I shall be told, 'You've *got* to have them, you must learn to accept.' I will not alter my principle. And I will insist that those who deny me shall not do so without admitting, as they do it, this absolute truth: steps leading up or down to a stage are exceedingly dangerous. *Especially if they be few.* I would rather have my passage of approach interrupted by a flight of sixteen or twenty-five steps, if it must be interrupted, than by three or five, for I should then have to face a precipitous drop whose presence would be forced, by its size, upon the mind, even in panic, and where a sloping ceiling above and the warning of shadows and lights and the whole conformation of the surrounding structure would emphasize its presence. I would even prefer the immense sweated labour of shifting scenes and furniture up and down this mountain, than have the treachery of a little drop so small that the walls ignore its presence and its deceptive existence may be entirely overlooked.

But better, far better, to make it our job to see that there is no drop at all, and understand that one reason for our existence is to save those who commission us from such anomalies against the very nature of design, of which we profess to be trained exponents.

It is necessary for architects who have never been in a show to visualize what is behind all this. I have been at pains to give as shortly as possible some sort of picture of the atmosphere of a stage during scene-change. This mental picturing of what is to take place on his work is, of course, essential to an architect. He must know the sudden change in mood that flicks across the air a second after the curtain drops on a scene—how, on a well-regulated stage, the actors immediately drop their rôles and swiftly turn to quit the stage and leave it free for the irruption of stage-hands, who are already striking the set. He must follow a group of these hands as they run off a heavy, triple, hinged flat, and understand the lack of *smoothness* in action that interruptions of floor level entail. He must notice the hold-up that a piece of furniture, till that moment swiftly fleeing from the set, suffers as it reaches a flight of four steps, and its bearers turn to negotiate them sideways or backwards. And he must not forget that, though the difficulties which certain actions assume in the presence of steps are manifest, there may be still other systems of scene-change he may never see attempted because steps make them utterly impossible anyway—such, for instance, as the smooth rolling away of a complete built set-piece on a boat-truck, through high doors, off the stage, and into the concealment of a neighbouring dock.

These things he may clearly visualize. But he may forget to see, as I have seen, that occasion which never fails to tighten the muscles to a thrill, even in old stage-hands, and which may occur when no scene-change is in progress, and that is what is involved by an actor's quick change, or by the whispered cry passed-on 'Stage waiting!' There is nothing to resemble these moments of galvanic hurry—of trained action pressed to its utmost speed—unless it be the excitement of a dashing fire-engine in traffic. Now in this particular atmosphere of emergency, effort is strained to the utmost, risks are taken in a stride without a moment's consideration—they must be—the whole show, the whole tradition and prestige of theatre depend upon them: here is a man or woman straining every physical and mental faculty to the utmost in the service of the public and the job. It is a peak moment of speed.

And then there is a drop of a couple of feet in the path.

You must remember with almost nightmare clearness the whole of the situation—the player may be in hampering skirts or cloak, he or she may, a second ago, have been facing the glare of a dozen 500-watt spots or the shine of a brightly-lit make-up mirror: his mind is—and must be—undivided upon his object. Even fractions of seconds are valuable. He turns a corner and there are three stairs leading down.

If you imagine not only this but can hear, as I have heard, the instant's rustle and flirt that precedes the thud of the body—during which instant you might have saved him had you been quick enough, for you saw the whole consequence in a flash—you will realize, as we pick him up and call the already descending stage-manager, what we, in the theatre, think of variations in level in the working floor of our occasions.

You will not reply then that an actor must be careful in the corridors. You should know that no properly trained actor will ever stumble or fall *on the stage*—he has a kind of sixth sense of obstacles there—but off the acting-area, with other aspects of his job to think of, he puts his trust in you not to offer him the folly of a hole in his working floor.

The whole working area on which the business of the stage is conducted should be on one level. Failing that, the levels should be so distinct that lightning speed is frankly abandoned and normal stairs of lengths to which we are used should lead to upper dressing-rooms where the stage-manager will see that no actor who has a quick change is ever installed. But, remember, changes involving scenery and furniture are always, in effect, quick changes.

Clear access from the acting-area to all its adjacent offices is an essential, and though the accusation of actual danger cannot be fairly levelled against awkward corners in ways of access, the accusation of delay and inefficiency can, and so emphatically as to make the requirement for *straight* and *level* means of access to our stages one of our first demands.

(*d*) It would seem that few have ever had the courage to claim its rightful importance for the wing-space—the spaces at the side of a stage. The attitude is, 'Oh yes, we know it would be very nice to have plenty of room there but you can't have everything, and four feet is really enough to move about in.' We must economize somewhere so we economize on wing-space. We had far better economize on stage space. *Eight feet on either side is the very minimum of practical wing-space for the tiniest practical stage.* In a larger theatre the space rises in proportion. More will be said concerning the wing-space in the discussion of the sides.

(*e*) It is very useful if the construction of the stage floor be such as enables a long narrow portion of it to be lifted as a trap, for the dropping through of scenery to store. The trap need be no more than eighteen inches wide but should be as long as the length of the longest battens from which curtains or cloths are hung. It should run from side to side of the stage, whose floor boards should, according to ancient tradition, run up-and-down stage so that their bearers beneath may run parallel with the trap and thus allow the rolled cloths to be dropped between that pair of them over which the trap comes.

It is of great help in view of the valuable storage room here to sink the floor under the stage so as to give a clear six feet of height, then flats (whose maximum width is 6 ft.) can also be dropped down, and stored on their sides. The old stage floor had many of these traps, and a great cellar-depth.

Sometimes this space is also valuable as a passage under the stage when no other passage behind is available: for every stage should be accessible from either side.

Apart from this a door into the basement is necessary for human entrance to the store, and such a door should be accessible without going into the auditorium.

(*f*) There are two ways of bracing framed-up pieces of scenery on a stage floor: one, by putting a brace-weight on the end of the brace to keep it from slipping; two, by screwing the brace end to the stage with a stage-screw. The latter is the more practical method. A stage floor, then, should be capable of receiving stage-screws, and not composed of polished (and hence slippery) or choice wood. This is my own view: I should add that some authorities consider the brace-weight method safe enough to compensate for the wearing of the stage that stage-screws cause.

For Pure Curtain Sets alone a plain floor may be sufficient.

For Detail Sets a trap is valuable for the lowering of flat details of scenery.

For Wing-and-Cloth Sets the trap is very useful indeed, for a set of rolled backcloths is difficult to store and the suggestion sometimes made that they should be poked up through a door high in the back wall in the hope of storing them in a loft above the dressing-rooms is thoroughly unwise in more ways than one.

Not only may cloths be stored in such a trap but they can be struck directly into it, that is, lowered straight through in a scene change. The cloth may either be rolled on a roller below the stage as it descends or (if it is not too thickly painted) folded zig-zag into a long box, then its lines (with snap-hooks at the end) may be detached from the top batten and attached to that of another cloth waiting rolled-up under the trap, to be unrolled and pulled into view by the ascending lines. This is the system of the 'sloat box', or slot box, described in Peter Bax's very practical book on 'stage management',[1] and is the only way of getting rid of a cloth on a stage with no head room, beside the ordinary 'rising bottom roller' method.

Further the trap allows the revival of a nearly forgotten, delightful method of getting rid of groundrows by sinking them in sight of the audience.

For Box Sets the trap and basement are useful for storing rolled ceilings.

For Cyclorama Sets another kind of trap or 'trough' in the floor at the foot of the cyclorama, capable of being covered when not in use, offers a valuable housing-place for a cyclorama foot-row of lamps. The normal trap as described above is ideal for the packing of groundrows and low set-pieces.

Concerning the floor of the auditorium:

(*a*) In the auditorium the seating should be planned with gangways at the side—at least near the front of the house—for, in any case, the side-front spectators get a bad view of the stage, and the nearer-in they are with regard to the proscenium edge the better. Side gangways also allow exits in the side walls for emergencies.

(*b*) The floor of the auditorium should be raked for the better viewing of the stage. In a village hall this is generally impossible, but a great aid to the comfort[2] of the back spectators is to raise the last few rows of seats on a platform. This need not be high, indeed the lower the better, for once it surpasses the level of the stage it needs to be increasingly heavily raked or the back spectators are worse off than before. Six or nine inches is very well worth while.

THE SECOND SIDE—THE TOP, ROOF, OR GRID

Summary

(*a*) No roof above any stage should be of the plain pitch type unless the side walls of the stage are considerably higher

[1] Peter Bax, *Stage Management* (Lovat Dickson, 1936).

[2] The comfort of spectators is a vital factor in showmanship.

than the proscenium opening; otherwise a pitch roof must contain a dormer shape either side.

(*b*) Every inch of unobstructed headroom that can be contrived is needed.

(*c*) No system of curtain-hanging should be fixed, or built in so as to prevent, in any way, full variation of shapes of set.

NOTES

(*a*) It is in the roof that a little theatre or village hall finds one of the two greatest structural obstacles to its smooth working, so a note at length here will not be amiss.

A low pitch roof is utterly unsuited to the nature of scenery, because scenery is square and the roof triangular. And you cannot fit a square peg into a triangular hole without a great waste of space.

It is a truism that scenery must reach above the proscenium opening in order to mask and prevent the front stalls seeing up over the top. Similarly scenery must reach out beyond the sides of the proscenium opening or the sides will not mask. A set therefore occupies an area behind the proscenium opening whose elevational aspect exceeds that of the opening itself, at the top and at the sides.

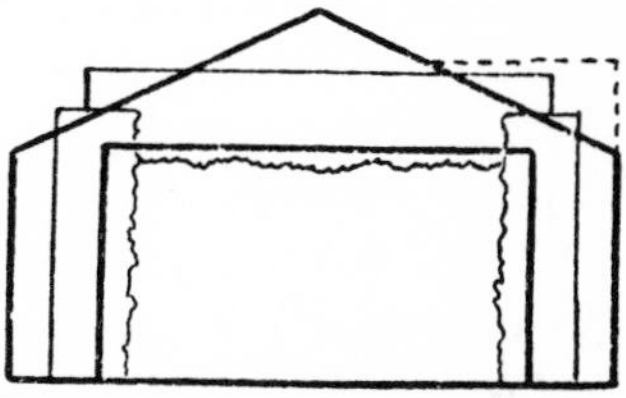

Fig. 6. The inadequacy of a pitch roof for scenery, and the need for a dormer.

It is the upper, outer corners of scenery that foul a pitch roof, and if you do not lift your border so high as to poke the ends of the batten through the tiles (Fig. 6), nor push your wings so far off that their upper, outer corners break through in the same way, then your near spectators can see over or round them.

Not only is this true, but the natural movement of scenery during a change is centrifugal—the top goes up and the sides go out. A pitch roof even just sufficiently high to allow the border enough depth and the wings enough width, when each is in place on a set, is therefore not properly adequate, for the border cannot fly even the minimum few feet nor the wings be run off to the sides to pack.

What is very obvious from Fig. 6 is that an inexpensive small-scale remedy for this is the use, on the roof above the stage, of the simple dormer form.

I would advocate the building of a pair of dormers in every pitch roof put up over a stage.

Ideally the face of this dormer shape should carry up the face of the external wall of the stage and should not be set back from it, but its top need not necessarily be as high as the ridge of the main roof. Five feet—even less—of extra headspace here is sometimes quite enough in a small hall, though it may leave little margin for full flying of scenery.

The essential places for the dormer shape are at the back of the stage (where the back of the set comes), and at, and just in front of, the centre depth of the stage (where the borders mostly come). These places should at least be relieved. But by far the best is a dormer running the whole depth of the stage.

It is worth while noticing that the space in the dormer need not for our purpose be entirely free of roof spans, and that if a dormer is added to an existing pitch roof no cutting of the rafters is involved. Any beam or system running parallel with the proscenium is tolerable across the dormer space. But any purlin or member traversing the space at right angles to the proscenium will cross the path of the battens of the scenery and immediately destroy the value of the dormer.

(*b*) The pulleys over which run the lines supporting all hanging scenery on a full stage are placed in an open grid of beams covering the whole stage area and at a sufficient height above the stage to allow full-size backcloths to be drawn up to a distance at least equal to their own height. Much headspace for the flies is impossible on a small stage, but because here backcloths can never be flown there is no reason to overlook the boon of a few feet of headspace in which to fly borders or 'booked' ceilings. It is too generally supposed that if full flying space is impossible, nothing extra above the set height need be thought about. But even five feet of headroom can be an inestimable boon, and it is just that boon that can be conveyed by an architect who thinks to place a dormer on the pitch roof above a small stage.

On the scale plan and longitudinal cross section of any stage project the system of sight-lines should be applied to discover the height of scenery and length of borders necessary for the given circumstances, so that it may be seen if such scenery is permitted by the pitch roof or whether a dormer shape should be added to avoid the various indirect tricks and shifts necessary to mask scenery that is in principle too low.

Point (*c*) in the above summary will be covered in the following notes concerning the roof of a stage considered in relation to the five types of set.

The Pure Curtain Set. Because of the wide use of curtains as setting on small stages, a certain belief is current that you provide a means for hanging the setting for any possible show by fixing permanently three battens to the roof so as to take a back curtain and two side curtains. But nothing is more misleading than the statement that you 'can play *anything* in curtains', and to be of any real general use curtains must be capable of many different arrangements on plan, and must be supplemented by many different types of 'detail' scenery as described in *Stage-Setting.*[1]

It is then unwise for an architect to make any provision for the hanging of curtains that is immovable or difficult to modify in shape. It is almost better to make no provision for curtain-hanging at all and let the company put in its own pulleys and find its own salvation; but then they are certain to come upon some limitation that could have been avoided with forethought, and the only wise way with a design for a stage roof is to subject it constantly, in the making, to the unequivocal tests of sight-lines.

The Detail Set. For Detail Sets (by far the most generally useful type) the architect has the discussion of their nature quoted above to guide him, and with that knowledge, the help of sight-lines, and the suggestion of the dormer, his problem can be worked out because its features are clear.

[1] Richard Southern, *Stage-Setting for Amateurs and Professionals* (Faber and Faber, 1937).

In both the preceding types of set all the curtains are hung from the roof or from a variable frame suspended from the roof, when a minimum of four points of suspension is demanded. In the second type there may be additional points of support needed for the hanging of traverse curtains.

Wing-and-Cloth Sets. In Wing-and-Cloth Sets the cloths and borders hang from the roof each from its independent set of lines. Each set of lines generally involves three ropes (from the two ends and the centre of the piece), three single pulleys in the roof to take the separate lines, a triple pulley or head-block at the side to gather the lines together and return them to the stage, where they are made off together to a cleat on the side wall. Sufficient sets of lines will be needed to hang all the borders that the sight-lines show to be necessary for each scene, and, further, a separate set for each border or cloth used in the other scenes of the show. It will be apparent from this that very few stages in this world can have too many sets of lines available, and that on the other hand their paucity often conditions and limits the scene design for a show.

The wings to-day are nearly always stood and braced on the stage.

The Box Set. For the Box Set little is hung beside the ceiling and that needs two sets of lines if it is plain and three if it is to be booked and folded.[1]

The Cyclorama Set. With the Cyclorama Set in its fullest form overhead lines at any part of the stage, except the very front, are precluded, for the top curve-forward of the cyclorama cuts them off. Overhead lines are so useful, however, that at present, while the cyclorama system is still in its infancy, it is better to truncate the dome and preserve some at least of the lines.

For all these types of set the roof must, of course, supply means of hanging certain elements of lighting.

[1] I hope in the future to give an account of ceilings and flying methods generally; till then illustrations to this paragraph may be found in Kranich (cf. note, p. 38).

THE THIRD SIDE—THE BACK WALL

Summary

Concerning the back wall,

(*a*) its central area should *never* be broken by doors;

(*b*) it should be plastered;

(*c*) it may often very usefully be curved forward at the ends or top, in the plastering, provided the amount of curve has been subjected to sight-line tests;

(*d*) there should be a passage behind from side to side of the stage.

Notes

Few notes are necessary here on these points. The plastering of the back wall gives a very valuable permanent sky backing or basis for a backing of coloured light. It forms a step towards the cyclorama. Any opening in the central part of the back wall, of course, prevents one from ever using it in this most advantageous and economical way. The points affecting the curve of this wall will be discussed later in Section 17.

In relation to each of the five types of set a back wall treated as suggested above is: for a Pure Curtain Set not of great importance; for a Detail Set very important indeed; for a Wing-and-Cloth Set a great potential help in economizing scenery and developing the style, as shown in Section 16; for a Box Set is of considerable use as a backing for any window in the back wall of the set; for a Cyclorama Set it is essential (or practically so, though it is possible to build a canvas cyclorama of sorts which may be reasonably efficient).

THE FOURTH SIDE—THE FRONT

Summary

(*a*) The sides of the proscenium opening must be wide enough to mask adequate wing-space behind them.

(*b*) The proscenium opening should not be too high.

(*c*) Proscenium doors may be considered again as useful features.

(*d*) The edge of the proscenium side should be designed so that the ***proscenium corner*** comes on the ***proscenium line***. Failing this the narrowest part of the proscenium opening should never fall along any but the proscenium line.

(*e*) The relation of proscenium edge to the two outermost seats must be very carefully considered indeed.

(*f*) The systems of the false and inner prosceniums should be studied and their installation carefully considered.

NOTES

(*a*) The necessity for adequate wing space will be discussed in the consideration of the side walls later. An alternative, in small theatres, to wide proscenium sides is to keep the sides narrow but to plan the stage so as to be wider than the auditorium (see, for instance, Fig. 10).

(*b*) An application of the sight-line method will show the best height for the proscenium opening in any given circumstances. Scenery becomes very difficult to mask at the top if the proscenium is too high. Only in special circumstances is the proscenium of normal full-size theatres raised higher than 16 feet—just below the height of a full-size stage flat. However high the actual arch may be in fact it is cut down in practice by a pelmet or a proscenium border. In a small stage it may well be so low as just not to spoil the proportion of the actors.

How low that is depends upon the width of the stage opening—if it were only 12 feet wide, your actor might pass in an opening 7 feet 6 inches high, but if it were 24 feet wide he would look cramped in anything under 10 feet high.

(*c*) Doors in the proscenium side are an old and typically English tradition, and useful to-day, whether placed facing the auditorium and giving on to a forestage, or set facing on-stage in the thickness of a deep proscenium (the traditional way), especially for Elizabethan and Restoration plays or revues or any many-scened shows where forestage scenes are played while the main stage is being changed for the next scene.

(*d*) A full explanation of item (*d*) will be found in Section 11. The subject concerned is the shape or splay of the proscenium thickness at the sides of the opening. This question of splay is so intimately connected with sight-lines that no attempt will be made to explain it now.

(*e*) The relation of proscenium to side seats is discussed throughout the treatment of sight-lines. It should be emphasized here that no plan of any stage is complete or capable of just criticism *unless the two outermost seats of the auditorium are marked upon it in their proper positions.* We ought no more to think of making the plan of a stage and omitting the outermost seats than of making a drawing of a face and leaving out the eyes.

(*f*) False and inner prosceniums are dealt with in Sections 15, 16, and 17.

Finally, on the stage side of the proscenium wall is accommodated the prompt corner and (generally) the switchboard, though there are advantages in having the latter at the back of the auditorium if an adequate system of signalling can be maintained between electrician and stage-manager.

THE FIFTH AND SIXTH WALLS—THE SIDES

Summary

Concerning the side walls of the stage our three equally important first requirements are that they and the strips of floor adjoining—the wing spaces—be high enough, wide enough, and sufficiently equipped to allow packing, working, and waiting.

Notes

Here is the most congested part of a stage. The three functions of the sides—to accommodate packing, working, and waiting—must be very well studied.

To begin with, for proper working, the stage-manager must see the stage from his desk, where the log and prompt books are kept, where times are recorded, whence calls are sent, and where the signal switchboard is situated. This desk is on the stage side of the stage-left proscenium wall, and belongs perhaps more to the proscenium than to the side wall, for it is round the down-stage corner of the adjacent side of the set that the stage-manager watches his stage. It is an essential part to plan.

The descending ends of the working lines come down the side walls, but against the walls are also the packs of scenery. So congested is the wing space in a large theatre that the functions of packing and working are often divorced, and the packing of scenery will remain on the stage while the working of lines is taken up a story and put on a special gallery (called the fly-floor) built above the wing space high enough to be clear of the packs below.

In a small stage the fly-floor is impossible, so the lines are worked from the stage. It is generally better to have a pack of scenery on either side of the stage; it makes for quicker striking if the left side of the set is struck to, and packed against, the left wall, and *vice versa*. Hence it is often useful to divide the lines and to have the up-stage half on one side of the stage and the down-stage on the other, so that on either side a space is left clear for the packs.

It is further very useful to have a *live* pack and a *dead* pack each side so that, half-way through a show, the 'dead' scenery, which is not wanted again, is not confused with the 'live', still to be used. But two packs and a group of lines on each side wall are generally too much for a small stage if the pack is made in the most convenient way, that is with the flats leaning upon each other parallel with the wall, so a pack case (a reversion to an old system) may be useful, where the flats are slid in like books in a shelf at an angle to the wall, then the live flats can be kept at one end of the case and the dead at the other—but at least nine feet clear wing-space is needed for this.

Fortunately it is only in Wing-and-Cloth Sets and Box Sets that many flats are used, and these are types of set less to be recommended for village stages.

But the chief difficulty of packing on a village stage even with the simpler styles of set comes from the old bugbear, a pitch roof, for if, as is often recommended, the height of the house walls, to the spring of the roof, is 8 ft. 6 in., and two feet of that is cut off by the height of the stage, it is immediately clear that on the sides of the stage the walls affording packing space are only about six feet high, and the problem becomes impossible. Again the dormer shape is needed—and a dormer shape that, as was emphasized earlier, in its face carries up the walls of the house.

But it is not only flat scenery that must be packed, there are also rostrums (which must be made to fold), and steps (which can rarely be made to fold), and fireplaces and other built pieces.

Further, there are furniture packs and property packs, and though props may be carried to a prop-room in each strike, the shifting of furniture for long distances holds up a scene change, and furniture is best kept on the stage.

In all this congestion space must be left to the actors for their entrances, their exits, and their reasonable waiting for cues—reasonable, for though no actor should be on the stage unless his cue is imminent, he must not on the other hand leave his preparation too late.

Lastly, there still has to be found space for the electrician to set his side lamps and carry their cables to the nearest connecting point (which itself must not be buried beyond his reach—too often he finds his dip unreachable under a thoughtlessly assembled pack).

Entrance doors to a stage are generally best placed at the very extremities of the back wall—on the side walls they are too often buried under packs—but the 'dock doors' or scenery doors by which the stuff is got in from the workshop are best placed in the side walls: they are closed during a show and may well be buried. In a small stage scenery may have to be introduced by way of the auditorium when that is nearest to the street and no space for a back way is to be found; then the dock doors are unnecessary.

For Pure Curtain Sets little wing space, beyond that for occasional furniture and that for actors, is needed.

For Detail Sets more is needed, for working lines and small scenery packs in addition.

For Wing-and-Cloth Sets much is needed, for many lines and bigger packs.

For Box Sets some space is generally needed for a few flats and lines and a great deal for furniture.

For Cyclorama Sets the wider the cyclorama the more it will mask, so little packing space is usable up-stage on the sides. The packs have to be concentrated down-stage.

In summary, we may tabulate the points to be watched in stage plans as follows:

Stage
- Floor to be flat
- Floor correct height
- *Floor continuous to sides*
- *Very wide wing space*
- Possible traps
- To receive stage-screws

Roof
- *No pitch without dormer*
- *Every inch of headroom*
- No built-in means of curtain hanging

Back
- *Unbroken back wall*
- Plastered back wall
- Curved ends to back wall
- *Passage behind*

Front
- Wide proscenium sides
- Proscenium right height
- Proscenium doors possible
- Proscenium edge properly splayed
- *Outer seats properly placed*
- Inner and/or false proscenium

Sides
- *High enough, wide enough, and clear enough* to allow packing, working, and waiting

SECTION 7

THE OUTLINE OF A SPECIFIC 'STAGE BAY' FOR SMALL HALLS

Conceived solely to show that a hall cannot truly be said to possess a stage if you merely put a platform in it

It has been suggested that some firm of building contractors should put on the market a village hall in sections (e.g. Fig. 7), so that one could buy one, two, or more according to the size of hall required, or could add a section to an existing nucleus when occasion presented itself. There are many objections to such a project, but the idea does offer us an opportunity of discussing in a convenient way some of the desirable points in the stage of a small hall.

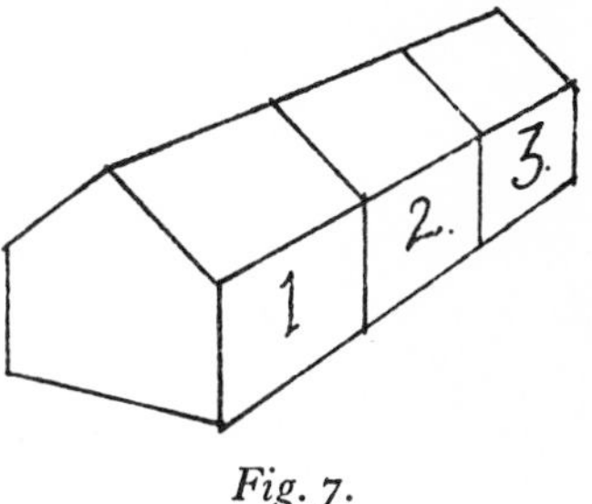

Fig. 7.

The idea in principle is not so modern as it may sound. According to Dr. Addy[1] the dawn of our whole domestic architecture passed through a not dissimilar phase when houses were not only built but valued 'by the bay'. The bay was an area of about 240 square feet, comprised between two neighbouring pairs of roof supports—crucks or crutches, or inverted 'forks', or gavels or gables. An extension of the house could be made by removing the end wall, adding another bay, and walling up again.

But what is interesting for us is that in this visionary, expansible, unit village hall we would recommend a specific unit for building-in should the hall require a stage.

[1] S. O. Addy, *The Evolution of the English House* (enlarged edition, Allen & Unwin, 1933).

This fact, together with a glance at the design of the unit, will probably do as much as a longer dissertation to emphasize the fact that to make a hall capable of use as a theatre it is not sufficient to build a platform—any more than the installation of a sink turns an attic into a photographer's darkroom. Instead, in the hall a complete 'workroom' must be

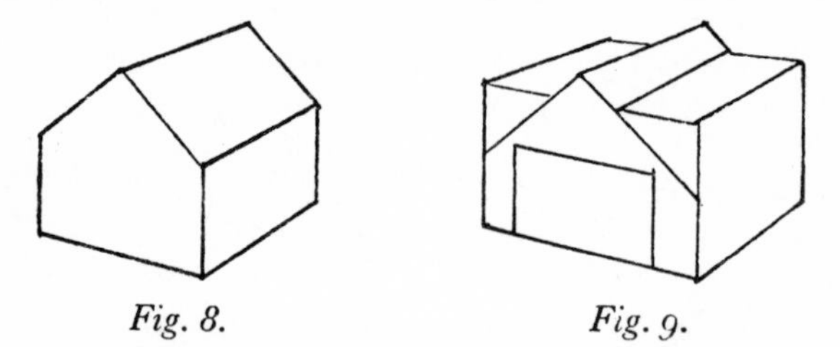

Fig. 8. *Fig. 9.*

planned and equipped, its four walls, its ceiling, as well as its floor, all designed and built with their use in view.

If now the shape of the normal unit were as in Fig. 8, then the 'specific stage unit for village halls' might be as in Fig. 9.

The height to the ridge is the same, the pitch of the roof the same, the depth or 'thickness' the same, but the width is

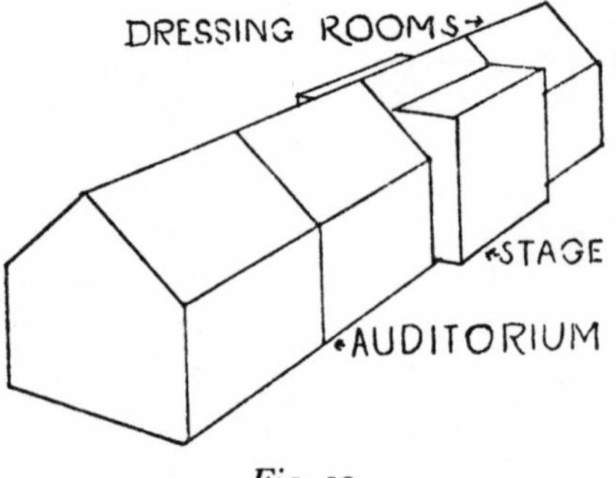

Fig. 10.

greater and the dormer shapes are now present in the roof. The proscenium is nearly as wide as the body of the hall to give better sight-lines, hence the extra width over all to allow adequate wing space.

Such a specific stage unit might be built directly on to the end of a normal unit, or set up with a gap of two or three feet and the gap walled in and roofed, so providing space for a forestage. Were a further normal section added after the stage, it again might be built directly on to the back or with a gap between, which would now serve as a way across behind the back of the stage, into which give the dressing-rooms.

In its simplest form, then, the normal exterior appearance of a village hall containing a stage could be conventionalized in the formula in Fig. 10.

And if that arrangement emphasized throughout British villages that a theatre is something more than a hall with a platform, its introduction into this book will have served its purpose, and the reader is ready to go on to consider the main theme.

CHAPTER TWO

Preliminary Points Concerning Sight-Lines

SECTION 8

THE PROSCENIUM AND ITS EFFECT

The outer spectators—the opening to be masked—the sides of the opening that mask

---

We now turn from generalities on stage planning to our special subject, the system of sight-lines. Since I leave generalities I must perforce narrow my approach. It was from the point of view of the designer of scenery that the system was worked out, and it is in those terms that it is most suitable for me to discuss it. For readers with another approach, the preliminary generalities should have offered some aid to reading from their particular point of view and making their own application of the system to their particular problems. I shall discuss the system; its application to special problems will be made best by those most familiar with them. In order to make the treatment complete in one place, two or three basic ideas will be touched on again.

No proper attitude towards the design of orthodox stage scenery is possible without an understanding of the proscenium opening, for, clearly, all scenery must be seen, and if it is outside the sight-lines it is out of the range of vision—and all sight-lines are dependent on the proscenium opening.

The proscenium is an obstacle to vision, and there are two ways with an obstacle: to circumvent it or to abolish it. To abolish the proscenium (in principle as well as in fact, for some abolish the arch and straightway return to its principle by putting up a substitute) is to necessitate a fresh theatrical style. There are certain types of show for which the accepted style is more suitable than a fresh one; for these it is not wise to abolish the proscenium, for suitability is the sweetness of an art.

The proscenium, then, is an accepted fact of the theatre to-day. It was not always so, and it may not be so in the future, but it is a feature of our own times. As such it behoves us not only to accept it but to understand it. Only then shall we be in a position to decide for or against experiments upon its nature and even its existence, and if we turn to them we shall go with surer steps.

The proscenium wall is a mask, it forms with its arch a frame. The proscenium is the fourth wall of a stage, dividing stage from audience, and through its opening the show is seen and is designed to be seen. Perhaps it is because one sees only what is through the opening, when the auditorium is dimmed and the show is on, that one is inclined to forget that there is a solid part to the proscenium wall as well as an opening, and that the stage is wider than the opening and lies behind the solid walls as well as behind the arch. This hidden or masked part of the stage is just as important for the working of the show as the acting-area. Every *acting-area* must be flanked by adequate *wing-space*, and that wing-space must be properly *masked*: part is masked by the proscenium, part by the setting. One of the functions of a setting is to mask all that part of a stage which is not at the moment 'acting-area'. But a set of scenery must stop somewhere, it cannot go on masking upwards and sideways for ever, so the proscenium arch is built to frame it, and behind the proscenium walls, out of sight of the audience, the scenery may stop. The arrangement is like a peep-show but with one important difference, that here is no tiny hole through which one eye may look, but maybe a sixteen by thirty foot opening through which many hundred eyes may see—eyes that must, be it noted, each one look from a different position and see from a different angle. The diversity of those angles of vision is a factor in set design; the most extreme angles govern the size of the scenery we set behind any given proscenium opening.

The principle of the proscenium arch then resembles that of a magnified peep-show where, through an opening in a wall of curtain or something more solid, a picture is seen of just so much of the multitude of materials behind as makes the setting for a given scene of the show. The scenery for other scenes, the apparatus used to move and support the scenery, the workmen, the waiting actors, and the furniture and properties of earlier and later scenes, will all be there behind the wall, but the spectator sees, through the opening, only the current scene. Its elements mask all the rest.

Let us see what this means: Imagine a square cardboard box with a rectangular opening cut low in one of the sides, Fig. 11. Just behind that opening is the acting-area, on which

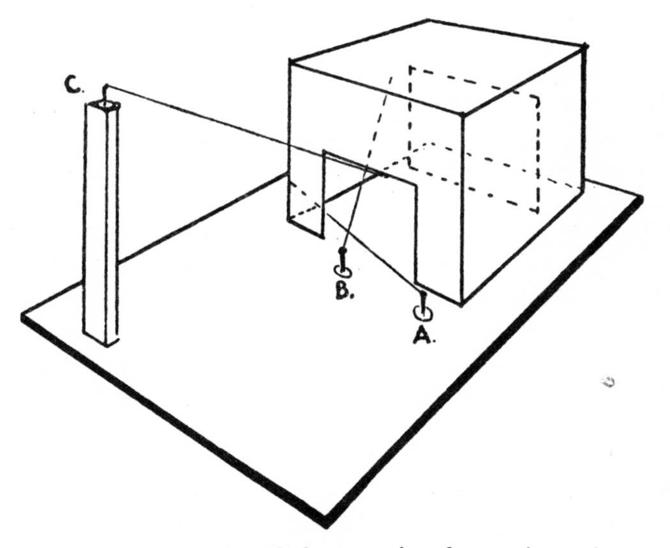

Fig. 11. The view through the proscenium from various points.

the players move. But the scenery for this stage must be something more elaborate than a backcloth behind the actors. Let us diminish ourselves to a couple of inches in height and walk to this box and stand at position *A*. Now, clearly, were there only a backscene behind the actors, we should be able to see, situate as we are at the side, diagonally across the stage and should have a clear view of the side wall of the box beyond, which has no connection with the set at all. A set designed for such conditions must have provision for masking the sides, yet the beginner tends constantly to overlook side-masking. One must learn to 'look sideways' at all scene designs.

Before we leave position *A*, another important point may

be made. Although we can see more than we need of the far side of the stage, what of the near side? We find that not only can we see nothing of the near side of the stage, but that our view of the background itself is restricted by the near side of the proscenium opening; this is true of all stages and we discover that the proscenium 'gets in the way' more than anything in the theatre. It is truly an obstacle and we begin to realize how rarely circumstances allow a set to present an equally good picture to every seat in the house.

We learn from position *A* that although we need to mask-in the far side of the stage, the near side on the contrary is masked from us. We have therefore to provide side-scenery, but we must work very carefully if we incorporate in its design any essential part of the set that needs to be seen by all, and we must seek to reduce the masked areas in the back corners of the set as much as possible, taking care that no important property or piece of furniture shall be lost in a masked area, which area, of course, differs in extent in different theatres according to the placing of the side seats.

Now let us walk to position *B*. We will forget the problem of the sides for a moment, but looking upward we are confronted with a still more difficult problem, for unless the background is exceedingly high we shall see over the top of it. There will be lights, battens, ropes, and what-not up there, that have nothing to do with the appearance of the show and are untidy distractions as far as the audience is concerned. It follows that in designing a set we have to mask-in the top as well as the sides.

Lastly, if our theatre is provided with a balcony, let us take a position relative to the highest seat and look down at the stage (from *C*). From here we are much more conscious of the stage floor, and may find that we shall have to incorporate the stage-cloth, or floor cover, into our set and paint a pattern on it. Looking up to the background of the set we find that the upper part of it is cut off—masked by the proscenium border, or top part of the opening—and it may be, in certain difficult theatres, that only the feet are visible of the actor who moves up-stage. Summarizing our knowledge, we find that the setting designer, beside thinking of a background, must think in at least two other dimensions—sideways and upwards (and perhaps downwards). From any but a certain number of centrally situated seats the vision of his set is restricted.

The proscenium, then, offers a difficulty that must be considered and solved in each individual case.

SECTION 9

THE NATURE OF A PLAN AND A SECTION

(*A note for those who find the language of plans obscure*)

Plan and section—the correlation of plan and section—the elevation—conventional plan-symbols

---

(To many people the language of plans and sections is clear; to many it presents stumbling blocks that they have never mastered, so that they are left with inconsistencies in their means of expression that may remain all their lives, a permanent confusion to themselves and to others. It is for the latter that the following section is inserted.)

It is with the study of the proscenium that we shall concern ourselves, and the whole principle of this book is that our study is made by means of a scale *plan* and a scale *section* of the proscenium wall and certain points relative to it. These two drawings will proffer, upon the application of sight-lines, answers to all questions concerning the dimension and placing of scenery.

To draw an object *in plan* or *in section* is to make a representation of it according to certain, very simple, accepted conventions. Though simple, they must be observed; and to ignore them may lead to hopeless confusion, yet some designers and many producers are quite incapable of stating themselves clearly in a plan or section and nearly as incapable of reading them.

A *ground plan* represents a version of the floor upon which an object stands, with the areas and positions of the various elements marked upon it. It is further to be noticed that a ground plan may also include representations of objects situated, not on the floor, but above it. Here at once is an asset, and a stumbling-block, to beginners. All relevant objects can be represented on a ground plan whatever their height above the ground. Once one is familiar with this convention one accepts it for its very usefulness and soon learns to avoid confusion, but at first it is disconcerting to discover two apparently similar rectangles drawn on a plan, one of which stands for a hearthrug and the other for the top of an eight-foot rostrum—or to find two similar lines, one representing a groundrow and the other a border sixteen feet above it. But in practice little confusion arises—and where it might occur there are, as we shall find, clarifying symbols to set the matter right.

Fig. 12.

All things on a plan are stated in terms of length and breadth. Everything is seen as it were vertically from above. With the aspect from the horizontal level the plan never concerns itself.

So far as the walls of a room are concerned, it is generally fairly well understood how their lengths, their corners, their breaks-forward and breaks-back, are represented. It is rather with such elements as doors and staircases, which in everyday life are generally thought of in terms of height, that the beginner's difficulties come; it is about these that he must control himself, not trying to put too much in his plan. *On a plan only horizontal planes are fully represented.*

In making a ground plan of such a detail as Fig. 12, the kind of sketch represented at the top corner of Fig. 13 is practically useless, yet one is again and again handed instructions for set-plans in just such equivocal terms, even by experienced producers in whom ignorance of the language of plans is scandalous. The proper statement is shown in Fig. 14. To the uninitiated 13 may seem to convey more than 14; he may observe, and truly, that in 14 no representation is made at all, that the opening is arched—but that is the way of plans, they only represent horizontal planes. We are concerned, however, not to show in what respects 14 fails to give as much as 13 but in what respects it shows more, and speaks more clearly, than 13, which respects far outweigh the others. To begin with, it is not clear in 13 whether one is to follow the evidence of the steps and put the opening in the side wall, or the evidence of the opening and put it in the back wall, or whether or not there is a landing at the top of the steps with the door opening

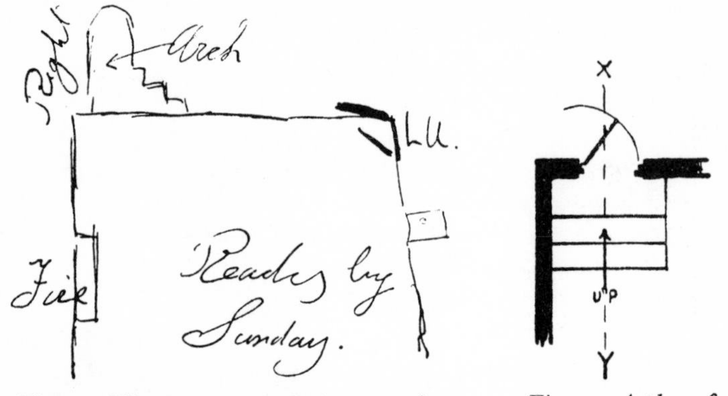

Fig. 13. The wrong method of representing Fig. 12 in plan.

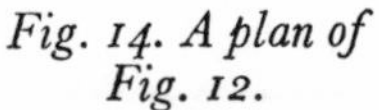

Fig. 14. A plan of Fig. 12.

off the side of it. Moreover, in 14 the length of each step is shown and the amount of floor-space the whole stair takes up is clearly seen. That the opening has a thickness is also stated in 14, so is the side on which the door hinges and the floor area the door covers when it swings. It may be objected that it is not clear in 14 whether the door sill is situated below the floor level with the steps leading down to it, or above the floor with the steps leading up. This is one of those points concerning relative levels about which it is useful to have an explanatory symbol on a plan. Here we settle it by the arrow and the word UP. Finally it may be objected that 14 shows neither the height of the steps nor of the opening. The answer is that it is not the purpose of a plan to be concerned with heights, that is the affair of the section, and it makes for very much clearer thinking if the functions of the two be never confused.

We shall concern ourselves with the language of plans in more detail later; here we need only notice one further point in Fig. 14: an architect's plan of a room differs at first sight from a scene-designer's plan of a room, because whereas the walls of a house have considerable thickness, those of a setting rarely exceed one inch; so the architect represents a wall as a thick black line corresponding in width to the thickness of the wall, the scene-designer's wall is a thin line and the thickness-pieces which show at such places as door openings are false thicknesses—mere boards screwed on behind to give an effect—and are represented as in Fig. 15.

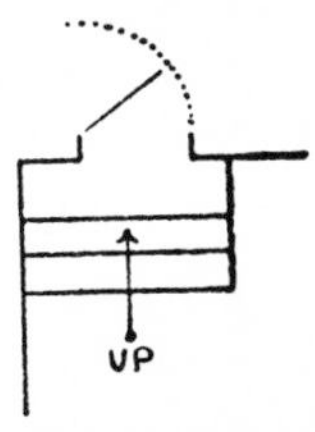

Fig. 15. A scene-plan of Fig. 12.

We are, however, concerned to establish only one point, that a ground plan deals with horizontal planes; it deals with flat things.

A drawing in section deals with upright things and with heights primarily. A plan shows always both the length and breadth of an object; it is from the section you read its height (incidentally, from the section you may also read, if you wish, *either* its width *or* its length—but not both—according to the way it is placed).

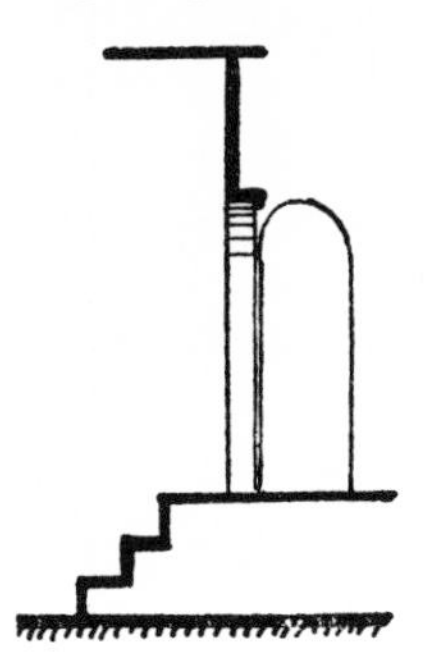

Fig. 16. A section at XY *on Fig. 14.*

In the sense in which we shall use the word in this book a section, or drawing in vertical section, is, roughly speaking, the representation of an object as it would be if sliced in two, longitudinally and vertically, opened, and looked at from the side. The line along which the slicing takes place may be the centre line or main axis of the object, or it may be an arbitrary line drawn across the plan in such a position as will give the most information about the object to an inquirer. For instance, if the designer wishes to show the height of the door, wall, and stair in Fig. 14 he may decide to make the section at the centre line of the door, which he indicates as *XY*, say, on his plan, then he makes his sectional drawing which he calls 'the section at *XY*'.

This drawing might be as in Fig. 16. Notice here that the door has been opened wide and so helps to show the shape of the doorhead. Further, that the opening itself is arched, is summarily indicated by the horizontal lines across the thickness of the opening which begin at the spring of the arch and grow increasingly close together as they approach the summit. Occasionally it is useful to show the edges of such parts as are cut through in thicker lines, corresponding in thickness with the thickness of the part.

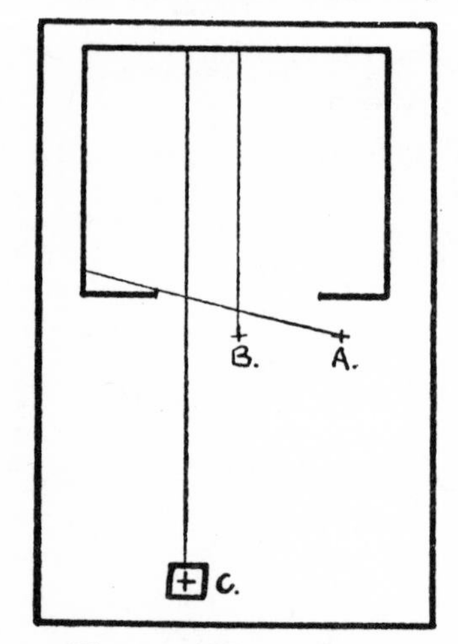

Fig. 17. A plan of Fig. 11.

Turning back to Fig. 11 we can represent the effect of those sight-lines in a more useful way now in this plan and section language, as shown in Figs. 17 and 18. Notice in Fig. 17 how clearly the plan shows the sight-line from *A*, because that is in the horizontal plane, but how, for any adequate representing of the lines from *B* and *C*, we must turn to the section in the other figure, because these are in the vertical plane. It is impossible to represent line *A* legibly in section at all.

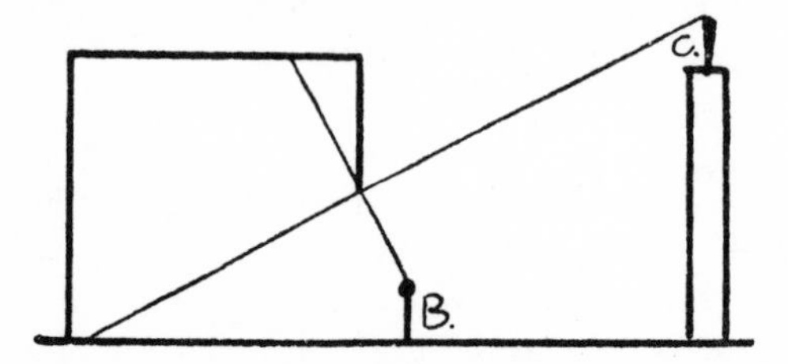

Fig. 18. A section of Fig. 11.

It is useful to notice (Fig. 19) that a section bears a particular relation to a plan drawn to the same scale if the plan be laid sideways beneath it. Certain information can then be projected from one to the other and the parts will correspond.

By comparison (or *correlation*) of these two complimentary two-dimensional drawings an understanding of the three-dimensional nature of an object is gained.

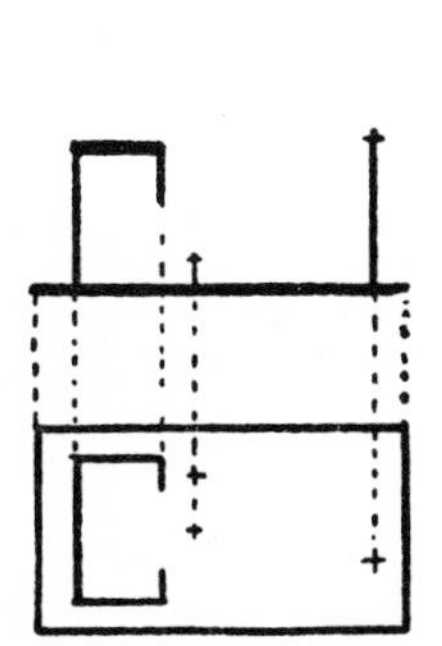

Fig. 19. The relationship between plan and section (correlation).

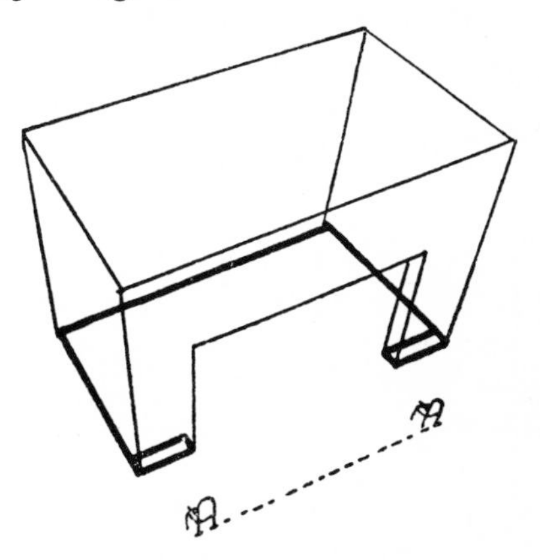

Fig. 20. Diagram of a stage seen from above.

We shall be so frequently concerned with the plan and section of a stage in the following pages that it will be convenient to reduce each to a symbol where the essentials are retained, and which can become as intimately a part in our consideration of the theatre as a form of speech in our daily life.

Fig. 20 gives the evolution of our plan-symbol. Here a stage is viewed from a high angle and emphasis is laid upon those lines which go to form our ground plan. In Fig. 21 those lines are abstracted from the rest and seen now, as it were, flat from above. With the thickness of the back wall and the side walls we are not concerned, but with the thickness of the proscenium wall we shall be very much concerned and so it is represented in double lines. This is our conventional plan-symbol of a stage.

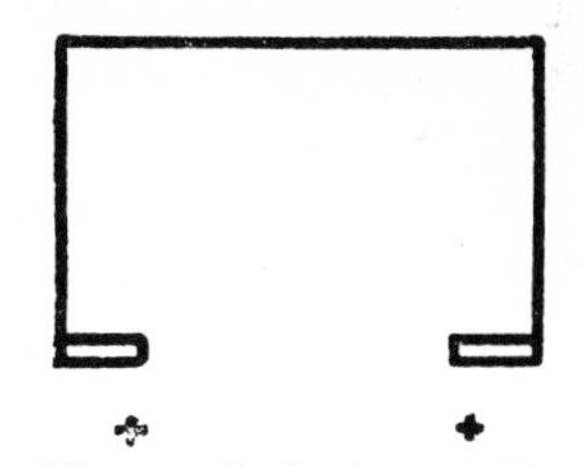

Fig. 21. Reduction of Fig. 20 to a conventional plan-symbol.

Fig 22 is a view of a stage cut down the centre line, and Fig. 23 a reduction in the same way as before to an essential section-symbol, representing the floor of the stage, the back wall, the roof above, the top part of the proscenium above the opening, with its thickness, and the nearest spectator's eye exactly at the intersection of the cross.

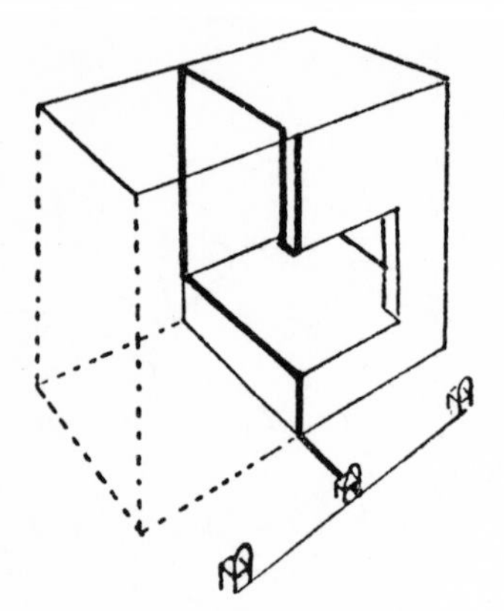

Fig. 22. Diagram of a stage cut vertically down the centre line.

These two symbols properly made and used are our essential companions in our study of stages and settings.

To complete this note of the conventional representations of an object we may include a third form of drawing, the drawing *in elevation*, but this is more rarely needed in the design of settings (Fig. 6 showed a stage in elevation). It is of considerable use, in designing sets containing several rostrums, to indicate the relative heights of these, but for straight sets the elevation may seriously lead astray, since it deals with an aspect of an object that is far too easily thought of as a 'view'. It is too easy to form a false belief that the elevation shows the *appearance* of an object. The elevation is a combination of parts of the information in the plan and section so as to give them again this time as they might, under certain very limited conditions, appear from the front (or back or side, if it is a back or side elevation) and it includes all dimensions of height and of width but does not in any respect represent depth. It is a view of the elements, *but with no perspective relation.* It is therefore a very misleading view to those who suppose it conveys the actual appearance of a set or building. In an elevation, strictly

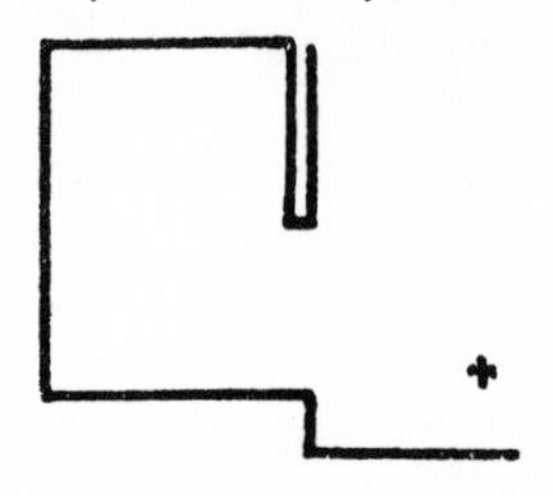

Fig. 23. Reduction of Fig. 22 to a conventional section-symbol.

speaking, only one plane should be represented; even if it is extended to show objects in different planes, all objects of the same size are represented the same size as if they were on the same plane even though one may be much farther from the spectator than another; just as in a plan, all is reduced to the same plane. A drawing in elevation, then, is merely another conventional method of stating about an object or group of objects all the facts concerning two out of the three dimensions:

the elevation covering height and width but not depth;
the plan covering width and depth but not height;
the section covering height and depth but not width.

The elevational drawing is, in scene design, mostly used to state the elements and sizes of a single piece or row of pieces of scenery for the carpenter, not to give an appearance of the whole set on the stage. It carries no information at all relative to sight-lines.

I have mentioned the slovenliness and confusion that surrounds the language of plans in the theatre. The following 'vocabulary' of symbols (Fig. 24) for objects most widely used in plans makes some attempt to clear this up.

A. B. C. D. E. F.

Fig. 24. Conventional plan-symbols of scenery.

The line indicating a wall or row of flats (*A*) should bear indications of the joins between the flats so that their number and the size of each flat can be clearly seen.

A fireplace (*B*) is generally set on the on-stage side of the flats and a window (*C*) on the off-stage side: the symbols for the two can be clearly distinguished if each is represented on its proper side of the flat. A bay in a wall is simply represented as in *G*, and a bay window as in *H*.

A plain flat is more clearly stated if a tick at either end marks its length (*D*), and this good habit becomes a necessity in representing a profiled wing flat (*E*), when the point at which the profile joins the flat is of vital importance to the drawing of sight-lines, for the sight-lines must be taken, not through the outer limit of the profiling, which may of course be cut back at some point right to the stile of the flat, but through the point at which the profile joins the solid flat.

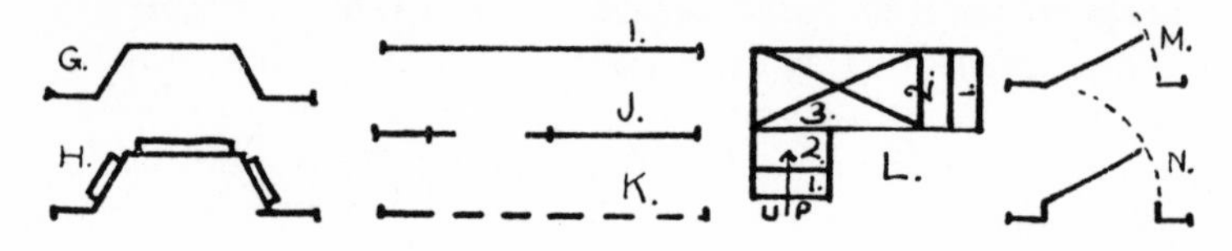

Fig. 24 (cont.). *Conventional plan-symbols of scenery.*

Similarly a backcloth or groundrow is a straight line (*I*), but a cutcloth should be represented by a line broken to show the narrowest part of the opening, and ticked to indicate the widest (*J*).

A border (*K*) is best represented exactly like a backcloth but in dotted lines (a useful convention always for signifying that any object on a plan is in a considerably different plane from the rest).

SETTEE
TABLE
SMALL TABLE
LAMP
ORDINARY CHAIR
ARM CHAIR

Fig. 25. Conventional plan-symbols of furniture.

In representing a rostrum it is often useful to put in the diagonals across the rectangle for clarification (*L*). When steps are represented it is very useful to number the different treads, otherwise it is always uncertain whether the top tread is level with the rostrum (as in the steps at the end in *L*) or one step below (as in the steps in front).

It is highly desirable that doors, flush or revealed, should be represented as in *M* and *N*, instead of by some semi-elevational anomaly. The dotted line illustrates the swing of the door edge as it opens, and warns one whether the door will strike some adjacent object in use.

Curtains (*F*) are distinguished from cloths and flats by representing them with a wavy line.

The commonest elements of furniture are simply represented, Fig. 25. The symbol of a complete rectangle should only be used for stools and tables, chairs should be represented by back and sides only, so that it may be clear which way they face.

It would most materially make for clarity if the above very simple symbols were used consistently in the theatre as the basis of a logical plan-language.

SECTION 10

THE NON-MASKING TRIANGLE

The elements of a typical small set—the placing of the border—on estimating the amount of curtain for a set

To begin our study of sight-lines let us take the simplest set of curtains upon a small stage. Besides providing a useful introduction to our subject, it will bring us more clearly than any other approach to the *non-masking triangle.* The non-masking triangle we must learn to recognize immediately the sight-lines betray it, for it always indicates a fault in our arrangement. It will come cropping up even in our most advanced work. A wary eye must be kept for its danger-signal and its warning must never be disregarded.

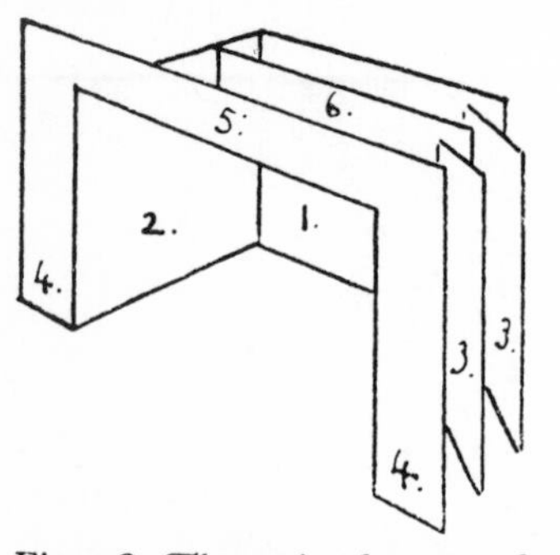

Fig. 26. The main elements of setting.

The elements of a typical setting that concern us in the study of sight-lines are as follows (Fig. 26):

The *background,* which may be a curtain, a wall of flats, a back-cloth, or a cyclorama (1).

The *sides,* which may be of curtain, of flats set in a continuous wall, or of flats or curtain strips set at angles to form wings (2 and 3).

Masking the front edge of these 'sides' come the two uprights of the proscenium, the *proscenium sides,* which may be, in a simple fit-up, of curtain and mere 'returns' of the set sides, and in a full theatre are the lower parts of the proscenium wall itself (4).

Connecting these across at the top and so framing the set is the *proscenium top*, either a curtain border in the case of a fit-up, or the built arch or transom in an equipped theatre (5).

The *border* (or borders) of the set itself, which prevent spectators seeing up (or, in special cases, a *ceiling* designed for the same purpose) (6).

We begin by taking the simple sectional statement of a stage as in Fig. 27.

It will be clear that, instead of drawing it freely and with little regard for the proportion and relation of its parts, one can draw it to the scale of a given stage, so as to represent in exact relation the depth of that stage, the height of the proscenium opening, and the position in regard to these of the spectator's eye in the front row of the stalls. If, on such a scale drawing, we find (according to the method I am going to outline) that the ideal positions of a border and a back curtain are here and there, we have only to mark them and measure them and we have, not only their depth or height, but their necessary distance back from the proscenium, and so we know where to hang them; and any further line we may make according to the principle of sight-lines can be measured on the drawing to a degree of accuracy sufficient for all practical purposes.

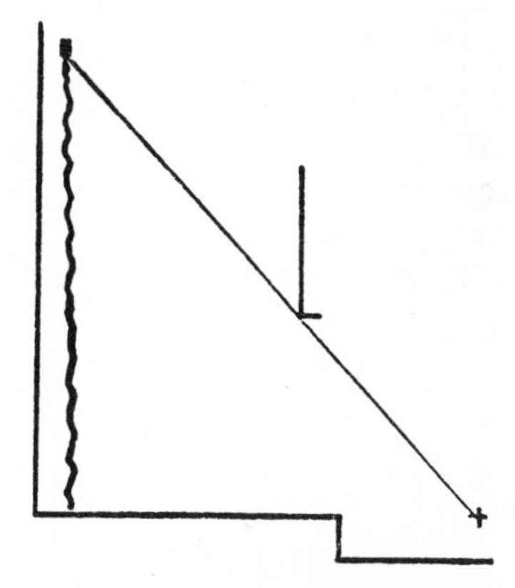

Fig. 27. The upper sight-line conditioning the height of the back curtains.

If, upon this scale-symbol of the stage, we draw a line from the spectator's eye-point through the edge of the top of the proscenium opening we have the *upper sight-line*, which would give the height of curtains for any position on the stage, near to the footlights or far back (Fig. 27), though this is modified by another factor as we shall see in a minute. We have to ask now: What governs the position on a stage of the back curtains? A variety of factors in each case, but speaking generally we may say that they should be at least 2 ft. 6 in. from the back wall of the stage to allow for entrances from the back. We can represent them at this position on a section and read off the height of curtain for any given stage. At present, however, we are being extravagant in our length of curtain. If we can afford such a length and if our stage headroom is sufficient to allow our hanging it, very well and good, but if either of these considerations presents an obstacle we must shorten our curtains and add a border.

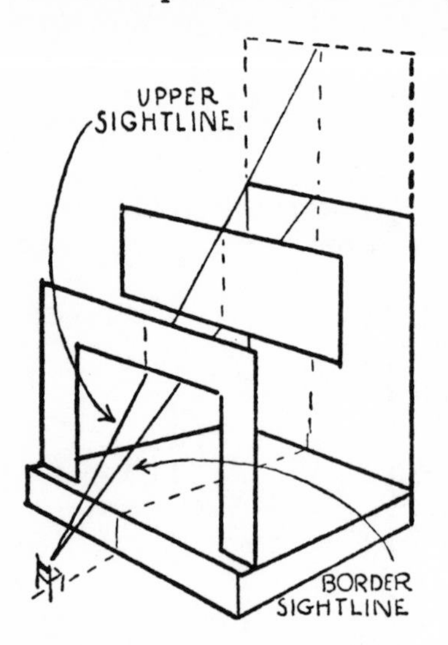

Fig. 28. The significance of a border.

Fig. 28 gives an idea of the effect of a border. It is clear that the upper sight-line without a border demands back curtains of a height indicated by the dotted lines; but the border's edge gives a *border sight-line* that enables us to use a lower backcloth. And notice that the amount of material we save on the backcloth is more than the amount we spend on the border, and the nearer the border is to the proscenium, the narrower it need be to mask the same amount of backcloth.

If we return to the section, however, we should find, after some practice, that there are certain features to preclude our bringing the border too far down-stage. To begin with let us mark the border at about half-way up-stage, as in Fig. 29, and consider the position.

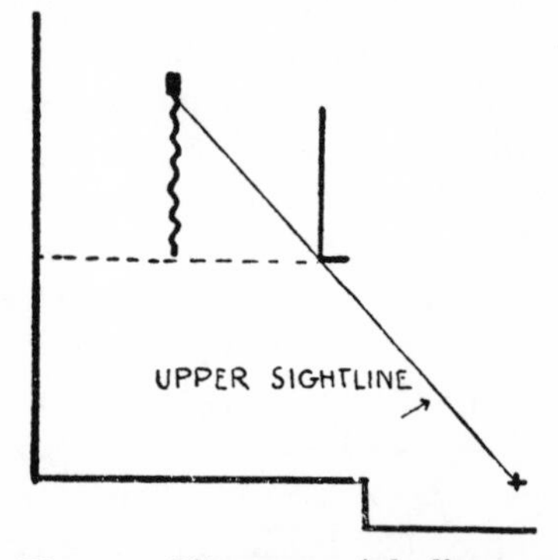

Fig. 29. The upper sight-line conditions the height of a border.

It is important to note at this moment that *a border must*

reach, at its top, just above the upper sight-line or we shall be able to see over it. In the figures the batten on which a curtain is hung is shown in each case in section, as a small black rectangle at the top of the curtain. This batten must always be out of sight.

We have now to inquire: At what particular point in the upper sight-line is it most advantageous and economical to hang a border, and what is the most useful depth for that border? *To be most economical the border must reach down to about the level of the proscenium arch.* If it is higher, the border sight-line is raised and the back curtains must be correspondingly longer. If it is lower we do not generally speaking economize because a lower border cuts off the back of the stage from the spectators in the gallery, and also it may cast an area of shadow up-stage from the lights in the proscenium or No. 1 batten. We may, then, make a rule that borders must be level with, or just about, the proscenium top, or with the proscenium border that fills in the top of the arch.

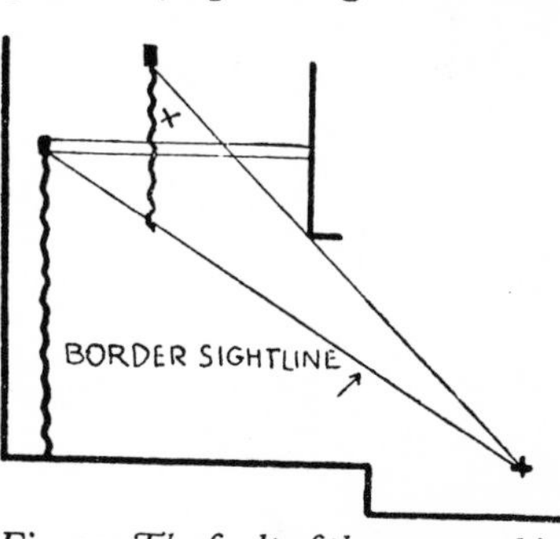

Fig. 30. The fault of the non-masking triangle. Note well.

If then the depth of a border is from a point just above the sight-line to a point about level with the proscenium top, what is the rule for its distance up-stage from the proscenium? Let us consider the border in the position indicated in Fig. 29, where the depth and the height above the stage seem satisfactory, and see if there are any faults in regard to its placing. In Fig. 30 we add the back curtains to Fig. 29; the height of the back curtains is decided by the border sight-line, they must reach up high enough to cut it. Let us indicate also the height of the side curtains, which, if we adopt the type of curtain-hanging described in *Stage-Setting*, will be the same as that of the back curtains, and is indicated by a horizontal double line drawn across, from back of the stage to front, at the level of the back curtain batten, in the figure.

We have now laid bare a most undesirable evil. We have drawn the scene-designer's bugbear: the non-masking triangle. Distinguish it carefully. There are three lines to watch, the vertical *line of the border*, the horizontal *line of the side-curtain-top*, and the diagonal *upper sight-line*. They form a triangle in front of the border. There is a cross in this triangle to mark it for your attention. The occurrence of this triangle, in any section you can draw of a stage-setting, indicates that there is an error in the arrangement of the parts which should be corrected at once. It shows that the set does not mask, and that the spectator would see over that part of the side that makes the base of that triangle.

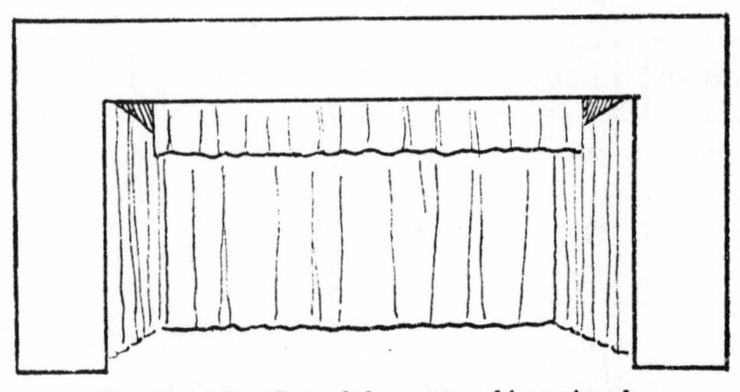

Fig. 31. The effect of the non-masking triangle.

Fig. 31 shows what the spectator sees if we set a stage according to the lines in Fig. 30. You notice the sides do not mask at the top in front of the border.

To avoid this non-masking triangle in Fig. 31, we must correct the lines in the section and there are three alternative remedies possible:

(1) To bring our border down-stage, that is, nearer to the audience.

(2) To increase the height of the side curtains.

(3) To do both.

To begin, let us bring our border nearer to the audience. This is represented in Fig. 32 where *A* is the old position of the border and *B* the new. The first result is that the upper half of our border is, in the new position, unnecessary—it is above the upper sight-line and therefore cannot be seen and may be cut away. But much more important is it that the movement of the border forward has allowed our border sight-line to rise, and now the top of the back curtain is exposed, and our set does not mask. So we must return and try the second remedy of increasing the height of the curtains. But before we leave Fig. 32 the reader may have this question: Surely, if instead of reducing the depth of your border, you were to move it uncut to its new position and then lower it, its top would still be above the upper sight-line and it would now be deep enough to mask the top of the back curtains; would not that solve the whole thing?

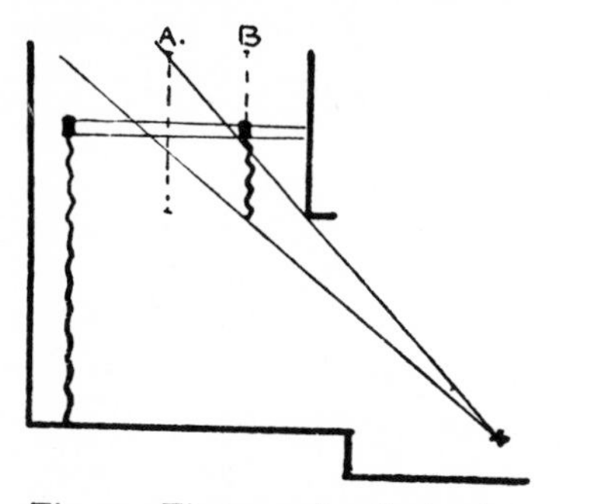

Fig. 32. First remedy: the border forward.

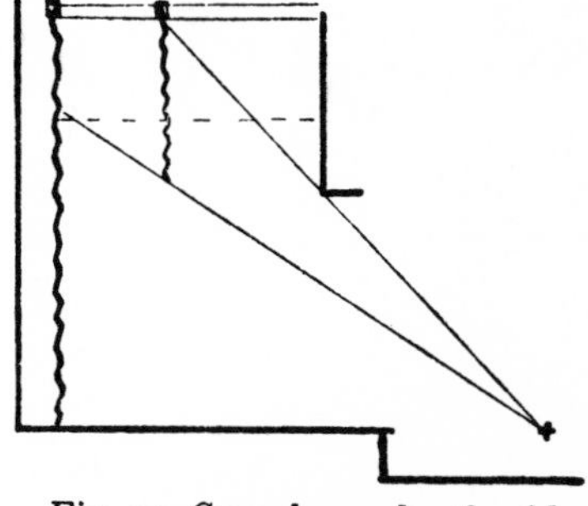

Fig. 33. Second remedy: the side curtains raised.

Almost, but not quite. It would entail the old difficulty of a border hanging below the proscenium arch. It would present a solution but not a perfect one, and only for such stages as were high enough to allow the border to drop below the proscenium arch and yet neither come uncomfortably near the heads of the actors, nor unduly restrict the light from No. 1 batten, nor cut down too much the sight-line from the gallery. It would be no more than a part solution because it would break our rule that the border should hang to about the level of the proscenium top. If the stage is small, one must grudge every inch that reduces it still further. Let us then look for a better solution, which will not entail a too-low border.

We turn to the second remedy of increasing the height of the curtains themselves to get rid of that non-masking triangle, marked *X* in Fig. 30.

In Fig. 33 we have raised the side curtains and the back curtains to the level of the top of the border, and again we seem to have a solution. But it is a wasteful solution. If we follow the border sight-line to the back curtain we remark that the upper part of the back curtain is never seen: it is higher than it need be. The reader may again suggest a point. He will say (perhaps impatiently) that the obvious thing is to retain the side curtains at this height and have the back curtains not so high. The patience he saves by this hurried solution would be more than offset by the patience he would have to spend later when he came to set up, on the stage, an arrangement for hanging curtains of different heights. No; there is one exact solution to the problem, and one exact answer for each particular stage; let us make a third essay for a perfect disposition of the parts.

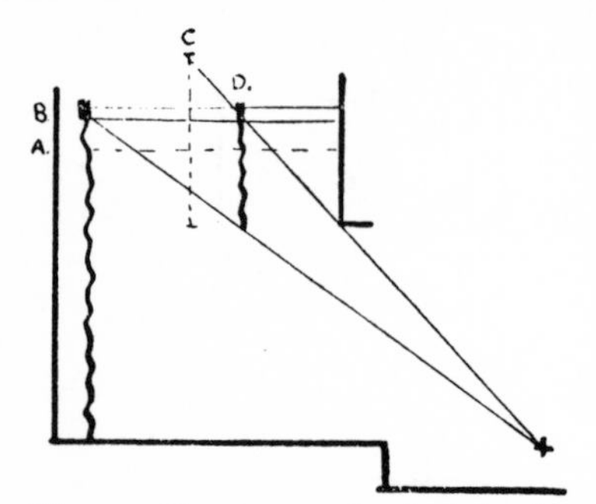

Fig. 34. Correct remedy: both border and side curtains adjusted.

In Fig. 34 we combine both these remedies: we raise the curtains a little, from position *A* to position *B*, and move the border forward a little from position *C* to position *D*.

Let us take stock. Comparing Fig. 30 with Fig. 34 we see we have eliminated the non-masking triangle, and have so arranged our parts that:

(1) The border top is just above the upper sight-line.

(2) The border top and the top of the side curtains intersect the upper sight-line at the same point (*D*).

(3) The border hangs down to about the level of the proscenium opening.

(4) The border sight-line cuts the back curtain at its top, and

(5) that top is level with the top of the side curtains.

Unless these five points are truly observed, any plan for the hanging of curtains on any stage is guilty either of not masking or of being wasteful of material.

In all satisfactory solutions we shall find that the place of the border is a little *below* half-way between the proscenium and the back curtains, that is to say, a little down-stage of the half-way line.

An examination of Fig. 35 will serve as a brief *résumé* of the above. It offers a comparative example of how arrangements that will turn out badly on the stage betray themselves on a sectional drawing to those who can read the evidence.

The appearance of a correct sectional drawing is shown at *A*, on the left. There nothing is wrong and the scheme strikes

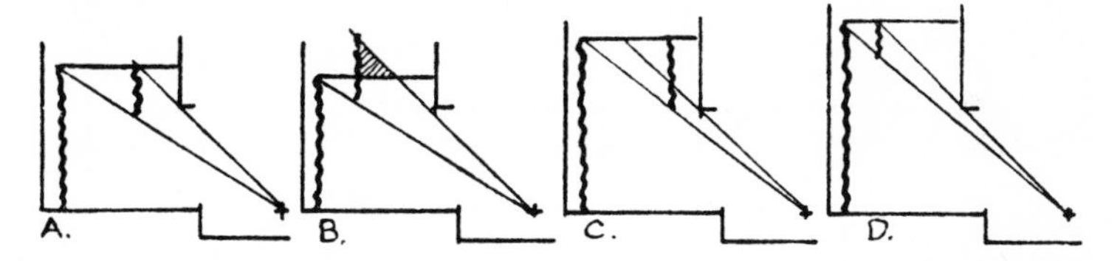

Fig. 35. A comparison of good and bad sections. The correct arrangement is on the left.

the knowing eye as sound at once. A section giving the configuration of *B* is condemned straight away; it shows a non-masking triangle, emphasized here with shading; the intersection of border-top with upper sight-line is not on the line of the side-curtain top. The appearance of *C* makes it suspect immediately, there is another triangle that ought not to be there, this time behind the border. It tells us there is a waste in this arrangement and that the curtains could be lower. You will notice that although the designer has arranged his border near enough to the front of the stage to make the border sight-line cut the top of the back curtain, as it should, yet he has been forced thereby to raise the border batten (and consequently the sides) above the upper sight-line in order to make them aline with the top of the too-long back curtains. He has broken the rule that border, upper sight-line, and side-curtain top should all intersect at the same point.

In *D* the border strikes the eye at once as being too far up-stage, and not 'just before the mid-point'; this arrangement masks all right, and the designer has made his border no deeper than it need be for masking, but were he to bring it down-stage and re-arrange his parts as in *A* he would save, even in a small set, possibly ten yards of curtain in the reduction in height of the sides and back. He has broken the rule that the border should hang about level with the proscenium arch.

On a large stage it will of course be necessary to increase the number of borders. Six or even more may be needed. But with any number of borders the principle still holds, see for example Fig. 36. Concerning this figure, it may be asked: Why not have only two borders and have them deeper?

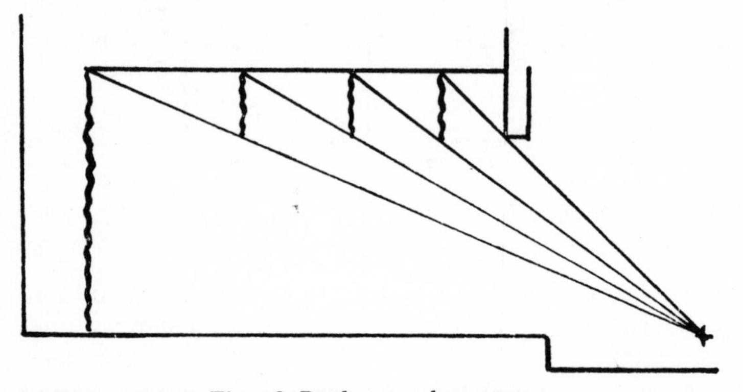

Fig. 36. Borders on a large stage.

If we hung such a stage with only two borders the height of the curtains necessary to avoid the non-masking triangle (Fig. 37) would be very much increased and would entail an expense increasing in a rising ratio with the increase in size of the stage.

There is one optimum position for any given set of circumstances. Notice in Fig. 36 how, on a large stage, the most economical arrangement gives us a set of borders hanging at increasing intervals as we go up-stage. All the intervals are different and this method allows each to be calculated to a nicety.

Though the general rule, especially for small stages, is to keep the borders as few as possible, yet in some circumstances it may be desirable to have more and shallower borders. On the professional stage travelling companies who visit a series of different theatres carry standard size borders of six feet deep. The number and height of these can be varied for different theatres, the principle being to use as little of them as one must to mask. This is occasionally wasteful in point of fact but it is quicker than making special borders every time to fit each set of scenes on each stage. It is the most practical and speedy way out, though every border involves the expense of a special batten of lights behind it to keep the next border up-stage lit in the same key as the first.

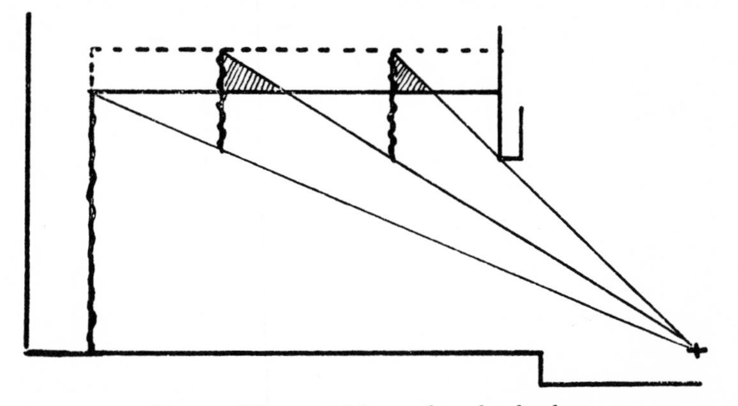

Fig. 37. The wastefulness of too few borders.

On a small stage we cannot often allow ourselves the luxury of a margin of safety, for even if we could afford it financially, rarely is the planning and the space adequate, and surplus material becomes nothing but an embarrassment.

From the above study of the section we are now in a position to decide, for any given small stage, the following points: the height and position of the back curtains, the height of the side curtains, and the best number and depth of borders together with the position of each, and we are able to be certain that these sizes are large enough to mask completely and yet small enough to involve no waste. What more information do we need to be able to draw up a full and final specification for the exact minimum amount of curtain that should be ordered for a given stage?

We need to measure the perimeter of the acting-area so as to get a width for our curtains. That perimeter or shape of acting-area can be examined very simply and fully if we turn from the section to the plan of the stage. We require, to represent this plan to scale, the width of the proscenium opening and of the wing-space. The depth of the stage we know already. We have decided on the position of the back curtains, and there remains their total width and the width and placing of the sides. We draw the plan to scale, and indicate upon it whatever plan-shape of curtains is most suitable to our purpose, Fig. 38, then measure this shape on the plan,

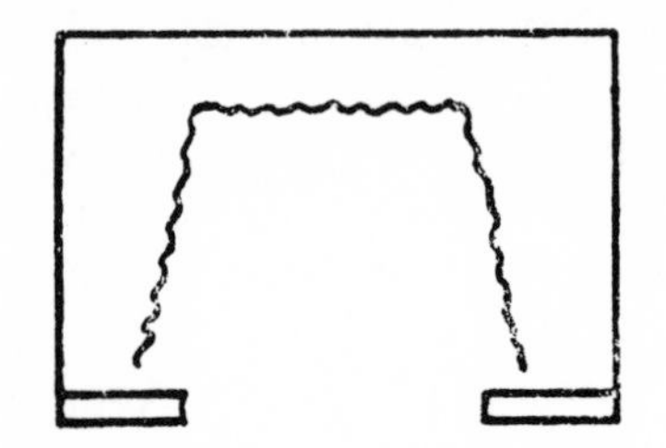

Fig. 38. Plan of a curtain surround.

reading off so much for the back, and so much for the two sides, adding these together so as to get the full length of curtain-run round the acting-area. Supposing our curtains are hung in strips as recommended in *Stage-Setting* and these are to be gathered in folds so that the resultant strips are each three feet wide, we have only to divide our length of curtain-run in feet by three and we have the number of curtains. We shall overlap each curtain strip upon its neighbour for a space of two or three inches, and the sum of these overlaps we must add to our length of curtain-run. There remains to calculate the length needed for border or borders, and for any extra curtains we may need for division into special narrow strips, or for backings, traverses, and so forth, and then we can add up the number of yards and find out the size of our order.

CHAPTER THREE
Sight-Lines and Small Stages

SECTION 11

THE EIGHT ESSENTIAL MEASUREMENTS

On measuring-up a stage—the rules for the Eight Measurements—notes on the rules—an interlude on the design of the proscenium edge

---

The foregoing was an introduction to the idea of sight-lines and the information to be extracted by their help from plans and sections. We have now to make precise and develop this method of working so that it shall give a sure and certain guide for the fitting of every style of setting to any size of stage.

We now leave the small hall with its simple curtain set and consider next a more fully equipped Little Theatre type and the styles of setting used there. It is clear from what we have seen in the last section that the dimensions of scenery and the number of pieces in a set depend on the sight-lines of the theatre, and that these in turn depend on certain measurements of the proscenium opening and of the distance therefrom of certain key points.

We have now to answer two questions: Exactly what measurements are necessary? How do we use them when we have them? It is the purpose of this and the next section to answer the first question, and of Sections 13 and 14 to answer the second.

It will be clear that, to make a full plan and section of a stage, there is needed a vast number of measurements, and the result may well be a set of drawings of considerable detail. Further, it will be clear that theatres differ in their architectural features and in their equipment, and some would need more measurements than others. We are not, however, faced with the need for a full plan and section (very useful though it may be to have them on one's studio wall), we may extract all that is necessary from something more simple. But we must know very clearly what may be safely left out, what is absolutely essential, and what may be in certain circumstances desirable but in others unnecessary.

There is in the general run of full-size theatres a certain number of features upon whose measurements the sizes of pieces of scenery depend and these features can be codified; they form a list of about twenty points, and with the rest we need never concern ourselves.

There is, moreover, in all theatres—not only in the general run of full-size theatres but in every theatre-building in existence, shaped on normal lines, down to the simplest army-hut with a temporary fit-up—a minimum group of eight measurements every one of which is absolutely essential to a scene-designer. If one of these is missing or inaccurate he cannot produce satisfactory plans for scenery. It will therefore be convenient to divide our measurements into two groups: those which are essential in any circumstances and those which are necessary in some. When we come to work on a job we must see that every measurement in the first group is taken; and the contents of the second group we must so arrange that we may easily see in any given set of circumstances which we shall need and which to omit.

Let us take the first essential group of eight measurements, leaving twelve for the second group. What are these Eight Essential Measurements?

For any given stage it is easy to supply in a few words the instructions for taking them. Because, however, there exist very marked differences between one stage and another, and because a designer must be equal to facing every variant of theatrical planning, the following rules have been couched with special care. Certain points in them may seem pedantically stated to anybody who has only one particular stage in mind; they are framed, however, to cover all the varieties of stage planning that the designer normally meets. It is even possible to find a number of Little Theatres in which the building is such that one of these measurements (the fourth) is not, in the true sense, essential, but in order to cover all cases it must be included in the eight.

The rules for taking these measurements will be given at first shortly, in bald simplicity, without remarks or definitions; after will follow full notes to show their application to special cases. The reader should not allow the fullness of these notes to obscure the simplicity of the main rules. Only a few, if any, of the 'special-case notes' are likely to apply to his own special case.

When we find ourselves suddenly presented with a strange stage and a long tape-measure, where are we to begin and how avoid wasting time? The most useful starting-point for measuring-up is the *proscenium line.* The proscenium line is a line taken across the stage from one side of the back of the proscenium opening to the other, Fig. 39. Generally it is upon this line that the proscenium curtains close. It is the junction between the stage and the fore-stage.

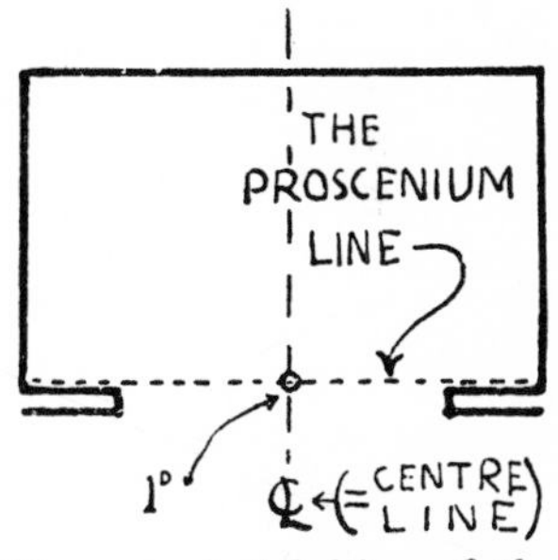

Fig. 39. A definition of the proscenium line.

Having established the position of the proscenium line, the designer should decide the *centre line* of the theatre running across the first at right-angles; it is the line from the back of the stage through the centre of the proscenium opening and down the middle of the auditorium. Apart from actual measurement, there are several aids to establishing this centre line; the footlights may be in two sections, with a clearly-marked central division; the 'carpet cut' may similarly have a centre join; looking up, one may be able to note the position of the centre lines in the flies; or there may be found on certain stages a brass-headed stud driven into the stage at the 'setting line' (which we will define later, but which for the moment we may take as being very near the proscenium line). Having established the proscenium line and the centre line, it will help the designer if he place some mark on the stage at their intersection (a penny is a very convenient object for this), and from this point he begins his measurements:

(In reading the following eight rules for the first time it may be more easy for the reader to ignore the word 'virtual'; its importance he will see a little later in the notes.)

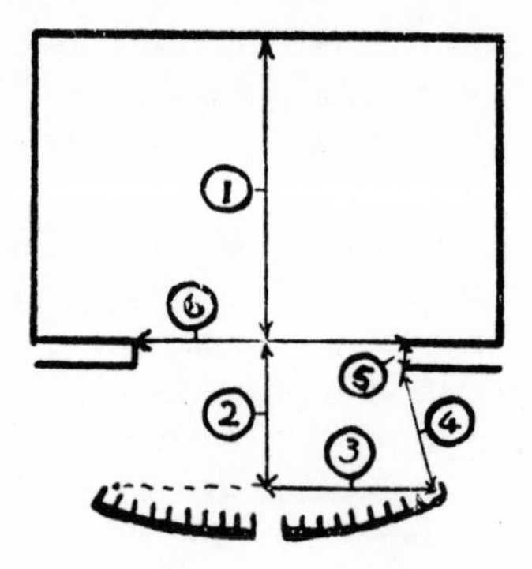

Fig. 40. The essential measurements, 1–6.

The First Measurement

The first measurement is the depth of the stage, measured along the centre line of the theatre from the back wall of the stage to the proscenium line, Fig. 40, No. 1.

The Second Measurement

The second measurement is from the centre of the proscenium line to the virtual centre of the front row of the stalls, Fig. 40, No. 2.

The Third Measurement

The third measurement is from that virtual centre of the stalls to the virtual outermost seat in the house, Fig. 40, No. 3.

The Fourth Measurement

The fourth measurement is from this outermost seat to the adjacent proscenium corner, Fig. 40, No. 4.

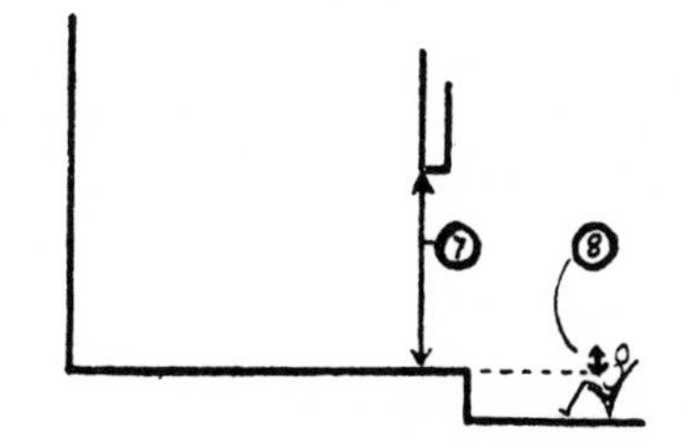

Fig. 41. The essential measurements, 7–8.

THE FIFTH MEASUREMENT

The fifth measurement is the direct distance of the proscenium corner in front of the proscenium line, measured at right-angles to that line, Fig. 40, No. 5.

THE SIXTH MEASUREMENT

The sixth measurement is the width of the proscenium opening, measured at the narrowest part, Fig. 40, No. 6.

THE SEVENTH MEASUREMENT

The seventh measurement is the height of the proscenium opening, Fig. 41, No. 7.

THE EIGHTH MEASUREMENT

The eighth measurement is the difference in level between the eye of the nearest spectator in the stalls, and the stage at the proscenium line, Fig. 41, No. 8.

It should be remarked in passing that the above measurements are placed in an order which affords a rough mnemonic for the designer: starting from the back of the stage (Fig. 42), the lines of measurement form a kind of figure '6' on the plan, and this, in some sense, emphasizes them as a knot of related points. The designer who follows the path of this '6', taking his measurements in this order, will be sure not to omit any of the first *six* measurements, and can then turn to the final two which are distinct from the others in that they are taken vertically and not, as those, horizontally.

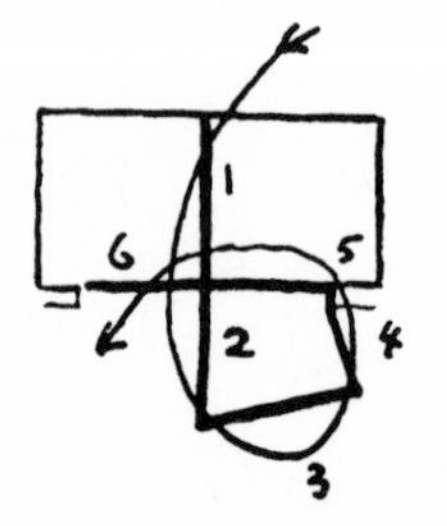

Fig. 42. A mnemonic for the first six measurements.

We have, then, stated in briefest summary the primary eight measurements with the view of making a concise and easily-memorized statement.

It will be clear that a rule so short, yet composed to cover so wide a use, will surely meet occasions where the conformation of the theatre is unusual and might lead the designer, unless he were keenly observant, into quandaries or even errors in measuring. It is to avoid such mistakes that the following notes on the rules are given in detail, showing how, once the definition of their terms is clearly stated, they apply satisfactorily even to complicated cases. I would again warn the reader that the fullness of these notes may be misleading, they will never all apply to one case; they are simply to prepare the designer for all emergencies. They are only to be kept in the background for drawing upon at need.

NOTES

ON THE EIGHT ESSENTIAL MEASUREMENTS

The First Measurement.

Rule. The first measurement is the depth of the stage, measured along the centre line of the theatre from the back wall of the stage to the proscenium line, Fig. 40, No. 1.

Definitions. For *proscenium line* and *centre line*, see p. 91.

Notes. It may occasionally happen that the back wall of the stage, through some special circumstance of the planning, is not parallel with the proscenium line, and so the stage is deeper at one side than the other. In such a case, take the measurement in the usual way to the centre of the back wall, but note also the distances from either end of the proscenium line to the opposite points on the back wall, so as to be able to record its slant on the plan.

The Second Measurement.

Rule. The second measurement is from the centre of the proscenium line to the virtual centre of the front row of the stalls, Fig. 40, No. 2.

Definition. The virtual centre of the stalls is the centre of a straight line drawn between the two outermost seats in the front row.

Notes. This second measurement should be taken from the proscenium line with the tape-measure horizontal. We find out how much lower or higher the spectator's eye is than this by the eighth measurement. Remember the measurement is taken to ascertain the distance of the spectator's eye, not his chair, therefore it should be taken to a point a few inches in front of the back of the seat. If the centre of the stalls is broken by a gangway, this should be ignored, and the measurement should be taken to the point where the spectator's eye would be were the seats continuous.

Why does this word 'virtual' creep into the rule? For many circumstances it need not be there. It depends on whether the rows of stalls are curved or straight. If they are straight no difficulty arises. If they are curved, where does one measure to? The 'centre of the stalls' must be defined in a constant way, whether the front line of seats be straight or curved, so we define it as the centre of a straight line drawn between the two outermost seats of the front row. If the stalls are straight then of course that is where the centre stall is situate; but if the row is curved you are left with a 'virtual' centre for measurement—regarding the row as a bow, you measure to the centre of the bow-string. We want to record the distance of the *nearest* spectator, and in curved stalls he is the man at the end, and if we measure to the centre of a line connecting the two end seats, we record what we want. Fig. 40 is drawn to show this.

The Third Measurement.

Rule. The third measurement is from that virtual centre of the stalls to the virtual outermost seat in the house, Fig. 40, No. 3.

Definition. The virtual outermost seat is that from which you see most of the opposite side of the stage.

Notes. The first thing to note is that the 'outermost seat' is not necessarily that at the end of the first row, it may be in one of the rows behind if the rows increase in length as they go back, see Fig. 43, where *A*, though farther from the stage than *B*, yet commands a wider view of the opposite side wall and so is, according to definition, the 'outermost seat'.

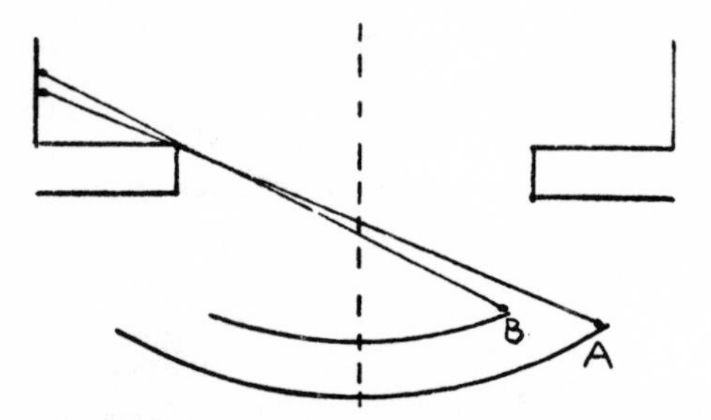

Fig. 43. Plan of a proscenium and two rows of stalls—the outermost seat is here A.

Secondly, the virtual outermost seat is not necessarily actually the outermost: note the phrasing of the definition—'the virtual outermost seat is the seat from which you can see most of the opposite side of the stage.' It may be only virtually the outermost, because actually some seats farther back in the house may surpass it in distance from the centre line: if from these a fraction less of the stage is to be seen beyond the opposite proscenium corner than from the one in front, they are to be ignored. Fig. 44 shows a particular case. This needs careful watching. Seat *D* may be the outermost seat according to measurement from the centre line, but from *D*, looking across, we can see the opposite side wall of the stage only from the back down to the point *H*, but there are other seats from which more of this side of the stage is to be seen, and so this seat *D* is not our virtual outermost seat. Clearly the seat we need is *E*, from which we can see to *F* on the side wall, for no seat in the house gives us a wider view than this. (Note well: the required seat is *not* here *C*; compare with the apparently similar but actually very different arrangement in Fig. 43.)

And as far as the principal measurements of scenery go, the point *E*, as it is the virtual outermost seat, is all we need, but there is a refinement in this particular case to which it will be useful to call attention.

So far we have been considering the opposite-wall sight-line or *cross sight-line*; let us, however, turn to the nearer *side sight-line.* This is the line through the nearer edge of the proscenium, and it governs the view obtainable of the near side of the scenery when we come to set it in place on the stage. *This side sight-line is to be taken from the seat from which we can see least of the near side of the stage.* In nearly all cases this seat and the seat from which we can see most of the opposite side of the stage —the virtual outermost seat—are one, but in this particular example they are not. So after taking the position of the virtual outermost seat (*E* in this example), it is as well to look back up the auditorium and notice if, behind you, there is another 'outermost' seat from which less of the near side of the stage is to be seen than from the virtual outermost, and if so, it is as well to take the position of that seat also, so as to avoid a plan of scenery on whose stage-left may be an important detail that you would of course be careful to make just visible from seat *E*, but which, when you get it on the stage, you find is after all masked from certain other seats.

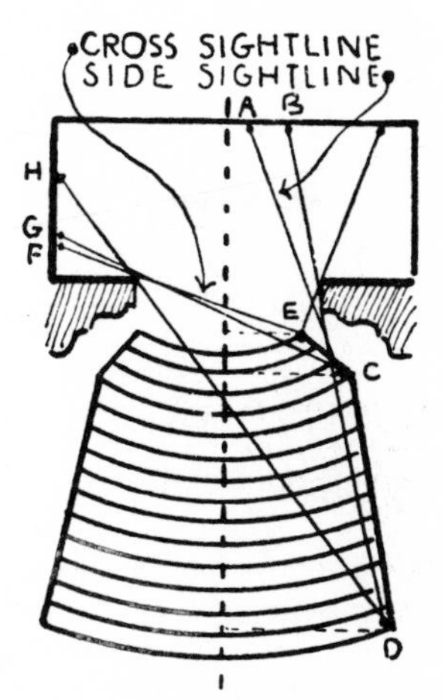

Fig. 44. Plan of a theatre— the outermost seat is here E.

In a case like Fig. 44, then, after establishing *E* upon which to base his cross sight-line, the designer must settle on another point from which to take his side sight-line. This point is by definition 'the seat from which least of the near side of the stage can be seen'. Remember that it also is not necessarily the outermost seat from the centre line, for, referring to Fig. 44 again, we know that the actual outermost seat is *D*, but from *D* we can see to *B* on the stage, while a walk down the side gangway of the theatre will show us that from seat *C* we can see still less—only in fact to *A*. *C*, then, is according to definition the seat from which to take our side sight-line.

Thirdly, a very difficult situation arises when the outermost seat is not in the stalls or pit at all, but in a box. In such a situation we must exercise a great deal of judgment and also some tact, even in talking about it. For the truth is that, though the occupants of the boxes pay the highest price for their seats there, they have some of the worst positions in the whole theatre. A man in a box can never see a show, for though the designer has spent great care to make a set consistent with the sight-lines of the stalls, he generally throws up the sponge when he comes to the boxes, and lets his principles go to the devil.

Frankly, there is no way of facing the situation if the boxes are thoroughly badly placed. Although the rule is so framed that, if there is a box, the third measurement is generally taken to the deepest seat in that box, for that is most likely to be the 'seat from which most of the opposite side of the stage can be seen', yet it is as well to measure also the outermost seat of the stalls, so as to be able to establish the more normal sight-lines as well, especially if (as is likely) the box is rarely used. In such an event you must be careful to note that you may occasionally have, with some shapes of proscenium side, a different *proscenium corner*—see note on the fourth measurement—for each of the 'outermost' seats, as shown by the two arrows in Fig. 45. The arrangement here is rank bad proscenium design but it occasionally occurs. The establishment of these four points—two 'outermost' seats and two proscenium corners—must then be made by whatever measurements the circumstances make necessary: they are generally additional lines to measurements 3, 4, and 5.

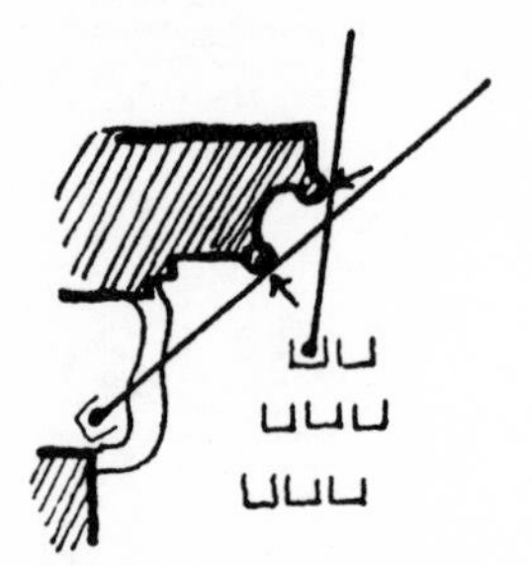

Fig. 45. A badly-arranged proscenium side, having two proscenium corners.

Though it is nearly impossible satisfactorily to design, with regard to a box seat, a plan for the scenery on the near side of the stage, because that scenery must be irretrievably hidden from the box and can at most be designed to suit the sight-lines of the outer stall seats, yet it is incumbent upon the designer to see that the scenery on the opposite side of the stage from the box masks not only according to the stall sight-lines but according to the box sight-lines: though the box cannot see the near side of a set, that is no reason why it should be allowed to see through the far side, even if it does mean an extra three feet on every backing.

In all cases the third measurement is to be taken directly between the two points mentioned, irrespective of whether the direction is at right-angles to the centre line (as in Fig. 40) or not (as in Fig. 49).

Lastly, if the auditorium is not symmetrical about its centre line, the position of the outermost seats may be different on the two sides and must then be measured separately.

The Fourth Measurement.

Rule. The fourth measurement is from the outermost seat to the adjacent proscenium corner, Fig. 40, No. 4.

Definition. The proscenium corner is that edge of the proscenium side that cuts off the field of vision of the stage from the outermost spectator.

Notes. This measurement is unnecessary in those very straightforward theatres where the outermost seat is on the same level as the virtual centre of the stalls, in other words, when the line of measurement 3 is at right-angles to the centre line (for example, in the theatre described later in section 14). But it is useful always to take it as a means of verification. In all other situations than the above-mentioned, the measurement is essential, so that it is good to get into the habit of recording it in any case.

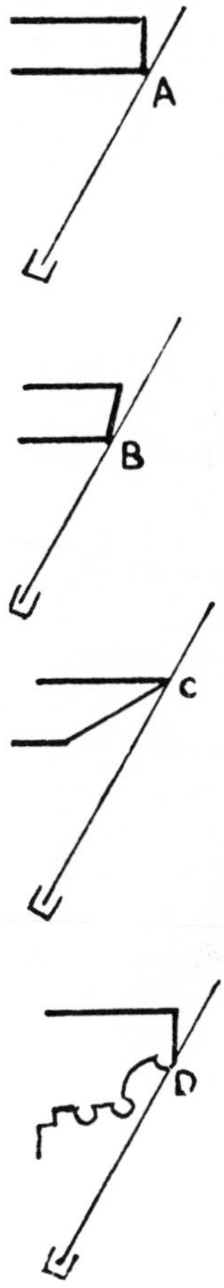

The term 'proscenium corner' must be defined with some care, otherwise in an elaborately moulded proscenium arch it will be difficult to decide. It is that corner or edge on the side of the proscenium opening which cuts off the field of vision of the stage from the outer spectator, and in a simple, unmoulded proscenium arch, cut cleanly across the thickness of the wall, the proscenium corner will be the front corner where the thickness of the arch joins the face, Fig. 46, *A*. But those who build prosceniums, so complicate and elaborate this thickness that the vital point may occasionally be found in an unexpected position. If the thickness of the proscenium is simply splayed, the proscenium

A

B

C

D

Fig. 46. Different positions of proscenium corners.

corner may be at the near (Fig. 46, *B*), or at the far (Fig. 46, *C*) edge of the splay, according to its angle and the position of the outermost seat. If the thickness is not only splayed, but elaborately moulded or rounded, the proscenium corner may be in the middle of the thickness (Fig. 46, *D*). The deciding factor is the point at which, when you are sitting in that outermost seat, the proscenium wall turns round and finally vanishes out of your sight on to the stage. It is the last point you can see on the turn.

The Fifth Measurement.

Rule. The fifth measurement is the direct distance of the proscenium corner in front of the proscenium line, measured at right-angles to that line, Fig. 40, No. 5.

Notes. The fifth measurement is the smallest on the list. We make it so as to establish the position of the proscenium corner with regard to the proscenium line and to see how much nearer the proscenium corner is to the audience. So it is the direct distance between the proscenium corner and the proscenium line measured at right-angles to that line.

This is the simplest measurement in the world when the proscenium is properly designed: for example, when the thickness of the proscenium opening is a straight line at right-angles to the proscenium line then the measurement is equivalent to the thickness of the wall, Fig. 40; moreover, when the proscenium is splayed, but splayed properly, exactly on the same angle as the sight-line from the outermost seat, then measurements 4 and 5 may be bracketed (see later, Fig. 48, *B*).

The edge of the proscenium opening, however, may not be designed on the proper angle, it may be splayed less than it should be, or it may be elaborated with decoration; then a difficulty arises and there is only one way to solve it. Let us first examine the position and then give the solution. So important a point arises here that we may interrupt our notes for a moment.

On the Design of the Proscenium Edge

So far as sight-lines are concerned there is only one satisfactory way to plan a proscenium opening and that is to splay its thickness on the same angle as the side sight-line (or at a greater angle than the sight-line, the centre line of the theatre being taken as a normal). This is represented in Fig.

47 in thick lines. The most logical angle of splay is of course that coinciding with the sight-line marked *A*, though the three other more acute angles suggested in thick lines do not in any way hinder or alter that sight-line. But, going now to splays of lesser angle, shown in thin or in dotted lines, we find that for each step a further fraction of the stage is masked, a little more of our view impeded, a virtually narrower stage enforced, and a less-favourable, more-oblique sight-line occasioned. It is worth while noticing that an inch or two of bad proscenium here will hide a foot or two of the stage beyond.

Passing through the decreasing angles we reach a point where the edge of the opening is square. Beyond that point the splay begins again but now facing towards the stage and no longer the audience. This latter arrangement in its crassest form is rare but we frequently find what is as bad, that some column or ornament has been placed against the edge of the proscenium and has the same effect (as in Fig. 48, *E*).

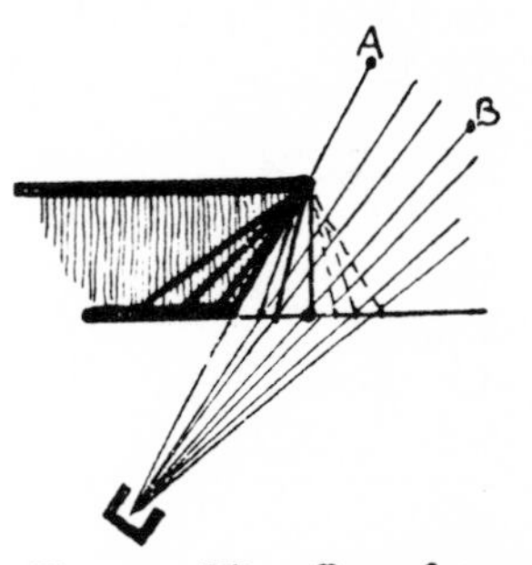

Fig. 47. The effect of proscenium splay on sight-lines.

Of these less satisfactory angles perhaps the one that has the most excuse is when the edge is square. This is the simplest form to build and so found oftenest in small theatres, and so far as taking measurement 5 is concerned it is simplicity itself—the nearer corner of the edge being the proscenium corner and the measurement being equivalent to the thickness of the wall. These excuses, however, do not alter the fact that, as the difference between sight-lines *A* and *B* on Fig. 47 shows, a square edge may cut off a great deal of stage from the corner spectators.

The conclusion to be drawn is that:

Ideally every proscenium should be so planned that the proscenium corner is situate on the proscenium line, then measurement 5 could be for ever cut out (see Fig. 48, *C*). An arrangement exactly the same in effect is that in Fig. 48, *B*, and in Fig. 47, *A*.

Notes on the Fifth Measurement (cont.)

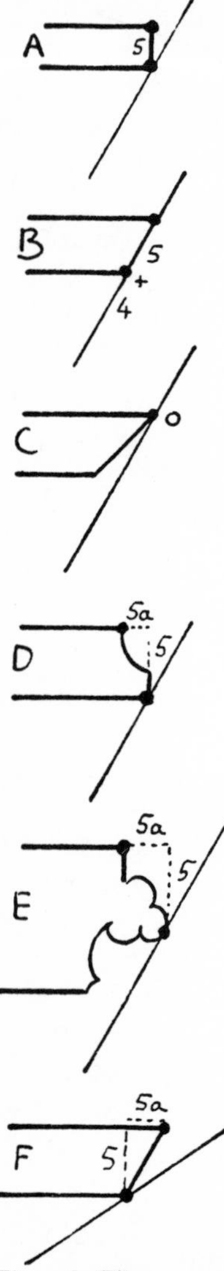

Fig. 48. The proscenium corner and the stage corner.

Our main concern at the moment is that, if the proscenium edge is neither correctly splayed nor square, measurement 5 is complicated. Let us make it clear.

Remember, all we seek is so to measure the proscenium corner that we can mark its position on our plan in correct relation with the rest. We need it because it is the 'pivot' upon which our sight-lines turn.

Consider now Fig. 48: here are plans of six proscenium sides of different types. On each proscenium two dots are placed; the nearer dot to the reader in each example is the *proscenium corner* as defined above, the farther dot we may for the occasion name the *stage corner* of the proscenium opening; it marks the junction of the proscenium line with the proscenium. In *A*, *B*, and *C* we should have no difficulty in establishing the proscenium corner on our scale plan with no more help than the information in our usual measurements; in *A* the proscenium corner is directly in front of the stage corner and at an ascertainable distance away from it; in *B* it is an ascertainable distance away from the stage corner and the two points are on the same sight-line, in other words, on the line of measurement 4 produced; in *C* the two points coincide. All these arrangements we can dismiss without another thought, they are completely covered by our rules and will present the designer with no difficulty.

But in *D*, *E*, and *F* it is different. These are not satisfactorily designed proscenium sides and our usual measurements would not give us sufficient information to place the proscenium corner accurately on our plan, because the proscenium corner is neither dead in front of, nor coincident with, nor on the same sight-line as, the stage corner. It is either to the right or left of it and we need to know how much. This we learn by making a supplementary measurement 5*a*. *Measurement* 5a *records the lateral displacement of proscenium corner with regard to stage corner*—as measurement 5 records the linear displacement.

We have then in such cases, (1) to measure how far the proscenium corner is in front of the proscenium line (which is our normal measurement 5 according to rule), and (2) also to measure how far to the left or right of the proscenium corner position the stage corner is. The latter measurement, which is measurement 5*a*, will read 'so much *out*' (beyond the proscenium corner), or 'so much *in*', that is, nearer to the centre line.

The designer must use his ingenuity in taking these two measurements and note that in some cases (such as that in Fig. 48, *F*) the fifth measurement has to be taken theoretically through the wall itself. This is impossible, but it is quite easy to make the measurement not from the proscenium corner itself but from a point exactly opposite it and nearer on stage. Fig. 49 shows a case where measurement 5 has been ascertained by measuring not between the specified points but between points opposite them.

The Sixth Measurement.

Rule. The sixth measurement is the width of the proscenium opening, measured at the narrowest part, Fig. 40, No. 6.

Notes. The sixth measurement must always be taken across the narrowest part of the proscenium opening if that proscenium is splayed or decorated. In all properly designed proscenium openings, as we have seen, that narrowest part will be on the proscenium line, in which case measurement 6 will coincide with the proscenium line, as it should do, but if the rule is broken it may result that the thickness of the proscenium arch bulges toward the centre line as a pillar would or a diamond edge. Then the proscenium line, lying at its back extremity, is not the same as the line across the narrowest part of the opening, and then we are faced with a most troublesome blunder.

This knot of the six related measurements was carefully spun like a spider's line from point to point in unbroken web, and all the measurements were planned to be capable of direct calculation each from the last, and all in relation to a given cross, arbitrarily made, to stand for the intersection of the theatre's centre line with its proscenium line. But so nicely adjusted is the web that it will collapse if the narrowest part of the proscenium opening has been loosely disregarded when the stage was built, and allowed to come where it would, floating vaguely (it would seem) between proscenium corner and proscenium line but contiguous with neither. Then it is related in no logical conformation with the organism to which it belongs, and, like all untidinesses, it puts us to extra trouble.

Fig. 49 shows a 'horrible example' created purely from imagination to illustrate the difficulties of this measurement 6, and also of the last measurements 5 and 5*a*.

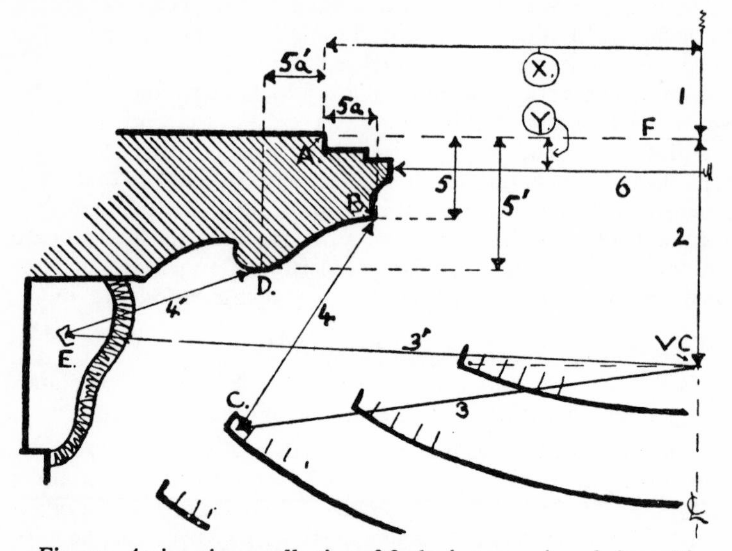

Fig. 49. An imaginary collection of faults in proscenium design with suggestions for measuring.

When the proscenium is so designed that the narrowest part of the opening (measurement 6) is neither coincident with the proscenium line (*F*), nor even drawn between the two proscenium corners (*B*), then our normal measurements do not give us any indication where to draw that narrowest part when we come to set out our plan on paper (according to the procedure in section 13). We certainly know the width, but it is now divorced from the line it should lie along, or the points it concerns, and we do not know where to place either it or our proscenium corner, which was measured relative to that width, so we must put some order into the chaos in the following way: *Whenever the narrowest part of the proscenium opening is neither coincident with the proscenium line nor contiguous with the proscenium corners we must, in addition to our normal measurements, take (1) the distance from the centre line to the stage corner of the proscenium (X in Fig. 49), and (2) the distance between the proscenium line and the line across the narrowest part of the opening (Y in Fig. 49).* Then we shall have the situation in hand again.

I, however, should probably cut such a tangle by deciding at once that, whatever my set design, I would first put in a narrow flat at the proscenium side wide enough to reach from stage corner to a point level with the proscenium edge at the narrowest part of the opening, so making the proscenium more orthodox. In any badly-designed, cut-back proscenium with a splay (or its effect) on the on-stage side it is best to make up this splay with such a masking flat because it will save you width in your first wing, and materially help your cross sight-line.

It must be added that there may occasionally be found a channel somewhat like that in Fig. 49 (see also Fig. 74 later), displacing the true stage corner but purposely designed to accommodate a safety-curtain and to act to some extent as a smoke-trap and provide a channel for the groove in which the safety-curtain runs. But in a well-designed proscenium this channel will be so deep, and the overlap of the safety-curtain on the proscenium so great, that it is completely out of the reach of any cross sight-line, and so it will be completely dissociated from the stage corner.

Returning to less tortured prosceniums, it will be clear that (instead of being at some unrelated middle point as we have just seen) the narrowest part of the proscenium may yet be in either of two positions—between the two stage corners, or between the two proscenium corners. These are the two normal alternatives, and if now the configuration is such that a measurement 5*a* is incurred the designer should note that when the measurement 5*a* reads 'so much *in*' (that is, when the stage corner is nearer in to the centre line than the proscenium corner is) it will follow that measurement 6 coincides with the proscenium line. But in the reverse case, when measurement 5*a* reads 'so much *out*', then measurement 6 will lie down-stage of the proscenium line by the amount of measurement 5.

The bearing this has on setting out a plan will be seen in Section 13.

The Seventh Measurement.

Rule. The seventh measurement is the height of the proscenium opening, Fig. 41, No. 7.

Notes. In a small theatre this is a fixed quantity and presents no difficulty, but in some larger theatres the arch may be so high that it is useless without a pelmet or a proscenium border of some sort. It is only in rare circumstances that the actual opening is ever higher than sixteen or seventeen feet. Those rare occasions are when flats higher than the regulation eighteen feet are to be used in the scenes, or when cutcloth scenes (which may be very high) are used. The proscenium border can be raised or lowered to suit various occasions and the record of its usual height should be accompanied by a note of its possibility of variation.

The Eighth Measurement.

Rule. The eighth measurement is the difference in level between the eye of the nearest spectator in the stalls and the stage at the proscenium line, Fig. 41, No. 8.

Notes. The last measurement is of the height of the nearest (and lowest) spectator's eye with regard to the stage. If the stage is raked (and there is no reason except blind tradition why it should be), the measure should be taken with regard to the level of the stage at the proscenium line. The eye of a spectator in the nearest seat may be above or below the stage, and this should be noted in the measurement so that it runs 'so much above' or 'so much below', or 'plus so much' or 'minus so much'.

It may be useful to notice, when sitting in this seat, whether there is any raised portion of the footlights which projects above the stage level, and if so to what extent it hides the feet of the actors and for how many rows of seats.

There must be very few normal theatres in this world whose configuration is so extraordinary as to call for the application of all the material in these notes at one time. The imaginary plan in Fig. 49 showed an extreme exaggeration of difficulties and how the rules are applied to them. It is to be regarded merely as a curiosity.

Fig. 50. How to measure a considerable height without a ladder: take a measured batten, lift it to the top of the height and measure the distance between its end and the ground.

SECTION 12

THE TWELVE ACCESSORY MEASUREMENTS

Measurements useful in special cases—a complete table of the Twenty Measurements

---

Upon the above eight measurements it is possible to base drawings capable of giving the sight-lines of any stage: each of these measurements is essential; if one is missing nothing can be done. But scenery has to be designed to fit more than the sight-lines. Ideally, stages should be so planned that if a set was made according to the proper sight-lines, the stage accommodation would inevitably be such that the set could be put up and worked with no other considerations. A stage should be planned to accommodate such scenery as fits that stage's sight-lines. But our stages are not ideal and there remain about a dozen points where scenery, though quite consistent with the essential sight-lines, may come to grief, measurements which, though not strictly speaking essential, it is generally very useful to check, and some of which one will find in certain circumstances imperative. These are the Twelve Accessory Measurements.

We will place them for consideration roughly in order of importance. To begin with, there are three subjects where measurements are almost as necessary as in our primary eight, but because one of them is not needed in all circumstances, and because the other two should ideally always be ample enough to offer a margin of safety for any arrangement that is itself consistent with the sight-lines, they cannot strictly be said to be essential in every case.

Concerning the first of these subjects the discerning reader may perhaps have been eager to ask a question for some time: What of the gallery sight-lines? We have put off the subject till now firstly because some little theatres have no gallery, and secondly because some larger theatres are so badly designed that even if we know the gallery sight-lines we are little better off, for the back of the set is hidden from the gallery in any case and we can do nothing about it, save when we make our set unusually shallow.

Nevertheless, we must delay examination of the gallery sight-line no longer. Even if our set is destined to be half-hidden, we may as well know exactly what little is visible; while in the better designed theatre knowledge of the gallery sight-line is most desirable.

To establish the point from which the gallery sight-line is drawn we must measure the position of the uppermost seat in the house. There may be cases where individual discretion is needed to decide this seat, but usually we are justified in saying arbitrarily that it is the highest seat in the theatre (ignoring those possible seats considerably nearer the stage but slightly lower, which yet have worse sight-lines, such as may be found on the extreme sides of the front of the gallery). The seat will then be in the back row of the gallery.

We need to know (*a*) the height of this seat above the level of the proscenium line and (*b*) the horizontal distance from the proscenium line out to a point vertically under the seat—that is, more shortly, its distance up and its distance out. These measurements offer some difficulty in the taking. Ideally one should borrow the architect's scale plans of the theatre and carefully measure these. But if, as is regrettably often the case, no one in the theatre knows where these are, the designer may proceed by the shift illustrated in Fig. 51. Here, upon a table placed centrally over the proscenium line, he lays a long straight batten, parallel with the centre line of the theatre. The batten must be exactly horizontal and tested with a spirit-level, and the table-legs packed if necessary. From the first balcony or circle an assistant now lowers a plumb-line until the designer, sighting along the horizontal batten, judges its plumb-weight level with the batten. A second assistant now lowers a plumb-line similarly from the second circle till it is level with the end of the first, and so on according to the number of circles, until at length the height of the uppermost seat above the last plumb-line may be calculated, and then the total height of that seat above the proscenium line is a simple addition—the table height plus the thickness of the batten (*A* in Fig. 51), plus the drop of each plumb-line (*B*, *C*, in Fig. 51).

Similarly the horizontal distance away of the seat is the addition—proscenium line to first plumb-line, plus distance to second, etc. (see *X*, *Y*, *Z*, Fig. 51).

The sum, $A+B+C$ we will call *measurement 9*; and the sum, $X+Y+Z$ we will call *measurement 10*. These two measurements establish the position of the uppermost seat.

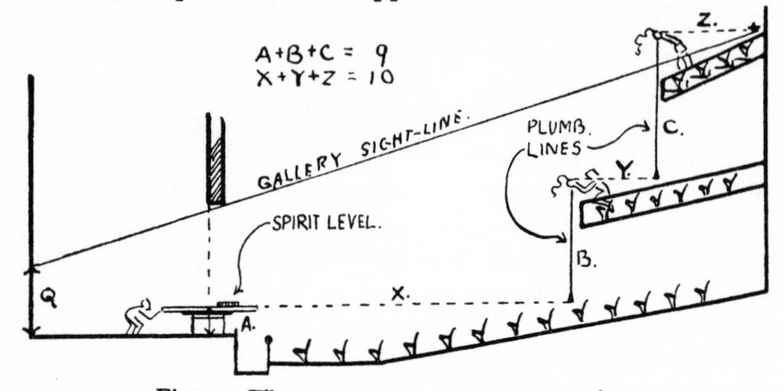

Fig. 51. The accessory measurements, 9 and 10.

It is always best to have the position of this actual seat when the gallery sight-line is needed, for from it supplementary sight-lines may be drawn to any object on the stage to reveal how much of the stage floor is visible behind it, and so forth—it is especially useful in ensuring that between two groundrows, or between a window and its backing, there shall not be visible a patch of bare boards. But it is possible to establish the gallery sight-line alone (without the seat) by a simpler method. This method only gives us the one sight-line and offers us no fixed point at the upper seat position from which to draw any other lines we need, but it may be sufficient for simple needs and it is an essential stand-by if lack of time or assistance makes the fuller method impossible.

By this method the gallery sight-line may be established by the designer single handed, and without his leaving the stage, as follows. Let him stand right at the back of the stage. Then, looking into the auditorium, stoop or raise himself on a ladder until the proscenium border just cuts his view of the topmost seat in the gallery; then let him measure the height of his eye at that point on the back wall of the stage (see Fig. 51, *Q*). This single measurement made to scale on the back wall of his sectional drawing will give a point from which to draw the gallery sight-line through the proscenium border. On a bad stage he may find that he must stoop so low that he must not only lie down, but move some distance from the

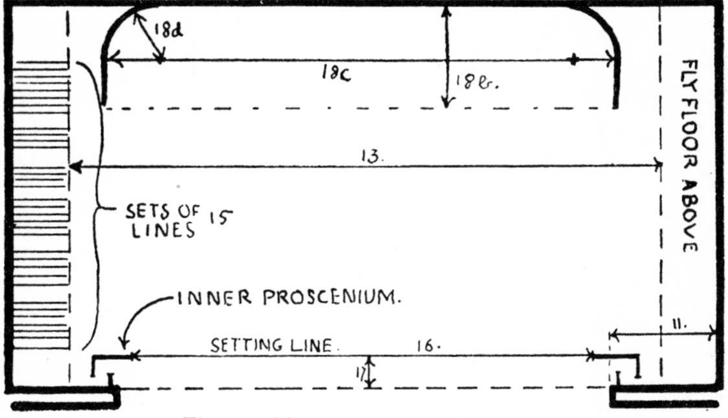

Fig. 52. The accessory measurements.

back wall of the stage before the gallery seat becomes visible. Then he makes his measurement along the stage floor from the back wall to the part that was his pillow.

The Eleventh Measurement, the next in importance, is the width of the wing-space, at the side of the stage behind the proscenium sides. This is taken from the edge of the proscenium to the side wall of the stage, Fig. 52 (11). If the stage is not symmetrical the wing-space each side must be measured separately.

The Twelfth Measurement, Fig. 53 (12), is the height of the roof or ceiling above the stage in small theatres, or, in theatres equipped with flies, more specifically the height of the grid.

The four measurements dealing with these three subjects,

gallery sight-line, wing-space, and grid, are of first importance among the accessories. The next three are of equal importance, but only in those cases where the stage is equipped with flies; even then, the first two may not come into consideration if the theatre-design is such that no *fly-floor* (see p. 52) is present.

The Thirteenth Measurement is the distance between the fly-rails of the two fly-floors if they are symmetrically built, one

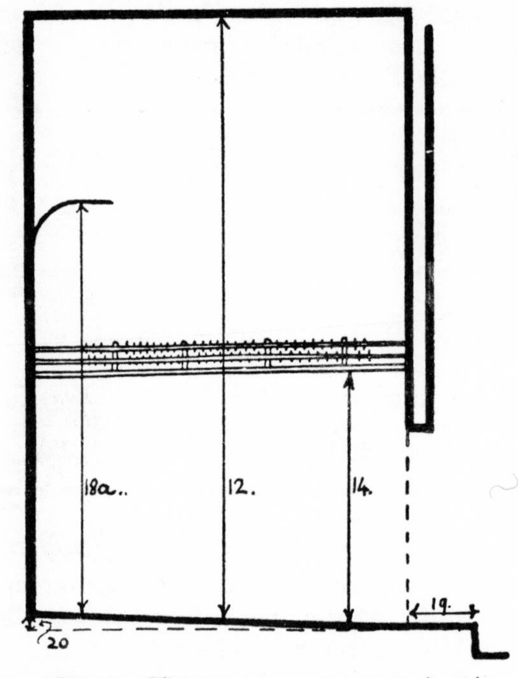

Fig. 53. The accessory measurements (cont.).

either side of the stage, or the distance between fly-rail and centre line if there is only one (Fig. 52 (13)). This measurement is important because the fly-floor, projecting as it does, limits the length of the backcloths and borders used on that stage. They must not be so long as to foul the fly-rails as they are raised or lowered.

The Fourteenth Measurement is the height of this fly-floor (Fig. 53 (14)), which similarly limits the height of such standing scenery as may be packed in the wing-space beneath.

The Fifteenth Measurement is the interval between the sets of lines in the flies, and should include the total number of sets, reading for instance, '25 sets at 9-in. centres'. But this measurement may not be constant throughout, and in some theatres the assistance of the stage-carpenter should be sought in making a specific scale plan of the arrangement of the grid. We will represent as a group the whole collection of measurements in Fig. 52 (15).

There now follows a pair of measurements necessary if a *setting line* is used on the stage. A 'setting line' comes into existence on those stages where some form of inner proscenium is used; it is, as it were, the proscenium line of this inner proscenium. A further discussion of it will be more in place later when we consider the inner proscenium in detail.

The Sixteenth Measurement is the length of the setting line (Fig. 52 (16)).

The Seventeenth Measurement is the distance between the setting line and the proscenium line proper (Fig. 52 (17)).

If the stage possesses a fixed cyclorama (or a track for a movable cyclorama), the width of this (Fig. 52, 18*c*), the depth (18*b*), and the nature of the curve must be noted on the plan, together with its position and maximum height (Fig. 53 (18*a*)) on the section. The cyclorama is, of its nature, curved, and the most useful way of measuring and recording a regular curve is to establish the centre of the circle of which it is a segment and measure the radius (18*d*). In Fig. 52 a usual type of cyclorama is represented whose centre and sides are flat and whose 'corners' are curved along the segments of circles of which the radius (18*d*) is necessary for recording the curve. It is more difficult, if one lacks the architect's drawings, to decide the centre of the curve forward at the top of a cyclorama, Fig. 53. Generally it is sufficient to fix the top of the cyclorama front by two measurements recording (*a*) its height above the stage at (*b*) such a distance from the back wall, as shown in Figs. 53 (18*a*) and 52 (18*b*) respectively. This data, grouped, forms *Measurement Eighteen.*

It may be useful sometimes to know the depth of the forestage or apron, that is, the measurement from the extreme edge of the stage to the proscenium line, together with a note of the curve, if any, of that edge. This measurement is rarely needed for calculating the size of scenery (*Measurement Nineteen*, Fig. 53 (19)).

Lastly, one may add a *Twentieth Measurement* concerning the amount of 'stage rake' (Fig. 53 (20)). In the old days stages were sloped up more or less sharply towards the back to help in providing a perspective vista. To-day, though the vista type of scenery is rarely used, stages are occasionally still built with a rake or slope, despite the fact that it is now far more of a hindrance than a help. If there is a rake it must be recorded, so that the measurement reads 'slope of so many inches up, in so many inches along'. In nearly every case the master carpenter will know this measurement and so make the difficult task of establishing it afresh unnecessary.

There is nothing beyond this that is needed for general work, though for special shows it may be necessary to make a careful plan of the stage floor to show the position and size of all traps, sliders, bridges, and fillets, together with a note of the working depth underneath the stage.

In certain big shows it may be necessary to remove large built pieces of scenery from the stage altogether when they are struck, and to pack them in a separate scene-dock. Should this be so, it is very important indeed to measure the dock-door and avoid constructing such a piece too big to get through.

Similarly it must never be forgotten that even if scenery has never to leave the stage during the run of the piece, it has yet to get into the theatre in the first place and the doorway by which it is to be brought in limits the size of the unit parts of any set, though they can of course be extensively battened out and built up once they are on the stage.

In addition it may be necessary to record certain oddities in a particular stage, such as a projecting staircase in the wings, or anything likely to affect the moving or placing of scenery, either on or about the stage, though if stages were planned according to the system of sight-lines such anomalies would be avoided.

SUMMARY OF THE 20 MEASUREMENTS

Let us now tabulate these measurements:

ESSENTIALS

1.	Back wall to proscenium line	*Illustrated in Fig.* 40
2.	Proscenium line to virtual centre of stalls	40
3.	Virtual centre of stalls to virtual outermost seat	40
4.	Virtual outermost seat to proscenium corner	40
5.	Direct distance of proscenium corner in front of proscenium line	40
5*a*.	Lateral displacement of stage corner, if necessary	48
6.	Width of proscenium opening	40
7.	Height of proscenium opening	41
8.	Difference in level between nearest spectator's eye and stage	41

ACCESSORIES

9.	Height of highest seat, Fig. 51 } or gallery sight-line	Fig. 51
10.	Distance of highest seat, Fig. 51 } or gallery sight-line	Fig. 51
11.	Width of wing-space	52
12.	Height of grid	53
13.	Distance between fly-rails	52
14.	Height of fly-floor	53
15.	Number and position of sets of line	52
16.	Length of setting line	52
17.	Distance between setting line and proscenium line	52
18.	Data for cyclorama	52 and 53
19.	Depth of forestage	53
20.	Amount of stage rake	53

If the designer takes that list as one of the essential elements of his outfit, he will be able to set down on a sheet of notepaper so much about his theatre that he can answer any question that is ever likely to be asked relating to the size, position, or working of any piece of scenery he may be called upon to design for that stage, and do it without leaving his desk.

Addendum. In some theatres it is valuable to ascertain how much the upper sight-line from the back of the pit is cut down by the edge or soffit of the ceiling of the first circle above; the view of an actor upon steps or a rostrum may be badly hindered in some theatres.

SECTION 13

ON SETTING OUT THE PLAN AND SECTION OF A STAGE

Scale-drawing on squared paper—correlation of plan and section—working on tracings—fitting set to stage

We may now leave consideration of the measuring of stages, and go on to extend the method of sight-lines, briefly suggested in Section 10, to suit the needs of all the fuller types of scenery used on completely equipped stages, and we pass from a simple curtain set to a province where the theatrical setting grows to include a large number of elements whose dimensions must still be intimately related with each other and with the stage on which they are to be set, if we are to escape (1) scenery that is too small and does not mask, and (2) scenery that is too big and is therefore cumbersome and costly. How can we make scenery fit? How big is a border? How wide is a wing?

The answers to these questions depend on the designer's use of the Twenty Measurements. How does he go about his work? How does he construct his scale plan and section, and how read from them the required information to plan his scenery?

A scale drawing may be made in two ways. We may elect to represent each foot on the stage by an inch (or any other convenient measurement) on our paper. For this we need a tee-square, set-squares, a scale-rule and a drawing board, all accurate and true. Or we may use a far simpler method which dispenses with instruments and needs only a pencil and a sheet of squared paper such as one uses when drawing graphs. Here we take one square (or more) on the paper to represent one foot on the stage. The accuracy of our results is ensured then, not by the accuracy of our drawing, but by the accuracy of the ruling on the paper.

It is material to see that the squared paper one buys is accurately ruled in true and equal squares. Whether these squares are themselves accurate divisions of an inch is, for our purpose, of less importance. One method of roughly testing the rulings is to lay one sheet of the squared paper sideways upon another and to see if what were the vertical lines on the first sheet exactly coincide all the way down with the horizontal lines on the second sheet. If not the paper will not give you true answers.

The most convenient squared paper is that said to be 'ruled in twelfths', that is, paper divided first into inch squares with heavy lines, then subdivided so that each square has twelve rows of twelve small squares marked in finer lines. Then if one decides to work on a scale of one inch to a foot, each large inch square represents a foot on the stage and each tiny square an inch. Similarly, with a scale of half an inch to a foot, each large square represents two feet and each small two inches, and so forth.

Having secured a sheet of accurately ruled paper we take our list of measurements and proceed in the following way:

First count the squares on the length and breadth of the paper and decide on a convenient scale for the drawing. The scale of half an inch to the foot is probably the most used and gives a reasonably clear drawing without being too big, but on special occasions larger or smaller scales may be more convenient.

Beginning with the plan, set the paper with its length across and select a vertical line near the centre of the paper, mark this 'C.L.' (the centre line).

Mark a position for the back wall of the stage on the centre line near the top of the paper.

From that point measure down the centre line to the proscenium line according to the dimension given in measurement 1, and mark its position.

From that point, measure down the centre line to the virtual centre of the stalls (measurement 2) and mark its position.

The next step is to place the proscenium corner. In all normal cases except one we do this in the following way: halve measurement 6, set it off either side the centre line and along the proscenium line, then set the proscenium corner in relation to the end of this line according to measurement 5.

We should note the one exception: When we have a measurement 5*a* and that measurement is *outward* (see p. 103), showing the stage corner of the proscenium is outward from the proscenium corner, we shall find that it follows that measurement 6 does *not* fall along the proscenium line, but lies in front of it at a distance equal (generally) to measurement 5. Then instead of following the order above we should halve measurement 6 and set it out either side the centre line as before, though now not at the level of the proscenium line but at a distance equal to measurement 5 *below* that line.

(I said above, 'at a distance equal *generally* to measurement 5'. That obstructive 'generally' I have, of course, to include in order to cover those occasional troublesome misarrangements in which the narrowest part of the proscenium is neither at the proscenium line nor between the proscenium corners. We have already noted the steps that must be taken to cope with this situation (in Section 11, the note on measurement 6), which were the making of measurements *X* and *Y* (shown in Fig. 49). When these have had to be made we shall, in setting out the plan, mark off a distance equal to measurement *Y* down from the proscenium line, and at that point set a line equal to measurement 6 symmetrically across the centre line. Next, in the same way, measurement *X* is set out symmetrically about the centre line, this time along the proscenium line. The ends of this line give the stage corners of the proscenium. Set out, to left or right of these, the measurement 5*a*, and from that, at right angles to it, measurement 5. This gives the proscenium corner.)

After establishing the proscenium corner there only remains the outermost seat and our essential points are in place. If the stalls are straight, and there are no boxes, the seat is at a distance equal to measurement 3 from the virtual centre of the stalls and at right angles to the centre line. In all other cases it is simplest to use the following way: set the point of the compasses, open to a radius equalling measurement 4, at the proscenium corner and describe an arc in the auditorium; then set the point of the compasses, open to a radius equalling measurement 3, at the virtual centre of the stalls and describe an arc. Where the two arcs intersect is the position of the outermost seat on the plan.

The further details contained in the Twelve Accessory Measurements may now be added, first the wing-space (measurement 11) to be set out from the corner of the proscenium, and establishing the position of the side walls of the stage, which may now be drawn in to meet the back wall. Next any extra measurements, or duplicates relating to the corner seats when the theatre is not symmetrical, may be drawn in. Next the fly-rails should be indicated in dotted lines running up the wing-space at positions determined by measurement 13. Then, within the fly-floor-spaces, indication may be made of the number and position of the sets of lines from measurement 15. Next the distance of the setting line above the proscenium line is marked from measurement 17 and the line set out symmetrically about the centre by halving measurement 16. Then the cyclorama (if there is one) is marked on plan, and finally, where necessary, the forestage.

Now turn to the sectional drawing of the stage. On another sheet of paper, working to the same scale, mark near the left hand edge the position of the back wall. At a distance equal to measurement 1 to the right of this, mark the position of the proscenium line, from this again mark temporarily the virtual centre of the stalls. Mark the stage level at the proscenium line a few inches from the bottom of the paper, and then, by measurement 8, establish the nearest spectator's eye, above or below the level of the proscenium line, at the virtual centre of the stalls. Next mark the proscenium height (measurement 7) above the stage at the proscenium line. And our essential points are in place.

The accessory points, if any, follow from the remainder of the Twelve Measurements: firstly the position of the uppermost seat (based on measurements 9 and 10) or its sight-line. Next the height of the grid (measurement 12) and of the fly-floor (measurement 14), the cyclorama (measurement 18), the forestage (measurement 19), and lastly the stage-rake (measurement 20), taking the original mark at the proscenium line as the basis and sloping the floor up from that to the back of the stage.

At this point the work should be roughly checked by laying the side of the plan along the bottom of the section, adjusting the two so that the back walls on each are in direct alinement, and then noting whether every feature that is represented on both plan and section is similarly in true alinement. This check is of the greatest value, and the method of *correlation* by which projection is made from one drawing to the other is, and will be again, of very great assistance to our work.

When on a sheet of squared paper we have such a plan of a stage, and when we have determined from the evidence of certain sight-lines which we rule on that plan that a piece of scenery must stretch from this point to that, we have only to

Fig. 54. A strip-measure marked to the two scales used for the squared-paper drawings in this book. Each square represents: above, six inches; below, one foot.

count the squares it covers to find the required size in feet of the piece. Similarly upon the section we may determine the height of a wing or cloth and the height or depth of a border. It is very useful, for this counting, to cut a strip from the edge of the squared paper, mark it to scale in feet (and inches if the scale allows), and use it as a measure. Especially is this strip-measure valuable when one has to measure plan-lines set diagonally across the squares.

In Fig. 54 I have prepared two such strip-measures, one for each of the scales used in the squared-paper diagrams in this book, that is to say, one strip to the scale of one small square to a foot, the other of two small squares to a foot. The reader, if he cares to make detailed study of Figs. 55 to 64, and 77 to 89, may like to cut this figure out to help his measurements.

Those who resent detailed preparation may suppose that the dimensions of scenery can be arrived at by trial and error, by bringing, say, borders of 6 feet wide and 40 feet long into a dress rehearsal and saying, 'I want to hang these borders in various positions to see where they go best, and then proceed to measure and cut them on the stage.' They are right, it can be done. The trouble is that there is a risk that such people will forget about borders altogether until the stage is set, and their design takes form not according to their vision but as a botched calamity. Let us completely abandon trial and error, and refer such people to the quotation at the beginning of this book.

From our two drawings we can obtain unequivocal evidence of the exact position and angle at which to set any piece of scenery relative to the fixed walls of the stage and the proscenium arch. Moreover, we can work out such alternatives as: we need *either* one border only at *such* a position (but then it will have to be *so* deep), or, if between the roof and the heads of the actors this will not fit, we can reduce the depth of the border to *such* a size (but then we shall need *two*, one so many feet back and the other *so* many). All these measures we may read off, without any 'perhaps', on our drawings.

It is useful to make plan and section in the first place with some care and detail and in black ink, to keep at hand for future reference. Working drawings can then be made by tracing the whole or part of either in pencil as occasion arises for studies and experiment.

From the measurements already in hand a front-elevation-drawing of the proscenium can also be made, but it will less frequently be needed to decide the dimensions of scenery. Its chief office will be served if you draw, in the proscenium opening, a man to the same scale and keep it before you as a reminder of the proportions of the frame behind which your scenery has to stand.

Upon these drawings of plan and section a designer will lay a sheet of thin paper, and trace the main lines of his stage and the positions of significant seats, so providing a reproduction of his conditions. On the tracing he can work out in comfort the size and placing of the elements he wishes to use for his set, striking sight-lines wherever necessary to test the adequacy of the arrangement from all points of view. If he works up this tracing to an inextricable confusion of lines by successive attempts, he has only to lay a new paper on the key drawing to begin 'with a clean sheet'; such parts of the earlier sketches as were promising are repeated on the fresh sheet, the rest left out, and he goes on with the unsuccessful attempts out of the way and no longer confusing his drawing and his thought.

There are two directions in which a scale plan can be of especial use to us when we set it on our desk and begin to extract its information. The first of these is in helping to explore a strange stage, informing us of its possibilities and warning us of its characteristic difficulties. It will tell us what sizes and types of settings are most practical and where we shall have to adapt, or invent a special treatment designed for the needs of the occasion, and what recommendations we may table for its future growth.

The second is, once the peculiarities of our particular stage are noted, in helping us to work out all the details of a specific setting for any given show, which will fit that stage as to its dimensions and suit that stage as to its mechanics of changing and as to the packing space.

The effect of the stage upon the setting-design is like the effect of the casting upon the version of a play. Neither the setting nor the characterization can be decided without reference to the stage and to the cast respectively.

This point is of the very greatest importance. Too often is it thoughtlessly assumed that the setting used on one stage for a given scene is the right setting to use on another stage for the same scene; and similarly that the shape of characterization that the cast of one production gives to a play is the shape to be adopted by another company presenting that play but drawing its cast from quite different material and talent. A show must be built out of the genuine material of a company and its form must be dictated by that material—never shaped by straining and twisting the material to an appearance of another company who have different demands to answer and different means to fulfil them.

When you have no Marie Tempest in your cast—and a real Mary Smith is more valuable in a company than an imitation even of Marie Tempest—you must produce a different version of *The Marquise*, for instance, from that first produced at the Criterion.

It is just the same with setting. If one can get full and detailed information of a method used for a certain special production of a play in a large theatre with a revolving stage, that knowledge will be something of a disadvantage, rather than a help, when one comes to present that play upon a fit-up stage in a town hall. We must avoid an attempt to reproduce the old methods of setting in the new conditions. We must banish the old from our mind altogether, and devise the show entirely afresh so as to be scenically consistent with the fit-up stage, just as cast and treatment of parts must be consistent with the company's abilities and the circumstances of the presentation and *with the type of audience*.

As the stage so materially affects the setting-design, it follows that before beginning the design the stage must be thoroughly examined and understood. Our measurements supply the essential data for a complete examination.

Let us take a typical set of measurements and see how much they can tell us in general about scenery and the requirements of their stage. We will take the example of a small 'Little Theatre' stage. The small stage offers the problems of sight-lines in an even more exacting way than a large one, but at the same time allows us to make simpler diagrams with less complexity of parts.

SECTION 14

THE APPLICATION OF SIGHT-LINES TO A SPECIFIC PLAN AND SECTION

The designer's notes of a specific small stage—a note on sectors of vision and the evil of 'perspective' sketches—'looking sideways' at a scene design—the lesson of an absurdity—wing positions and cross sight-lines—cloth positions and cloth sight-lines—border positions and upper sight-lines—'correlation' for wing heights and border lengths

---

			ft.	*in.*
1.	Back to pros. line		14	3
2.	Pros. L. to V.C. of stalls		10	8
3.	V.C. to outermost seat		12	0
4.	Out. seat to pros. corner		9	6
5.	Pros. C. to pros. line		1	3
6.	Width of pros.		20	0
7.	Height of pros.		10	4
8.	Eye-level		+0	8
9.	Gallery distance		—	—
10.	Gallery height		—	—
11.	Wings	S.R.	5	0
		S.L.	3	10
12.	Height of grid, or roof		18	5
13.	Fly-rails		—	—
14.	Height of fly-floor		—	—
15.	Fly-lines		—	—
16.	Setting-line length		—	—
17.	Setting-line distance		—	—
18.	Data for cyc.		—	—
19.	Forestage		2	9
20.	Stage rake		—	—

One doorway U.R. 3 ft. 3 in. wide, 6 ft. 6 in. high, 2 ft. 5 in. from back wall.

One doorway D.L. 5 ft. 3 in. wide, 7 ft. 6 in. high, 7 ft. 10 in. from back wall.

Back wall plain brick. No passage across. Fixtures allowable.

The above is a copy of a designer's notes for a certain small stage.

It is simple after the elaboration of our earlier study of the measurements. But being simple it is an assurance that the practice of measuring is not so difficult as it looks, and that this stage is a subject eminently suited for the next step in a study of sight-lines.

The notes have not been altered for publication. They concern a newly built small stage just as it was when the designer was first called in to study it and plan the fitting of scenery to it. It is an example of the usual error where a designer is called in to initiate the setting *after* the stage itself was finished building, and in the planning of which neither he nor any other technical expert has had a say. Any modifications he may make to the existing stage are slight. Of what nature is this stage? How does he approach the problem of creating the precedent which its scenery will follow?

The notes, as they are, convey something of the nature of the stage before any drawings are made. The eight essentials show us that it is a simple stage with no oddities to make us refer to the notes on the measurements, and as the proscenium thickness is square no measurement 5*a* is needed. The stage floor is not high, for the spectator's eye-level is a plus measurement, that is, is above the stage level. Only one measurement each is given for Nos. 3 and 4, therefore the auditorium is symmetrical. The measurements show there are no boxes. The proscenium opening is reasonably wide for a small stage, but the stage itself is rather shallow.

As we run down the twelve accessory measurements we see that there are no possibilities of flying in the full sense, as the ceiling is only 8 ft. 1 in. above the proscenium top (i.e. 18 ft. 5 in. less 10 ft. 4 in.). We notice that the wing-space is constricted and is wider on the stage-right than on the stage-left, and it is therefore likely that we shall find this a stage where it is more convenient to have the prompt corner on what is usually the 'O.P.' side, that is on the stage-right; where there is more room. There is no gallery, and the stage is flat, there is a tiny forestage projecting 1 ft. 6 in. (that is, 2 ft. 9 in. less 1 ft. 3 in., the proscenium thickness) in front of the proscenium wall. There is no equipment yet for hanging, but upon inquiry we find we are to be allowed to make fixtures in the ceilings and walls. There has been no inner proscenium installed and no setting line yet marked. It is a virgin stage.

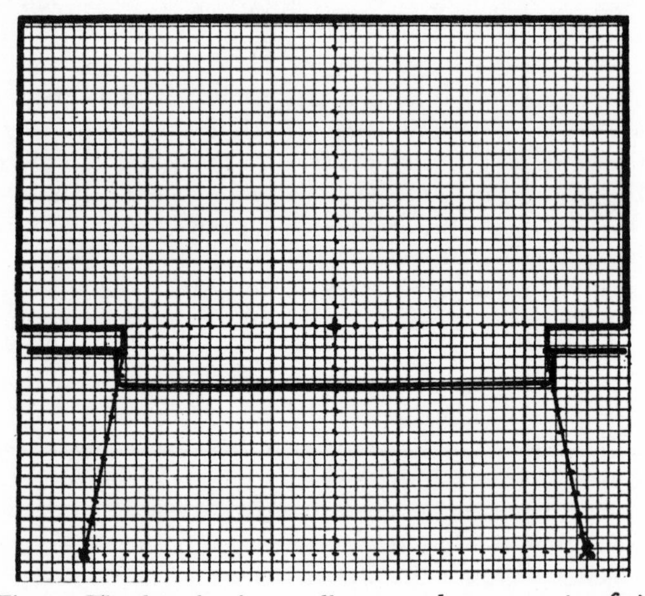

Fig. 55. The plan of a given small stage: scale, 2 squares to 1 foot.

On these measurements we make the scale plan and section on squared paper. Fig. 55 shows us the plan. (The ticks mark the feet, and the scale chosen for these illustrations is 2 small squares to 1 foot.) We have to make constructions in this plan according to certain principles; we have to establish the sight-lines and use them as evidence for the shaping of scenery. Let us make ourselves quite clear about these sight-lines, their direction, and the information they have for us.

Before we begin to take the short cuts of the experienced designer there are certain observations to be made on this plan.

Were we to draw upon it three 'cones' with their points on the seats *A*, *B*, and *X* respectively, we should have the appearance shown in Fig. 56. These three cones represent the sectors of vision of the spectators in those three seats.

Beginners always make the mistake of considering all schemes only from the point *X*, forgetting *A* and *B*. Indeed far too many scene designers who should know better produce perspectives of scenes viewed from the direction of *X* with no

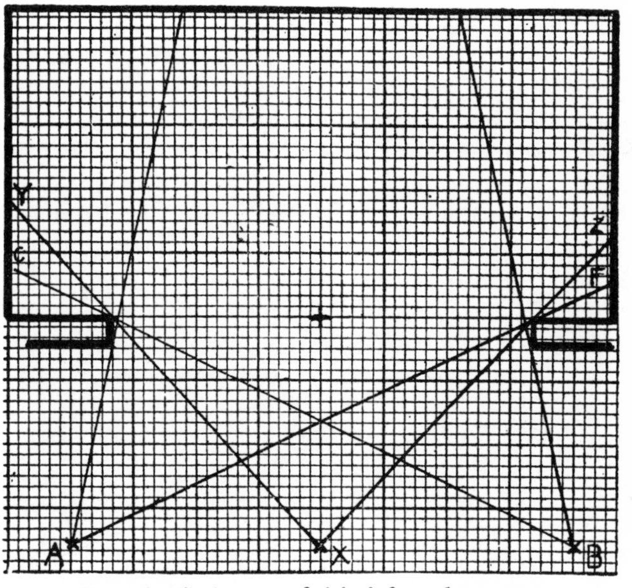

Fig. 56. The 'sectors of vision' from three seats.

signs in them at all of how the persons sitting in *A* or *B* shall be provided against seeing through the scenery to the side walls of the stage.

There is at present a vile custom among theatrical and non-theatrical people of judging a scene design purely on the evidence of a colour sketch showing the set (and possibly only the centre parts of it) in so-called perspective. These 'impressions' are utterly valueless as evidence. No serious person should ever treat them as anything but tentative accompanying notes to more solid work in scale plan and section, which alone bear any information of the facts of the scheme, and in which faults and inadequacies are betrayed with unequivocal evidence to any one who can read.

Some persons hold that this perspective vision contains the artistic germ of the set. But a germ in an ill-built body is the beginning of disease: where there is no practical health to control or nurture the germ, one kills the other, and neither germ nor frame can thrive, and an impractical basis is not only disease but death to a style.

Plan, section, and scale model are the evidence on which one should judge the project for a set. No colour perspective is of the slightest weight (except from a very experienced scene-painter) unless it is drawn *after* plan, section, and model have been made, when of course it is superfluous except as a convenient record or as the subject of reproduction in a souvenir programme or an art magazine (and indeed even for the latter purposes a model provides far more interesting material).

For, let it be repeated, a perspective sketch of a set can show no more than is included in the sector of vision from *X* —in fact it must show less, for the point from which these sketches are supposed to be taken is never in the front row, as *X* is, but somewhere vaguely in the middle depth of the auditorium. If the reader will now imagine himself in the dress-circle of a full-size theatre with the usual somewhat horse-shoe-shaped auditorium, and, looking over the rail, will fix his mind's eye on a seat in the stalls on the centre line immediately below him, and then suppose two long cords drawn from the back of that seat, each to one side of the proscenium opening, he will get a very vivid idea indeed of the vast majority of seats outside this cone of vision, at the back, at the sides, and above: that vast majority of seats does the designer of the perspective sketch ignore, for his set can only take the appearance shown if viewed from within that narrow sector (and that without raising the eyes too much). I am supposing even then that he is so competent a designer that the proportions of his perspective anticipate exactly the proportions of his building, which is nearly impossible unless plan and section have already indicated to him the relative size of every part.

So, in practice, we shall be wiser to cut the horizontal sector of vision from *X* for ever from our thoughts and never design a set from its point of view.

But before we turn our backs on it, it should be noticed that, even from this point, the end of the sector *YXZ* is not merely a straight line connecting *Y* and *Z* (in which case one could of course mask the stage merely by a flat backcloth as long as the distance between *Y* and *Z*), but an area going up to the back wall of the stage and with sides as well as back, into which three dimensions and the idea of separate planes must enter. Again, it is essential in the designing of scenery to think not in the flat, but in a succession of planes, to think, in other words, in three dimensions. The technical problem in the traditional wing-and-backcloth set is to know just how far these planes of scenery should stretch; they must end somewhere, and that somewhere must be beyond the edges of the proscenium opening, but how far beyond?

It is the sectors of vision from the two outer seats *A* and *B* that supply the answer. They indicate that if any piece of scenery stretches off-stage far enough to cut the outer side of one of these sectors of vision (to cut, that is, the lines *BC* or *AF*) it will mask, and we shall not be able to see round its side. But *BC* and *AF* are not infinite lines, they are restricted in length by the side walls of the stage. If those side walls were further out, clearly it is conceivable that we might have a piece of scenery in one plane (that is, a backcloth) at the back of the stage and so long as to stretch from line *AF* produced to line *BC* produced, and that in fact is what many beginners seem to suppose, judging by their lack of provision for masking sides and top, but this would mean a backcloth in this case approximately 74 feet long—over three and a half times the width of the proscenium opening and, if we may anticipate what our section would tell us, 22 ft. high, or 3 ft. 7 in. above the roof of the stage!

If these figures come as a surprise, it cannot but be a wholesome surprise, for it must emphasize that a setting design may not be conceived in one plane—even from considerations of space alone, for that plane would have to be enormous to mask. We must then, to state it in elementary terms, stand up on the stage a number of pieces of scenery, in various planes, designed to frame the view of the back scene and so enable us to restrict its area. This is the merest traditional truism, entirely obvious to any one who had a toy stage, or even a Victorian peepshow, as a child, and yet—perhaps because toy stages have been less common childhood-companions to the growing generation than they were to the established one—the student of to-day who remembers the fact is the exception not the rule. Perhaps, too, a partial reason is that the modern student wishes to go beyond the outworn limits of the wing-and-backcloth set. So he shall; but whatever territory he enters, the system of sight-lines, so clear to demonstrate in the traditional style, will still be his only guide to thinking about, and exploring, his project for a set.

This wing-and-backcloth setting is, in fact, an arrangement of just such a plane nature, the centre distance being represented on the back plane, and the side foreground on a nearer plane, upon a set of framing wings, with perhaps other trappings of the style.

Let us see how this principle may be applied to the present plan. Let us draw upon it tentatively a backcloth as wide as the stage will allow and mask the sides of this backcloth by a pair of wings parallel to it but in a nearer plane.

Before we look at the figure showing such a disposition, let me warn the reader. He is approaching an absurdity.

We shall take the innocent proposition above and execute it faithfully and literally and by logical steps. The sight-lines will, at one and the same time, help us exactly to realize the proposition and will pronounce as well the extent of its absurdity. We must examine it and then employ those sight-lines to lead us, as logically, to better arrangements and as impartially to demonstrate the lesser inadequacies of these.

Sight-lines inform us how to draw up an arrangement, and then, further, inform how practical it is.

Now we may look at Fig. 57 and see what the sight-lines say. Clearly, to mask the backcloth edges the wings must stretch to lines drawn between the edges of the backcloth (*G* and *H*) and the opposite outermost seats (*B* and *A*). Further, in order that these wings themselves should be masked at their outer edges by the proscenium arch, these outer edges must cut similar lines drawn from the same seats through the opposite proscenium corners (*BC* and *AF*), so occupying the position shown in the figure.

Some of the objections to this arrangement, such as the ridiculously small opening between the wings, will be obvious straight away, but let us consider it as a theoretical

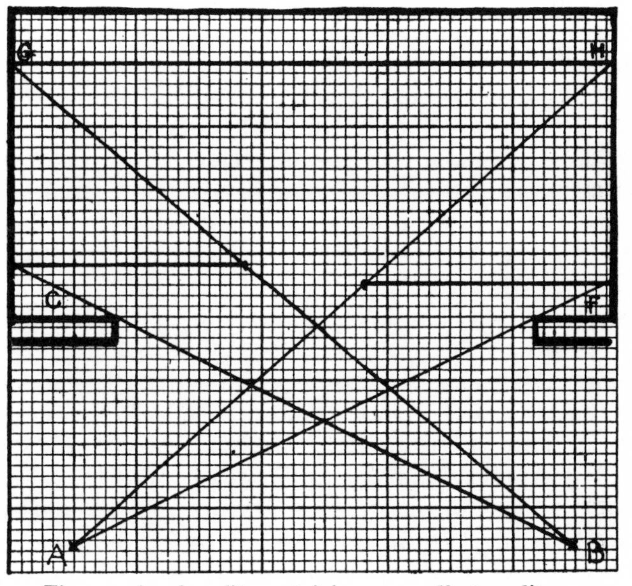

Fig. 57. An absurdity containing an excellent quality.

example. We have to note one (perhaps unexpected) very good point about this plan. It does mask from every seat in the house. The wings are not symmetrical—that is because, as our measurements told us, the stage is not symmetrical—but they do emphasize one especial point about which we will make a rule whose principle should never be broken: *The off-stage edge of the wing must just cut the cross sight-line.* If it did not reach that sight-line—imagine it stopping short, say two squares before it cuts it—then the piece would not mask and the man in the opposite side seat could see past the off-stage edge of it into the wing-space. The farther away that edge is from the sight-line, the wider the gap he could see, and, it follows, the more people on that side of the auditorium could see it with him.

Furthermore, we are able to count from our plan the exact width of each piece and the exact position of each with regard to the walls of the stage, and so are in a position to reproduce our lay-out exactly upon the stage, knowing that the real set will take form no less (and no more) adequately.

So two points of cardinal importance have emerged from the absurdity.

Keeping them in mind, let us take steps to remove the absurdity from the lay-out without losing its good qualities. We must rearrange; and this is part of a scene-designer's work on plans, in which the value of this method above all others is that, by it, he can examine the greatest number of alternatives and correctly assess their relative advantages and disadvantages.

Let us now ask what it is that makes these wings so wide—what conditions their width? It is (*a*) the size and (*b*) the position of the backcloth. A wider cloth would allow narrower wings, but a narrower cloth would demand wider wings still. A nearer cloth (keeping the size constant) would allow narrower wings, a cloth farther back would need them wider. How do we fix on the position and width of this cloth? Firstly, its position is governed by the depth of the set, the situation of the back wall of the stage, and upon whether any one needs to cross the stage from side to side behind the backcloth. We are supposing this to be a 'full' set, that is, one as deep as our stage will allow, and upon reference to our notes we see that there is no way of access from one side of this stage to the other save by crossing the stage itself. We must then establish our backcloth at least two feet from the back wall so as to leave a minimum comfortable passage between the two, since communication between the sides of a stage is essential in general practice.

So the cloth takes its present position on the ground plan. We shall have to consider its width in a moment, just now we will draw it as wide as our stage will allow, see Fig. 57. The excessive width of the wings now follows as a matter of rote:

draw a sight-line from the edge of the backcloth to the opposite front corner seat (*H* to *A* and *G* to *B*). This is the Cloth Sight-line. It is clear that the wings must be drawn so as to connect their respective cross sight-line with their respective cloth sight-line, else they will not mask.

We can then neither reduce the width of the wings as they stand, for they would then not reach their sight-lines, nor increase the width of the backcloth, for the walls of the stage forbid it; the opening between the wings is absurdly small; each piece of scenery reaches to the side walls of the stage and so allows no passage for the actors to get round to their entrances, and finally, the wings are inconveniently wide to build and handle, measuring 11 ft. 6 in. and 12 ft. respectively.

Our next move must be to increase the opening between the wings. One way to do this is to *splay* the wings, that is, keeping the off-stage corner in place, to push the inner corner up-stage so that the wings stand at an angle. Taken to its limit, this arrangement would of course lead us to wings leaning against the side walls of the stage, and touching the backcloth at right-angles—a sort of box set. Then any painting upon the wings would be seen edgeways by the audience and need to be specially designed. It was this problem of foreshortened painting that exercised the designers of the late seventeenth century. They had two solutions, either to use the principle of parallel wings that we suggest in our Fig. 57, but to decrease their width and increase their number, having several on either side the stage, one behind another, or to turn the wings at an angle, when they masked more effectively and had not to be so numerous. In the first arrangement, with the many narrow, parallel wings, drawing upon the wings was easy, as it displayed itself full face to the audience. In the second arrangement, with oblique, but fewer, wings, the painting was looked at from an angle and, especially when its subject was elaborate architecture in perspective, it presented to the designer some of the nicest problems because he had to calculate false vanishing-points in order that lines representing foreshortened horizontals should, on an oblique surface, really appear horizontals to the audience.

The task was so great, and the demand of the new mechanisms for moving scenery (among other reasons) so strong, that in spite of Andrea Pozzo's brilliant treatise on false vanishing-points for oblique-wing treatment in 1700, succeeding designers—even the sensation-loving Bibienas—used the easier parallel wings and accepted the extra amount of construction and painting which their greater number entailed. But the

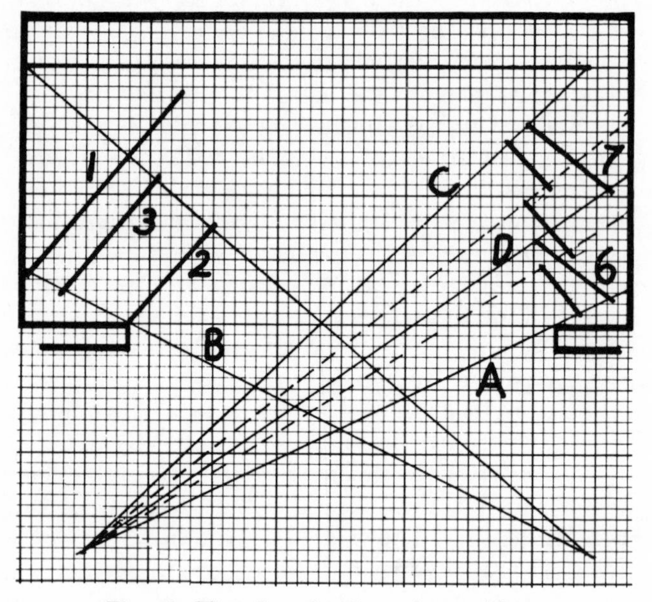

Fig. 58. The effect of various wing-positions.

more practical method won in the end, and with the passing of elaborate architectural perspective from the stage, the last objection to oblique wings vanished and they became the economical accepted method of to-day.

In Fig. 58 we may note the effect of oblique wings. Let us first consider those on the stage-right. The line marked 1 represents our original wing angled to a fresh position. It may, our sight-line tells us, in this position be reduced from 11 ft. 6 in. to 8 ft. in width (we measure it with a strip of the squared paper as on p. 120), and it will still mask the edge of the backcloth. Notice the economy of material brought about by improved placing of a piece. We can reduce its width still further by bringing it nearer to the spectator. The limit of this reduction is shown in the line marked 2, which measures about 6 feet. This is more nearly reasonable, for 6 feet is about the limit of wing-width for comfortable handling. But against positions 1 and 2 we still have the objection that the wing is jammed against a wall at its off-stage edge, preventing the passage of an actor round it and so forbidding any entrance in front of the wing. Further, in position 2 there is no room for the tabs to close. In position 3 we so arrange the wing that there is just sufficient room to allow the squeezing past of an actor. The wing here needs to be approximately 7 feet wide—still wider than is convenient.

We may set here, in passing, a tricky problem for the reader: the above arrangement may suffice at a pinch for the stage-right, but what arrangement can be made for the narrower side—the stage-left? Perhaps he may care to seek a solution of his own. It is such a problem as he may have to solve one day. For myself I shall put off the task till after the study of Section 17.

To the backcloth the same objection applies— that its edge adjoins the side wall of the stage and forbids the use of the passage we specially left behind it for the actors' crossing. Let us cut off two feet from each end of the cloth. Now this entails, of course, a new cloth sight-line and upsets the simple arrangement of wings that we have just proposed. Let us examine what rearrangement is necessary to satisfy this new condition.

For this we turn to the stage-left of the drawing. Here is represented the narrower cloth, giving line *C* as the new cloth sight-line. This new sight-line demands that our wing should be wider still. Setting it even in the easiest position, it would have to be at least 9 ft. wide—much too wide for practical purposes. This, furthermore, is the narrow side of the stage and an actor could not pass round the wing off-stage. So we are forced to a new move.

We must increase the number of wings, and as a result we shall be able to reduce the area of each. How wide must they be, and at what angle? If we roughly bisect the angle between the cross sight-line and the cloth sight-line we have the position of a third, intermediate, sight-line (*D* in Fig. 58), which we may call the Second Cross Sight-line. This regulates the positions of both the on-stage edge of the first wing and the off-stage edge of the one behind it. We select a point on the cross sight-line and draw a line from there to the second cross sight-line, this gives us our No. 1 wing. Next we draw a similar line from the second cross sight-line to the cloth sight-line and we have our No. 2 wing (lines 6 and 7 on Fig. 58). Now we can measure these and find that our system tells us that on this stage we can mask a 24-foot backcloth, hung 2 feet from the back wall, with two 5-foot wings stationed at angles we can exactly specify from measurement of the plan. And this is positive and useful knowledge.

But we can go further. What would be the minimum width of wing if we were to use three of them? We roughly trisect the angle between the cross sight-line and the cloth sight-line, and, marking-in our wings to suit the lines, we find that three 3-foot wings will suffice. And a three-foot wing is a very light and simple piece to handle.

Further, if we particularly wish to display any painting on the three wings and for this reason decide to turn them more to the audience, we could represent them between the same sight-lines at their new angle and discover what each would then need in the way of addition to its width to allow it to intersect the sight-lines.

We begin to learn much of a very practical value from our sight-lines; still their information is by no means exhausted.

In Fig. 59 we turn to the information the *Side Sight-line* can give. It is the line *BC*, from the corner seat through the nearer side of the proscenium opening. It tells us at once that three wings in positions *M*, *N*, and *O* would be completely hidden from that seat. Further, in the alternative arrangement 1, 2, 3, a sight-line from *B* through the edge of the No. 1 wing shows that it would completely mask the two behind; but if we set our wings as in *X*, *Y*, and *Z* (that is, draw No. 1 off, push No. 3 on, retaining No. 2 in position, and see that they still cut their sight-lines in their new positions), we have an arrangement where the edge at least of every wing on the stage will be seen from every seat in the house.

(It should be clearly noted that the width of wing indicated by the sight-lines in the above method is the minimum needed to mask. If the wing is, at any point, cut in for profiling *beyond* that indicated width, it will not mask. In calculating then, one must not think of a 6-foot flat with 2 feet of profiling as an 8-foot flat. The masking is only of so much beyond the six feet of the flat as the profile adds at its most

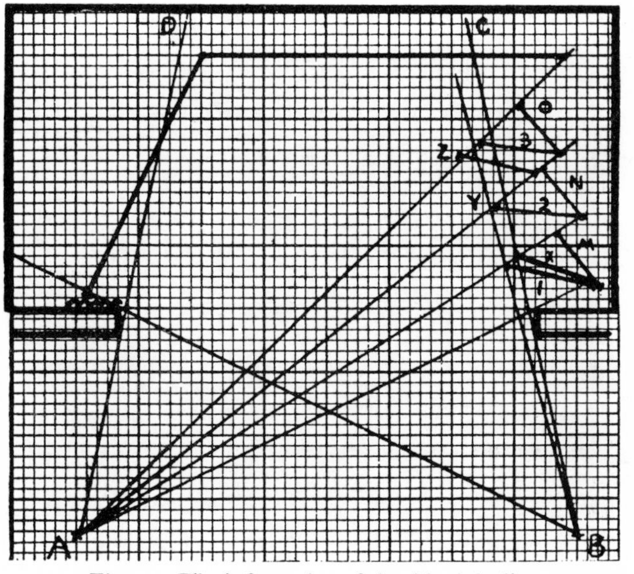

Fig. 59. The information of the side sight-line.

cut-in point. Hence the value of representing a profile wing by the symbol shown in Fig. 24, *E*.)

If we have to design a box set, we learn by the cross sight-line at what point to plan the down-stage edge of the side wall so as to be far enough away from the proscenium to allow the tabs to work and yet be near enough to mask, and how far out beyond the proscenium edge we must set it to suit these conditions; and we know by the side sight-line (*AD* in Fig. 59) at what angle to set the wall as a whole so as to preserve part of it at least in visibility from all seats. Finally, we can measure the length of the walls of our set and decide of what size flats we may make the sections of the walls, or how best to accommodate the material of some existing stock to the conditions of this particular set.

We turn now to the section, and our first step is similar to that on the plan, but simpler. An *upper sight-line* (see Fig. 60) drawn from the spectator's eye-point through the top of the proscenium opening shows that just over 5 feet of ceiling can be seen at the back of the stage. We must mask this. We do so

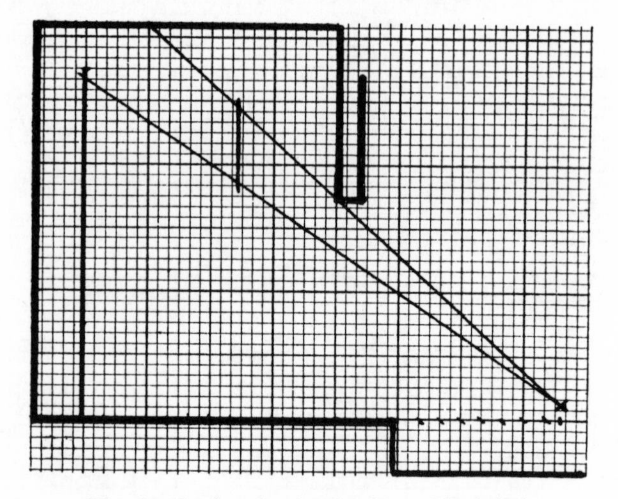

Fig. 60. Section showing border and backcloth.

by connecting a point on the upper sight-line with the cloth-top sight-line. This vertical line is our hanging border. How do we find the sight-line to the backcloth-top? By marking the position of the cloth 2 feet from the back wall as on our plan, and carrying it up to within a short distance of the ceiling, leaving a space of about 2 feet at the top to allow for the pulleys and gear from which the cloth is hung. A line from this point—situate 2 feet below the ceiling and 2 feet from the back wall—to the spectator's eye gives our cloth-top sight-line, and our border is easily drawn anywhere between the two sight-lines. We take a point according to the rule we made on p. 83, a little below the midway point of the stage.

The sight-lines now tell us that, for a backcloth 16 ft. 6 in.

high, and hung 2 feet from the back wall, we need in order to mask on this stage a 4-foot deep border, hung about 4 ft. 9 in. behind the proscenium, with its lower edge about 11 feet above the stage.

We may similarly calculate the requisite depth of border for any height of cloth, or the requisite height of cloth for any position or depth of border.

The section has told us now all we want to ask of it alone, but we must take a third step before our design is complete and, combining the information of plan and section, ask of the two together questions concerning the height of the wings, the length of the borders, and the relative suitability of placing for these two groups of elements.

In Fig. 19 we noticed that a plan has a certain relation to its section on the same scale in that, if the section be laid sideways beside the plan and carefully alined with it, a line may be drawn across from any object on the plan to the section and it will there mark the level of that object in true relation with the other parts of the section. This process of 'correlation' may be applied to our subject now, and we may turn from the two-dimensional aspects of our set to consider it in three dimensions. Upon Fig. 60 let us represent the wings, correlating Fig. 58 with Fig. 60 so that the stage-left side of Fig. 58 lies horizontally across the middle of Fig. 60 and the back wall of the stage in Fig. 58 is in the same line as the back wall in Fig. 60. Take first the pair of 5-foot wings; from the edges of each draw parallel lines to Fig. 60 and you will then have the virtual width of the wings projected on to the section as in Fig. 61, where they are labelled *P* and *Q*. Notice the lines do not represent the actual width of the wings, but only the apparent width which they would show, angled as they are and seen from the side, which is precisely what we need, as you will see.

To gain our specific information, we want to know how high the wings need be. The answer is simple: take *P*, produce the up-stage side of *P*—the edge on your left—until it cuts the border sight-line. That is the height of scenery needed to mask in that position: you can draw a line across there to mark the top of the wing. Take *Q* and produce the up-stage side similarly until it cuts the upper sight-line. You will find that by a stroke of luck it has to be exactly the same height, namely 14 feet. Wings do not always work out so neatly as this, but in practice the convenience of having all wings the same height so as to be readily interchangeable when required easily discounts the waste of a few inches in some, and we should always decide to make all wings equal in height to the tallest needed.

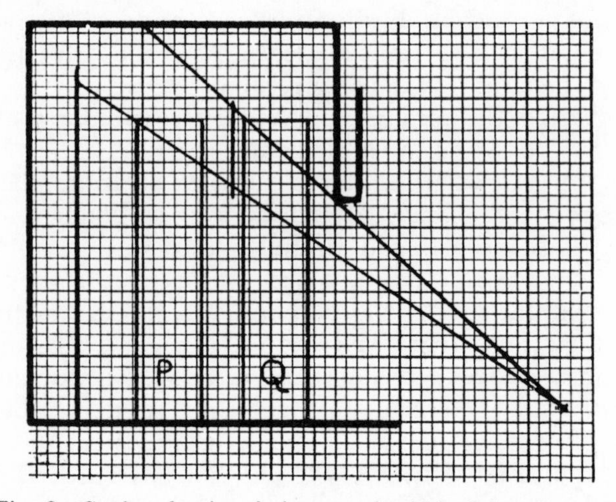

Fig. 61. Section showing the 'apparent' width of the wings, and how their correct heights and positions with regard to the border are ascertained.

We have next to decide a very important point. We have till now placed the borders and the wings without regard to each other; we must find out whether they interfere and whether the border hangs where we want a wing to go. Clearly the borders must hang *between* the wings—they cannot pass through them. We refer to our Fig. 61 and see that the border comes in the space between *P* and *Q* and we can consider the arrangement with satisfaction as one where our luck has held and where there will be no interference.

But let us examine the position where, instead of setting up our two 5-foot wings in the section, we take our three 3-foot wings.

I set them up as before, in Fig. 62, leaving the old wing lightly indicated for comparison. The three wings are numbered 1, 2, and 3. Producing 3 upwards to the border sight-line we find it need not be so high as *P* had been, and turning to 1 we find it may be considerably lower than *Q*, but, as before, we must have all wings an even height, and we have only to decide whether 2 needs to be higher than 3 to settle the height for the lot. Unfortunately, 2 presents us with a

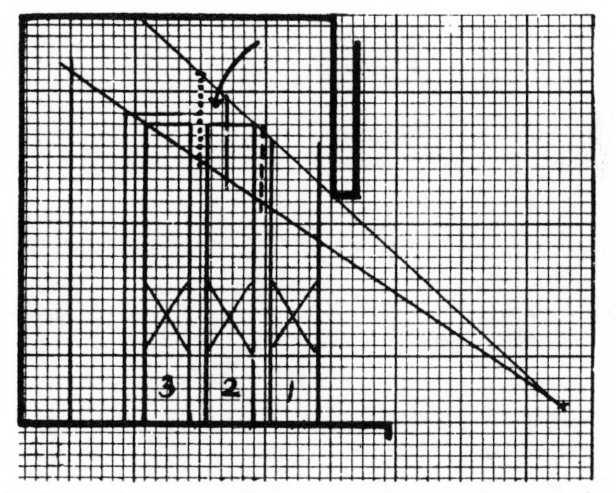

Fig. 62. Section showing how proper adjustment between wings and border may be attained.

dilemma—when produced it goes *through* the border. This is impossible, so we must move the border till it hangs in a space between two wings. We begin by moving it back to hang between 3 and 2 in the position indicated by the dotted border; we notice it must now hang a foot higher so as to mask at the top. But if we look carefully at this arrangement we shall find there a fault that we decided to avoid away back on p. 80. There is a *non-masking triangle*—marked with an arrow —just over flat 2. No part of the top line of this wing reaches the upper sight-line and therefore it is not masked. If we retain our border in this position we must increase the height of this wing (and hence, to keep uniformity, of the others) till its up-stage corner reaches the upper sight-line—that is to 16 feet.

On the other hand, if we bring our border down-stage so as to hang between wings 1 and 2 (indicated by the dashes), we could make the height of No. 2 wing the same as that of No. 3 and there is our solution right away.

Notice that if we increase the depth of our border an inch or two, we should lower the border sight-line and enable ourselves to reduce Nos. 2 and 3 wings to the minimum height of No. 1 and use a slightly shallower backcloth. It is

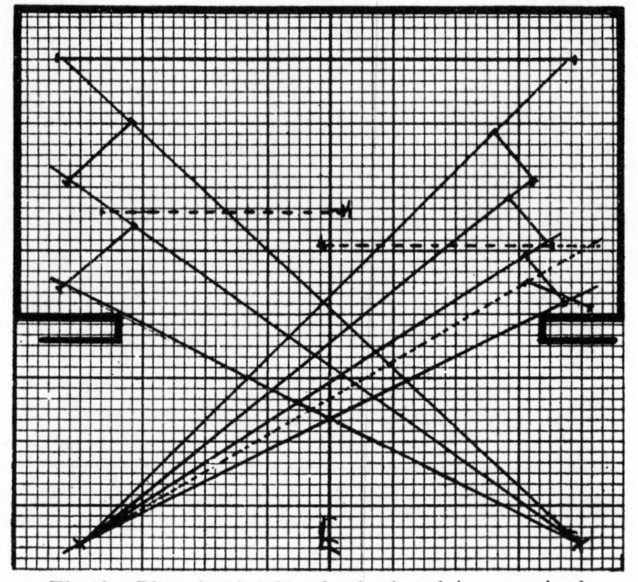

Fig. 63. Plan showing how border length is ascertained.

for the designer to decide whether the advantages of this move outweigh the disadvantages of reducing the height of his picture, as he must, of course, if he drops the border below the proscenium opening. He must watch against cutting down the view of the backcloth from the gallery if there be one.

In any case, the designer now knows a very great deal about the size and number of pieces of scenery and their most efficient placing on this stage. He lacks only one prime dimension—the length of the border.

To find this he returns to his plan and reverses the correlating process by which he decided the height of his wings; he now projects the border from the section to the plan. Let us take Fig. 63 where, upon the stage-right, is represented the arrangement with two side wings, and, upon the stage-left, that with three narrower wings. We aline the section (Fig. 62) with the stage-left half of the plan (Fig. 63) so that the back wall on the plan and the back wall on the section are in the same line. We then carry across the position of the correct border from the section to the plan and mark it with a tick.

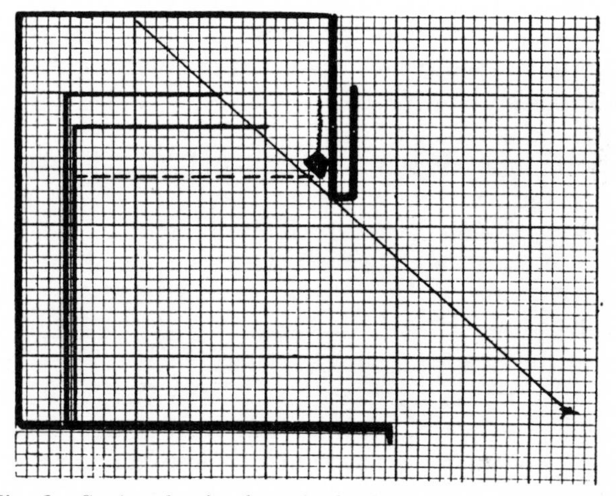

Fig. 64. Section showing how the depth of ceiling is decided for different heights of flats.

Remove the section and produce the tick into a horizontal line (a border is represented on a plan by a dotted line)—where should this line end? Clearly where it cuts the second cross sight-line, conditioned by the edge of the first of the three wings, and begins to disappear behind the edge of that wing. Upon measurement it is found to be 10 ft. 6 in. long from end to centre line. Notice how the shifting of the first wing to a flatter angle, as shown in the figure, may entail an addition of over 2 feet to the end of the border.

An exactly similar process, correlating the section in Fig. 61 with the stage-right of the plan in Fig. 63, will, as is shown in the figure, give the length of the border used with the two wider wings—it must be 11 feet from end to centre.

There is another valuable piece of information that the section can still give us, this time with regard to the box set and the relation of the height of its walls with the depth of its ceiling. Fig. 64 shows how a box set of flats 15 ft. high could be covered by a 7-foot ceiling, and how, if the flats were reduced to 13 ft. 6 in., a 9-foot ceiling would be needed. The dotted line shows that if the flats were only, say, a foot higher than the proscenium opening (that is, if they were 11 ft. 4 in.) the ceiling would have to be 11 feet deep and would have to come so near the back of the proscenium that it would cut off the light from the proscenium batten of lamps, an arrangement that must be avoided at all costs.

Even though this was a smallish and fairly simple stage, as befits an introductory example, every one of the principles formulated is directly applicable to large-scale work, with a number of wings and borders, or an out-size box set, or an elaborately built scene.

A brief *résumé* of the points touching on the length of borders and the height of wings, to decide which, correlation of plan and section is necessary, is made in Fig. 65 which gives us the appearance of a full set from a side seat: on the right, where the borders are too short—below, the little half-plan shows how the fault arose through the failure of the border-lines to cut their proper cross sight-lines; then, in the middle, the appearance of too-short wings, with, below, the way that mistake shows itself on the section by the presence of the non-masking triangle; thirdly, on the left it shows the neat arrangement where both faults are eliminated—with the correct plan and section below.

Such, then, is the principle upon which the parts of a scene may be correctly dimensioned and placed upon any given stage, and the whole setting worked out beforehand so that a model may be prepared, every element of which is correct to scale ready for painting.

Though we have as yet only touched the fringe of our subject and dealt with the simplest of setting arrangements, we have been round the whole of it, and however these arrangements are complicated by any developments of method, the principles outlined above include all the necessary groundwork for a full treatment of large and detailed sets upon the stage of big and elaborately equipped theatres.

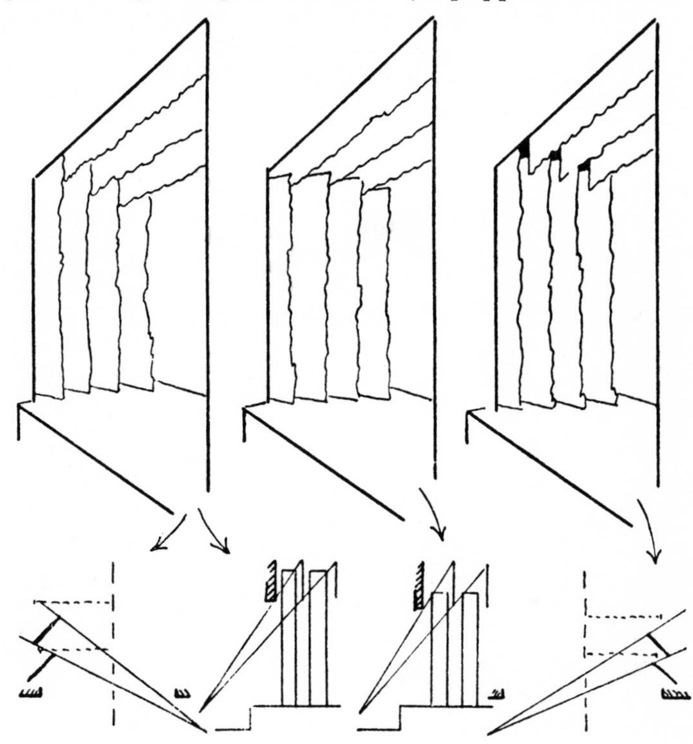

Fig. 65. Above, from left to right: correct arrangement; wings too low; borders too short. Below: half-plan and section showing correct arrangement; section showing too-short wings; half-plan showing too-short borders.

So much do the sight-lines teach the designer as he develops in their use that they begin to be themselves constructive, and suggest entirely new departures and the fresh handling of problems in design. They themselves sometimes supply inspiration by the conditions they impose.

Chief of these constructive contributions is what they suggest concerning the use of a *False* or *Inner Proscenium* as a masking agent. This subject of the inner proscenium we must now consider with those helpful sight-lines to guide us.

It will be convenient now to step a little more boldly into the province of the full-size stage, for the one we have been examining presents only an embryo of the situation we shall find there. Especially in connection with this inner proscenium is there an important new point to be considered affecting the lay-out of sets, in that all of them come to be pushed farther up-stage.

CHAPTER FOUR

Sight-Lines and Full Stages

SECTION 15

THE INNER PROSCENIUM AS A MEANS OF FRAMING SCENERY

The inessentials of scenery—the 'mantles of Harlequin' —the tormentor—on the stage-management's seeing a stage—the importance of including the inner proscenium in scene plans

---

I have explained elsewhere[1] that in dealing with full scenery we are facing the paradoxical necessity of including inessentials. It may often happen that all the scenery of a set is not really necessary to the presentation of a scene or to the design but has been included only to mask. Yet this too must be as carefully painted and as truthfully in key as the rest, even though it can only be seen from half a dozen seats in the house. And it is just as needful for that reason to remember that it must not, although it has to be in key, contain any element essential to the composition as a whole.

It may very well be, for instance, that a normal simple design does not call for more than a couple of wings, one border, and a backcloth to express all that it has to say, nor, possibly, does it need the full area of all of these, yet in practice it must be divided into elements sufficient in number and area to satisfy the requirements of masking the stage according to the sight-lines of plan and section.

It follows that for two types of company, that with limited means and that with artistic awareness, there is a search towards a method of reducing the individual pieces of scenery required on a stage to a minimum. If, upon occasion, the designer requires a set of many parts, these he can still employ—to profusion if he will, for you can play with more

[1] *Stage-Setting* (Faber).

scenery than is necessary (if you can afford money and space) and come to no harm, but if you play with less than is necessary, you are not able to mask.

Can we then satisfy the exacting demands of the sight-lines, as we develop our study to larger stages, in some other way than by the multiplication of pieces of scenery, each of which has to be changed for every scene?

We can. And here we touch the fringe of a movement in setting towards the gradual elimination of scenery. We may, to begin with, so standardize part of our setting that it is neutral in design, whereupon we have to paint and change only the remainder. In the touring theatre of the early part of this century it was common to standardize the Number 1 wings and border and turn them into a semi-permanent, painted-curtain frame—in other words an 'inner' proscenium behind the real one.

The value of such an arrangement is considerable in two directions. It gives a surprising saving in scenery (to what extent we shall see later), and it offers, in certain cases, a frame to the scene that has the merit of being variable in size. We can push on or withdraw the 'pros. wings' and raise or lower the 'pros. border'.[1]

This particular solution of the 'inner frame' problem is still obtaining in many of our provincial theatres. It gave us those famous 'Pros. Wings and Border'—those 'Mantles of Harlequin' as the French well call them—that have come to stand almost as a symbol of the theatre, with their supremely elaborate festoons and prodigal folds and swags of painted crimson velvet, and golden cords, tassels, and fringes.

It is important to realize that these were very real and true elements of theatre, and by no means merely ornaments. Their arrangement is most interesting and still offers a very practical method to-day. In detail the arrangement was this: the large, profiled pros. wing itself was duplicated by another, similar but a few inches shorter (for back view see Fig. 66).

[1] 'Proscenium' is a clumsy word to use often in technical conversation, and in the theatre it is frequently shortened to one syllable, especially when in combination with another word. Indeed the constant use of the fuller form in speaking such phrases as 'pros. line', 'false pros.', or 'pros. wing' would smack somewhat of the pedantic.

This second wing normally stood hidden behind the first when the full open stage was used; it was called a 'tormentor', and the name is sometimes applied to any pieces at the front of the stage which can be brought on or off to join up the side of a set with the side of the proscenium. The wing and tormentor ran in forks, and the tormentor was clipped to the wing by a cleat at the top fore-corner, in which it slid, when it was required to narrow the stage opening.

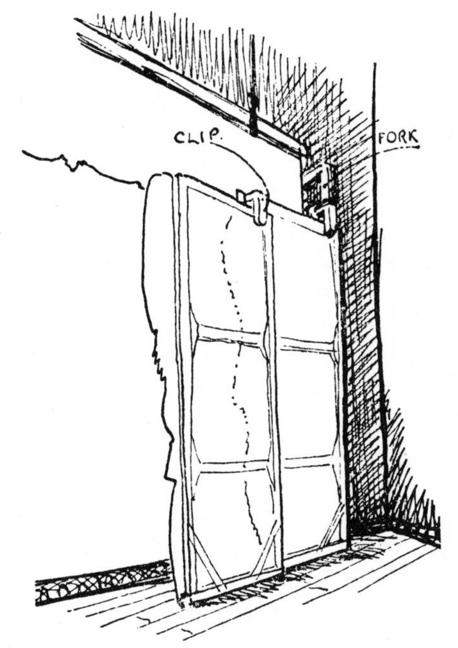

Fig. 66. A proscenium border, proscenium wing, and tormentor seen from behind.

In front (generally) of these, across the top, hung the great 'pros. border', similarly painted, and capable of being raised or lowered to accommodate the height of the set.

There is an alternative arrangement especially common in music-halls, where a shallow front scene is sandwiched between full scenes to close off the greater part of the stage, so that a change of scenery can be effected behind, while the show continues in the narrow space in front of the front-cloth. This alternative arrangement is to hinge the pros. wing and its extension together, and stand them at right-angles, the one straight up-and-down from the pros. wall, and the other on-and-off, parallel with the proscenium (Fig. 67). In this case a door is often put in the first flat (irrespective of the curtain design upon it) for the entrance of the actors. The front-cloth drops directly behind this and needs no other wings at all.

Fig. 67. Booked proscenium wings.

If a number of front-cloths is needed in one show, it follows that, because these must each be hung on a different set of lines, they are at varying distances from the proscenium, and so it is necessary, if the pros. wings are to mask them all, that they too should be variable in position, and this is achieved by progressively opening out the hinge and pushing the knuckle farther on-stage for each scene (Fig. 68). The down-stage wing of the two may be hinged to an upright batten braced against the proscenium wall. Care must be taken to see that these wings (especially the up-stage one) are high enough for their tops to be masked by the pros. border, even at their fullest extension.

In theatres visited by touring companies carrying their own scenery, of course, some such method of accommodating various sizes of sets was essential.

With the development of the box set and its straight continuous side, however, another problem arose: How were those off-stage in the 'wings' (now only called so by courtesy) to see what was happening on the stage? The question may be unexpected but it is a very real problem indeed. How, for instance, can an actor time a perfect entrance if he has to open a door in a continuous wall of flats (like that in Fig. 69) when he can rely on no other means of telling what is the situation and the moment upon the stage than his ears? With the old wings, he could see the stage wherever he stood but with the box set he is walled out.

In practice many solutions may be found, but among them is likely to be this, that an actor waiting behind the door watches, not the stage, but a signaller situate in some place where the stage can be seen, who gives him his sign at the

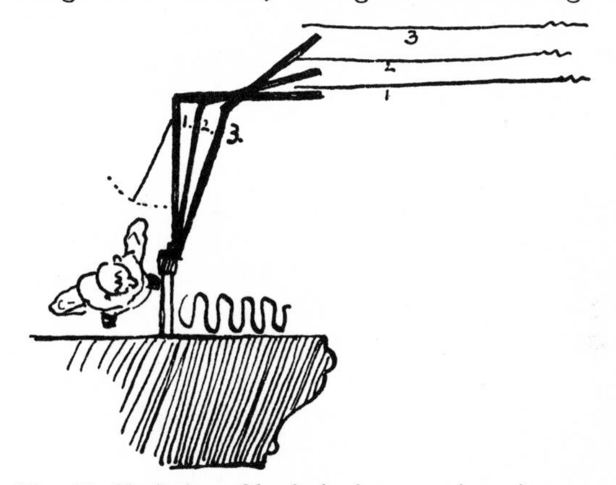

Fig. 68. Variation of booked wings to suit various positions of cloth.

psychological moment. Where is this signaller to be stationed to have a good view of the set?

Further, as conditions on the stage grow more elaborate, it is necessary to synchronize such things as the dimming of the lights when an actor on the set turns a dummy switch. Here again, his movements must be watched by some one capable of signalling to the electrician on the switchboard.

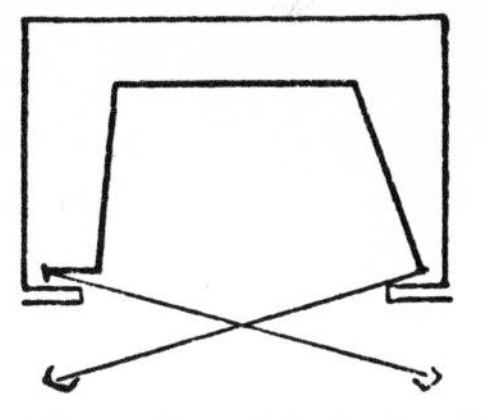

Fig. 69. Method of masking-in the sides of a box set.

Moreover, we know the superlative value of a well-timed curtain; how is this to be achieved if the stage-manager or his assistant has no adequate view of the stage?

The only break in the continuous walls of a box set—or at least the only place where you can depend on having a break in all cases—is down-stage, where the side-walls of the set join the proscenium. These side-walls you can either return with a sort of tormentor (Fig. 69, stage-right) or splay wide enough to reach beyond the proscenium opening and stop short of the proscenium wall (Fig. 69, stage-left).

So our 'inner frame' is now complicated by the necessity for allowing the stage-manager to see the stage he is managing, and to see it from a place where he may also house his system of signals and the desk for his prompt-book. For where he is, there should they be, not somewhere where he must leave his post to reach them.

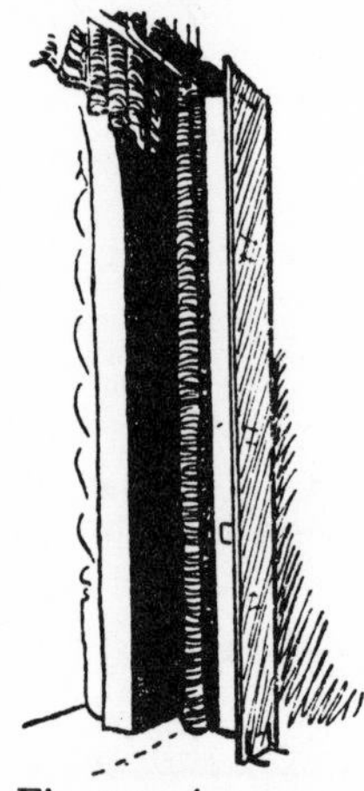

Fig. 70. A common form of inner proscenium.

A further point in accommodating the box set to the proscenium is that if the down-stage ends of the side wall of the scene are to be set a short distance away from the proscenium it is often useful to have some rigid structure intervening to which the first flat of the set can be cleated up.

Under these demands the old tormentor scheme develops into the more or less solidly-built 'inner pros.', whose arrangement may take several forms, but which is (see Fig. 70) in principle similar to the booked pros. wings set at right-angles. But it is generally composed of two much narrower flats, and these are now no longer richly painted but covered with black velvet. The two flats are generally about two or three feet wide and are, most usually, permanently fixed at right-angles to each other on the stage floor.

The angle or 'knuckle' formed by the two flats is in some theatres facing the stage and in some the wings. See Figs. 71 and 72.

The up-and-down flat is in either case provided with a hinged flap covering a peep-hole through which the stage-manager can watch the scene, and various arrangements may be designed to make his inspection more easy.

The presence of the trap-door is rarely noticed by an audience (unless the show loses its grip on them), for it is an unobtrusive detail competing for attention with a vast, brightly-lit stage, and is generally likely to attract the eye only when a bright light is carelessly exhibited through it.

As the front-scene went more out of fashion on the legitimate stage, so the need for entrances through the pros. wings diminished, and they are now mostly seen in the music-hall, where painted or black-velvet booked screens, as wide as the old pros. wings, are occasionally still to be seen, set with the knuckle pointing up-and-off-stage, and the old traditional door in the lower wing, while up in the air above it is a second opening, reminiscent almost of the balcony above the side doors in the Restoration stage. Behind the upper door the 'perches' are situate, whence an electrician controls the old 'limes', or the 'arcs', or the more modern 'focus spots'.

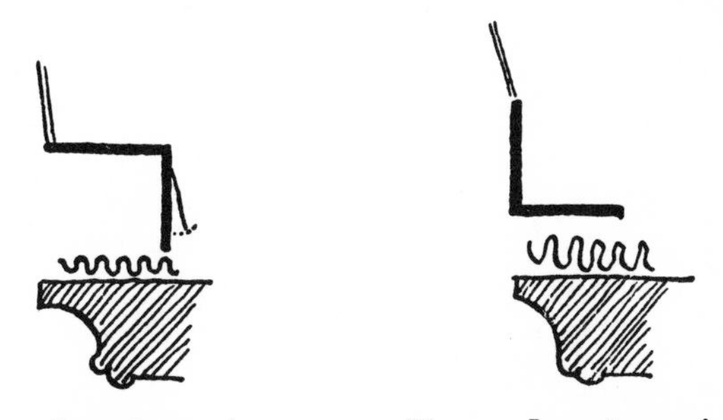

Fig. 71. Inner proscenium—knuckle 'up and off'.

Fig. 72. Inner proscenium—knuckle 'on and down'.

The stage-manager's view of the stage is through a peep-hole in the up-and-down-stage flat. In the arrangement with the angle off-stage, which is slightly more costly of space but is the more satisfactory on larger stages, the comfort and efficiency of the S.M. is increased by a handled mirror, pivoted on an arm from the proscenium wall, just beyond the drawn-back curtain, Fig. 73. The peep-hole may be gauzed with fine black net to make it still less obtrusive, and, to lessen the risk of lights behind being seen, it may be further masked with a backing-flap.

The function of the inner proscenium, then, is to be a sort of link between the architecture of the theatre with its permanent proscenium wall, and the set which the designer places on the stage. It adapts the proscenium arch to the set. The presence of this link is far too frequently overlooked by designers. They plan scenery to touch the proscenium, forgetting the stage-management's territory between, and when their scene is set up it has to be pushed two or three feet up-stage from the marks they had intended. They should carefully note the nature of the inner proscenium on each stage they work for, and see that their set is amenable to it, will join up with it properly, and will use to the full the advantages it offers. The inner proscenium is the affair of the stage and its staff, who will see that it is correctly set and masks; the designer's main concern is with the set proper based on sight-lines conditioned by the inner proscenium; and any suggestions concerning the alteration of the inner proscenium

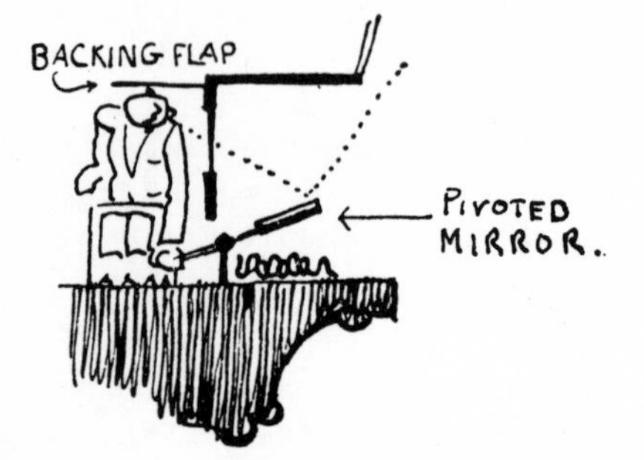

Fig. 73. The stage-manager's view of the stage is important.

are to be put before the resident stage-manager and his master-carpenter.

It follows then that with an inner proscenium the designer begins to set his scenery not at the proscenium line and adjoining the proscenium wall (as we have described him doing on smaller stages) but at a line further up-stage. Between proscenium and scenery there comes the inner proscenium. The scenery joins to that and begins from there. So we come upon the *Setting-line*. The setting-line is a line across the stage at the up-stage limit of the inner proscenium. Above that line the designer is free to set as he will, below is the province of carpenter and stage-manager, and the masking of that narrow area is their affair to be achieved by the neat arrangement of the inner proscenium. It is at the setting-line that the scenery begins.

This corner down-stage is then something that should be reckoned with and clearly understood; it is meant to provide the stage-manager with a place from which to work the show as well as being an 'adaptor' to fit the set to the proscenium. In a large theatre, there may be several important and separate elements functioning in this narrow part of the stage between proscenium and set proper. Most of these are part of the technical equipment of the stage itself and only partly related to the scenery of a show. They are summed up in Fig. 74.

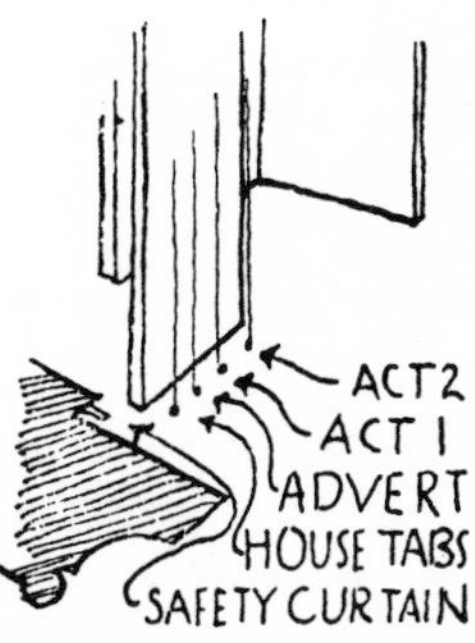

Fig. 74. Occupants of the narrow inner proscenium space.

Starting from the proscenium and going up-stage, we meet first the safety curtain, sometimes nick-named the *iron*, which, as we have seen, works generally in a channel set on the back of the proscenium wall, and far enough from the opening to be clear of any sight-lines and form an efficient smoke-trap.

Next above this we may find one or more *guide wires* to maintain the vertical descent of certain drops or cloths. These wires are fixed into the stage floor and strained up vertically to the grid, one on either side of the proscenium opening for each drop. The drop falls between its wires and is provided at its side edges with a set of rings or bobbins; the rings run on this wire. So the drop, as it is raised or lowered, is prevented from blowing forward or back and fouling other pieces or unmasking the proscenium opening.

So congested may be this little strip of space, of such importance to the working of a stage, that the drops flown within it may have to be set much closer together even than the minimum 6-inch intervals between the sets of lines for the scenery proper (space is valuable here lest the scenery be pushed too far up-stage), and so these guide wires are essential to ensure the drop's working dead in its true position and not catching its batten on that of another cloth as it passes.

There may be several of these drops. The *House Tabs*, or front curtains belonging to the theatre or 'house', may themselves be on such lines, in which case these are the first we shall meet directly behind the safety curtains. Next there may be that concession to impertinent finance—the advertisement curtain, a painted drop. Then there may be one or more act-drops, sometimes the property of the theatre and painted with a characteristic device, and sometimes specially painted for the current show and designed only for use during its run. These veil the stage in act-intervals, and so in some small degree serve to heal the breach in the show, which any wait occasions, by presenting the audience with a design relevant to the show, while the house tabs themselves are used, rather as full-stops than as commas, to signify the end of the spectacle.

When there is a number of such guide wires they become such an item as to involve a special masking-piece behind them. This special piece is set a little off-stage from the opening and at right-angles to it, as shown in Fig. 74. It is an especially useful aid to the clearer seeing of the stage by the stage-management, as it enables the inner proscenium proper to be set farther up-stage and still mask, allowing a wider space through which to keep watch. Such an extra masking-piece is suggested also in Fig. 67. It is a valuable adjunct in circumstances where one wishes to push the cross sight-line as far up-stage as possible, and it is a regular feature of several theatres.

When it is present this extra masking-piece in effect gives us a different *stage corner* for sight-lines, but on all such occasions the actually effective corner for these is, of course, that of the inner proscenium itself, which measurements 16 and 17 safely establish, whether the extra masking-piece is present or not.

SECTION 16

THE INNER PROSCENIUM AS A MEANS OF REDUCING SCENERY

The False Proscenium

So far, these additions to the proscenium frame have had for their purpose the fitting of settings of various types and sizes to a given stage and the maintaining of visibility from the prompt corner whatever the nature of the set wall. With the latest form, however, a new rôle for the inner frame becomes possible, the rôle of *an economizer* of the amount of scenery needed to mask-in a given stage, for, if we increase the depth of this inner proscenium we make a sort of bridge or tunnel with the set a shallower arrangement at the end of it.[1] It offers us therefore some aid towards the reduction of that area of 'inessential' scenery that is forced upon us by the nature of the Wing-and-Cloth Setting, whose possibilities for extravagant and realistic display upon occasion may be doubtful compensation for the great increase of work and expense, the complexity, and the consequent slowing-up of the show.

The inner proscenium hitherto described is an unobtrusive thing, indeed that is why so many designers forget it, but, as

[1] In how far one is justified in pushing the scenery away from the audience and burying it up-stage, one must decide in each individual case and according to the nature of the show. An intimate, realistic scene loses much by the use of a deep false proscenium, for the actors cannot come close to the audience without detaching themselves from their setting. But in shows where the conception of the set is on less photographic and more theatrical lines the false proscenium offers a help quite consistent with broader acting technique. The Restoration stage supplies a perfect example of the use of such a deep proscenium, and a study of the methods of the time is illuminating. (See, for example, Montague Summers' *The Restoration Theatre* (Kegan Paul, 1934).)

we deepen it, another entity is born and becomes more noticeable and steps over into the designer's province, requiring him to incorporate it in the visual pattern of his set. And this new element should rightly take another name to distinguish it and its function from its less emphatic cousin. For this purpose there is a possible term but modern stage usage confuses it somewhat with the first and we may as yet lay down no law, but in practice we find the term *False Proscenium* used most widely by designers to designate this fresh form. 'How are you setting your new show?' we ask, and the answer comes, 'I'm using a false proscenium. There are several scenes and we've got to cut down expense.' And so, beside the inner proscenium which is retained as an indispensable working link to join any set to the theatre, there may be set yet another 'proscenium', the false proscenium, and this one is definitely the affair of the designer and among his proper methods; if he use it in a design he must specify its size and nature and design it together with the rest of his set. It must come *above* the setting-line. Let us see what it is and why he calls it in as an agent in the economy of scenery.

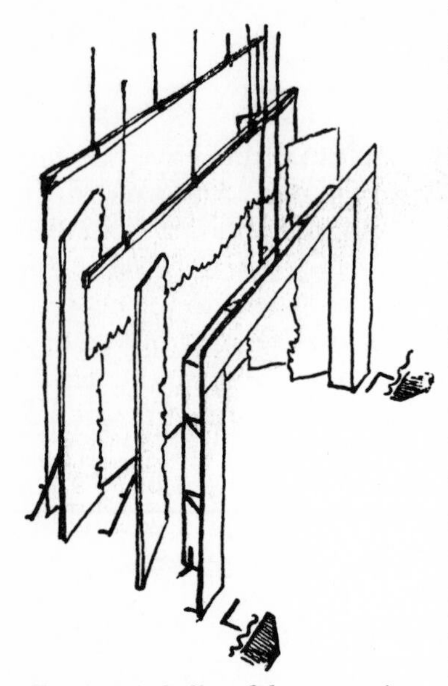

Fig. 75. A shallow false proscenium.

The false proscenium consists of two sides and a top, standing behind the real proscenium arch and inner pros., and virtually repeating their forms. It may provide a shallow or deep frame to the stage and its two most general shapes are shown in Figs. 75 and 76.

In the first example it is almost a twin of the inner proscenium. The upright sides consist of two narrow flats each, one of them set parallel with the proscenium proper, the other at right-angles to it, facing on-stage. These two columns of the side reach to the top of the proscenium opening and are connected horizontally at the top by a similar pair of flats: one face-down across the top, the other, at right-angles, at its front edge. The whole, from the front, looks like a solid square opening in the thickness of a wall.

Herein lies the difference from the inner proscenium if difference there be to occupy us at all: a false proscenium (which is generally related to a specific show, and put up only for that show) will almost certainly have a fixed top. An inner proscenium, on the other hand, is part of the theatre, remains useful for all shows, and must be more or less variable, at least in height, and so the more rigid top of the false proscenium type takes the place of the more flexible proscenium border. In a small theatre, however, where variability of height is probably impossible anyway, a form such as that in Fig. 75 may be built and go under either name with equal justification.

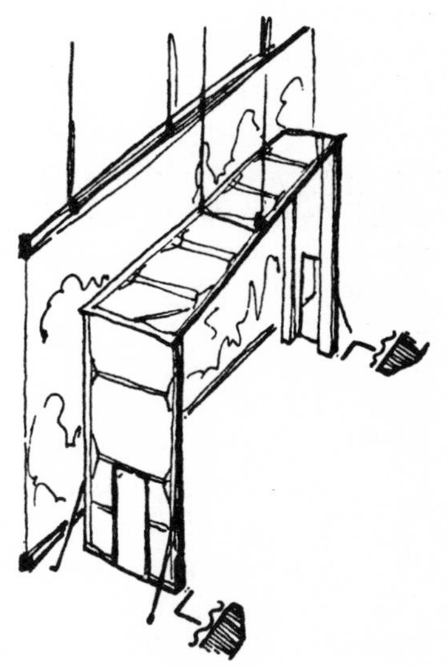

Fig. 76. A deep false proscenium.

But 'false proscenium' tends to be used to designate a fixed frame, while 'inner proscenium' suggests possibly fixed sides but almost certainly a variable top in the nature of a border.

The second form, in Fig. 76, economizes still further on scenery but is perhaps more suitable for larger stages. It presents a deeper arch and consists merely of a couple of 6-foot (or wider) flats, one either side, at right-angles to the footlights, with a third flat laid ceiling-wise across their tops, to form a kind of bridge. The side flats will generally contain doors.

The value of these arrangements is that a stage whose sight-lines normally demand, say, two wings a side and two borders, may be converted into one needing only one wing a side (even if that be slightly wider than before) and no border —or even, with the deeper sort, no wings at all and no border, merely a backcloth. If any set should come along demanding for its pictorial effect two wings or more a side, that can be as easily contrived on a stage with a false proscenium as without, merely by making the wings narrower. With a shallow false proscenium you are limited very little more than before in the maximum number of wings you can crowd on a stage, but you are able to reduce your minimum when economy in material, time, or style restricts your scheme.

The plans and sections on a later page will show upon what arrangement of sight-lines the dimensions of a false proscenium may be calculated and how its addition to a stage allows an ascertainable economy of scenery.

The building of a false proscenium presents only one slight difficulty, in the means to be taken to prevent the long ceiling flat at the top from sagging. This is almost always best done by suspending it from the roof above by ropes, or by wires (which do not stretch like ropes). The wooden frames of the component flats may be covered with a composition board instead of canvas, for there is no quick striking to be faced, and consequently no lightness to be sought.

The up-and-down-stage flats of the first variety are butted cleanly against the back face of their front neighbours and screws are put through the latter into the thickness of those behind. Struts may be screwed across the angle at the back. The whole may be fixed to the floor with angle-brackets. Such a structure is not so permanent that, if occasion demands, it cannot be dismantled and taken away in half an hour's time.

SECTION 17

THE FALSE PROSCENIUM AS A MEANS OF ELIMINATING SCENERY

Flippers—the plaster back wall—curving the plaster—an ideal stage masks itself

---

Part of the modern movement in setting is towards the elimination of scenery. To what extent we are now to see.

In Fig. 77 we have the first of another series of plans on squared paper. The stage shown in this series is considerably larger than the last, and the scale used is now one square on the paper to a foot, instead of two squares.

This stage, then, is 20 ft. deep and has a 28-ft. wide proscenium opening. Wing-space is 8 ft. a side. Part of the equipment of the theatre is a small inner proscenium composed of 2-ft. flats, giving us a setting-line 3 ft. up-stage. There are no boxes and the sight-lines from the corner stalls are well placed in easy positions.

Of the 58 theatres listed in the 1936 *Who's Who in the Theatre*, 45 are deeper than this and 13 shallower: 36 have a wider proscenium opening and 22 have a narrower. We are, then, treating of a small-medium stage, and one especially favourable to a demonstration of the effect of a false proscenium.

In Fig. 77 we have the normal wing-and-cloth arrangement, but one that offers a special point to our attention which as yet we have not fully discussed. Upon the stage-right, two 6-ft. wings are set before a 36-ft. backcloth, and set so as to mask most efficiently, that is to say they are set at right-angles to the sight-lines. *A wing set at right-angles to the spectator's line of vision masks a greater area.* It is, in effect, so far as the masking is concerned, a wider wing than if it were set at any other angle, but when we have appreciated the point and turn to design a set upon this principle we come against the dilemma that a wing set at right-angles to the cross sight-line is so obliquely set with regard to the body of the audience that the painted design upon it may appear to poor advantage and be badly foreshortened. Further, if the wing is profiled with a shape that the designer has, we may suppose, drawn with some care so as to frame pleasantly his background,

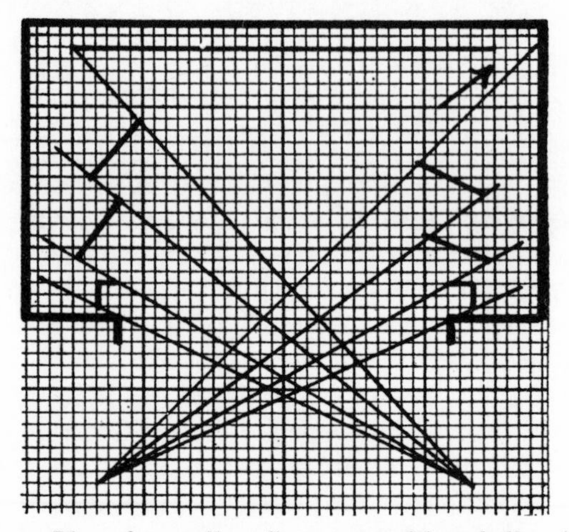

Fig. 77. Plan of a small-medium stage with a shallow inner proscenium, at the scale of 1 square to a foot; showing how flat-angled wings mask less than more obtusely angled ones.

those cleanly cut, irregular edges will be to some extent spoiled of their framing effect, because their projections and indentations will be virtually reduced and 'diluted' through the wing being set so that they are seen obliquely and not, as intended, from the front. Something of the deadening effect is suggested in Fig. 78.

In order, then, to display the design on a wing satisfactorily it must be set at a flatter angle, in which it is less efficient as a mask. On the stage-left of Fig. 77 you may see how a flatter arrangement of the same-size wings may display their shape better to the audience, but unfortunately in one respect it ruins our scheme; the No. 2 wing has had to be brought somewhat down-stage and now no longer masks the backcloth.

It is here that we find one of the great advantages of *flippers*. If the profiled area on the on-stage edge of the wing can be turned full to the spectator so that the full value of the edge can be appreciated, while the body of the wing is still set in its most useful position at right-angles to the sight-lines, we settle both difficulties. All we have to do is to make the profiling in a separate piece and then hinge it on to the body of the wing. This hinged addition is termed the flipper.

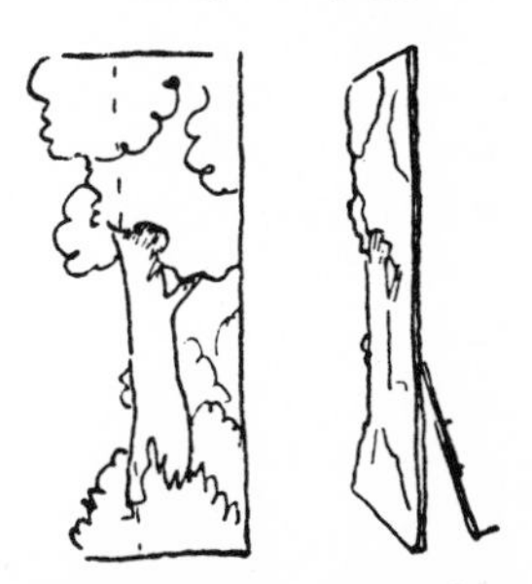

Fig. 78. The weakening effect of an obtuse angle upon profile.

We have already suggested that the off-stage half of each wing is scenically an inessential area in the sense that only few spectators see it, and it follows that a good designer never places an essential detail of his composition

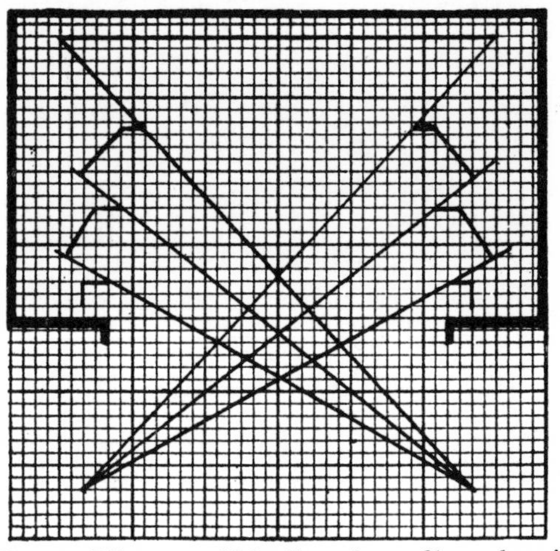

Fig. 79. Flippers, which allow the profile to show its true shape.

in these areas, and only paints on them mere repetitions or extensions of the main scheme. His important details and his profile he reserves for the on-stage part of the wing and the hinged flipper, then he may set the wings at the angle the sight-lines demand but fold his flippers to the angle that suits his design.

Our wing-angles, then, on the stage-left of Fig. 77, which are such as best display the painting and the profile, had seemed at first to incur an increase in the number of wings needed to mask. Our first step in the elimination of scenery has been negative, or at least preventive; we have put the profile on flippers and returned them on-stage, retaining the wings themselves in their old, most useful angle, and so

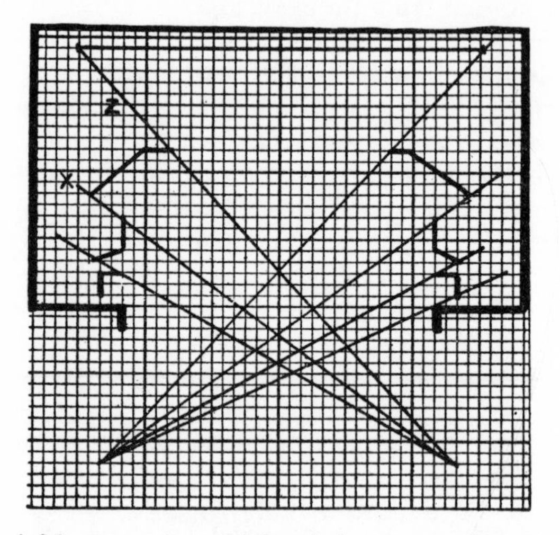

Fig. 80. A false proscenium added to the inner proscenium eliminates a pair of wings.

avoided what seemed an inevitable increase in their number. Fig. 79.

Our next step is positive. We are actually to decrease the number of wings.

In Fig. 80 a simple false proscenium has been added, just up-stage of the orthodox inner proscenium. The sides of this new false proscenium consist as usual of two flats at angles. This time the *knuckle* is on-stage, that is to say the angle is pointing on and down, whereas the angle of the inner pros.

points up- and off-stage. Moreover, the up-stage false pros. flat on each side is 3 ft. wide and the off-stage one 2 ft. 6 in. and in the placing of them care has been taken to splay the off-stage flat in each case instead of maintaining it at a right angle. This has allowed the whole structure to be set farther up-stage, and so to push farther back the cross sight-line *X* occasioned by its edge; had the lower flat been set at right-angles, the upper flat on either side would have needed to be a foot wider to mask the same extent. Further, a wider view of the stage from the wings is allowed by the splayed arrangement.

A question may raise itself here: Why not connect the outward extremities of the two flats of the false proscenium side, so giving a line about 4 ft. 6 in. long, set like a wing and at right-angles to the line of sight? This would allow a single 4 ft. 6 in. piece to do duty for the false pros. side instead of two pieces angled together. The question is legitimate, the move is quite possible, as the sight-lines show, and its economy of those twelve inches of flat is real. The decision rests on the visual effect. The nature of a false proscenium is to frame a set; it is generally more in the architectural nature of a frame to place the pieces as shown in the figure than to set a narrower piece exactly as a wing, when its distinction from the set it should frame is not so sharp, and when, in fact, one would merely revert to a reduplication of the old pros. wing system. The architectural nature of the side is not spoiled by the slight splay of the nearer piece; it will scarcely show as more than a firm right-angle. But, in fact, either method is practicable.

Another point in favour of the arrangement illustrated is that it combines more consistently with a false proscenium top with which we wish to replace or supplement our pros. border, for, as our sections will show us later, the ceiling-like top is a far better masking agent in these circumstances. But the method is flexible. Different means fit different occasions. The sight-line system presumes to do no more than clarify the dimensions for any suitable arrangement, or point out the faults of an unsuitable one.

This new proscenium now occasions, of course, a fresh

cross sight-line, *X*. We draw it from the opposite corner seat through the up-stage extremity of the false pros. If we next draw our cloth sight-line, *Z*, as before, we find we need only one wing a side to mask, and that wing must be 6 ft. plus 2 ft. wide (the 2 ft. is the flipper), though we must be careful to set such a wing at its correct angle, for at too flat an angle it will not mask. We should notice that the farther up-stage we go, the flatter will be the angle of a wing set at right-angles to the sight-lines.

A carefully-planned, 3 ft. plus 2 ft. 6 in. false proscenium, then, may eliminate a 6 ft. plus 2 ft. wing. So much for our initial move against the profusion of inessentials in the set. We have begun to economize on the wings, can we turn our attention with equally good results towards the backcloth?

Here modern developments have evolved a recognized technique, tending towards greater simplicity, more flexible effect, and reduction of scenery. Let us ask ourselves how much of a backcloth is essential. For masking, clearly its whole area is essential, but if we could settle the question of masking-in the back of the set by other means, how much of the cloth remains essential to the scene in the show itself? Often very little. Often, all that is needed could be stated with a small groundrow or set piece. Even though the set be, for instance, a realistic or simplified-realistic exterior, generally only the landscape at the bottom of the cloth is essential, the sky is only there to fill up. If in such an exterior set we cut out the low line of landscape from the bottom of the backcloth and stand it in front of a plain skycloth, we can set a hundred different landscapes with one permanent skycloth, variously lit, and a hundred groundrows.

Not only would that be an immense saving of time in painting, and an arrangement a great deal easier to set and strike, but it would definitely increase our atmospheric effects and the number of shades of expression we could get into each individual scene by suitable modifications of our lighting.

The new conditions, then, include a permanent sky back against which various groundrows or set-pieces are placed. But if the sky backing to the stage is to be permanent it need be no longer lightly built of canvas. It may, instead, be built permanently of whatever material we choose, whatever (other things being adequate) takes the light best and gives the best effect. The great requirement of a sky backing is that it should not show seams or joins, and should never pucker or wrinkle, but should be a clear, perfectly blank surface upon which we can play with light, and where no mark exists to break the effect and betray an inkling of what the 'sky' is nor where it is situate. If there is a pucker or spot the spectator's eye can fasten and focus on that and judge therefrom the distance of the surface; if it is perfectly blank, if its edges are masked, and if it is bathed in light, there exists no visual clue to betray its situation this side the clouds. It can be used to convey a sense of space, and so to avoid that cramping effect of a shallow stage upon a would-be open scene. It is for this reason primarily that shadows cast on a sky are bad; they allow the audience to judge where the sky is and to see it is only eighteen inches behind the balustrade, or the line of distant hills.

So much admitted, we may begin to see as we pass that the possibilities of a good back far exceed the mere representing of a convenient sky—that we are in fact on the verge of a new style in setting. But practical considerations are before us at present, let us return to this sky and its material; and the ideal material for a sky backing is plaster. Plaster your back wall and you quadruple the value of your stage. Look again at Fig. 80. The sight-lines through the flippers show that the wings mask the corners of the back wall of the stage. Now suppose that wall to be smoothly plastered and painted, and suppose that the line in front of it, which we have hitherto been considering as a backcloth, no longer marks the position and length of a full cloth, but of a low groundrow. We may thus take a further step towards the elimination of scenery by getting rid of four-fifths of the backcloth and framing-out the remainder to stand on its own.

And we may continue the process, for a new means comes to hand in this plastered wall, a means to eliminate even those wings left.

Consider, in Fig. 80, the sight-line that cuts the up-stage

edge of the false proscenium *X*. If we could only arrange the back wall to cut that line *our stage would mask*. This is by no means impossible. As a first move let us push that sight-line farther back by increasing the depth of our false proscenium to 6 feet.

At this point it behoves us to pay attention to every possible means of pushing up the sight-lines, and to watch for their every suggestion of assistance. We see that if we merely extend our 3-foot, up-and-down-stage flat to double its width, we shall mask to such-and-such an increased extent; but if, as well as widening that flat, we angle it slightly on-stage we shall mask even more.

We have then to consider the pros and cons of this question of splaying the false proscenium sides. Clearly they would mask most effectively (were masking our only concern) if we follow the rule and angle them so far on that they are lying at right-angles across the sight-lines. But this would bring them so far on-stage as seriously to narrow the acting-area—it might be reduced to a mere 18 feet wide. We have constantly to keep this exchange of advantage and disadvantage in mind: angle on your side more and you improve your cross sight-line but decrease the width of your stage. To what extent may we compromise here? Generally, in practice, a guide is offered by the side sight-line: angle your piece on till its up-stage edge touches this line. You then have the satisfaction of knowing that even had you angled it less and preserved a more open stage, actors at the extreme side of the area would have been masked in any case from the side seats. If, then, these are blind corners anyway, there is more excuse for cutting them off with scenery.

In Fig. 81 the false proscenium side upon the stage-right is extended and angled on to cut the side sight-line—the stage opening is then 23 feet, a not especially noticeable narrowing.

But another point concerning the placing of the parts of the false proscenium now arises. We may perhaps allow ourselves liberty with the supposed right-angle between the two pieces provided we keep one at least parallel to a main axis of the stage. Now, however, we are proposing to splay the other flat, and it must be carefully considered whether such a universal lack of conformity in the sides with the main lines of the stage will not weaken their general sit and bearing. Should this be so, we may arrange the smaller down-stage flat parallel to the footlights and splay the up-stage one from its inner edge. This will mean increasing the width of the small flat to at least 3 feet, to mask. The splay inward of the larger flat we will for the moment leave undecided, noticing that, whatever its position, it conditions a sight-line which it is our purpose to

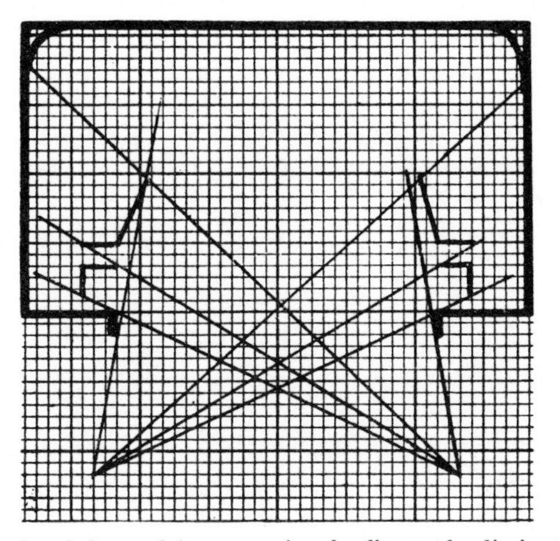

Fig. 81. A deeper false proscenium leading to the elimination of all scenery.

have strike the back wall of the stage, so eliminating any need for wings.

Considering now this sight-line we shall see that it still fails to reach the edge of the back wall, and still leaves some feet of the side wall unmasked. But now, if the wall is to be plastered, we can bring the edge of the wall forward to meet the sight-line.

It follows that, as plaster may be as smoothly laid on a shaped wall as a flat one, consideration may be given to the shape of this stage back wall. Need it be flat? It need not. It can be curved. It can be dome-shaped like the inside of a quarter of a sphere.

Upon a larger stage a false proscenium can, with the best will in the world, only reduce say four pairs of wings to three, unless it be made deeper than is convenient. But if the back wall is plastered and, in plastering, the outer corners are filled in and brought forward in a curve for some distance along the side walls, a second pair of wings may be eliminated straight away; and after that, by increasing the encircling arms of the back wall, any others you like until the stage is completely masked again, but now with no wings at all. Fig. 81.

On the stage-right of this figure it is shown that by setting the false pros. side in the indicated position, the back wall may

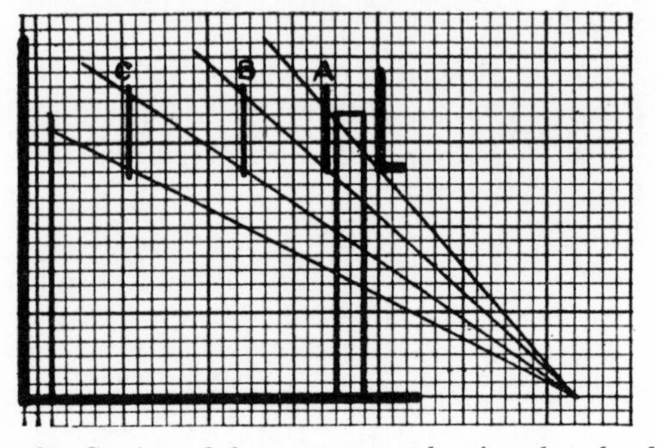

Fig. 82. Section of the same stage showing three borders.

be masked provided its ends curve forward for the short space of 4 feet down the sides of the stage.

On the stage-left of the same figure a very clear example is given of the value and information of sight-lines. We see that if we use exactly the same shaped pieces for our false pros. sides, but make the very slight adjustment of carrying the up-stage corner of the large splayed piece 12 in. farther off-stage, we shall make it necessary for the plastering to be carried nearly 3 feet farther down the stage sides than before.

There are, behind the placing of the elements of a setting on plan, two notions: to set the piece at the angle most becoming to its appearance, and to set the piece at such an angle as will condition the most favourable sight-lines for economizing the pieces beyond it. Frequently, designing consists in reconciling a conflict here.

Turning now to the section of the stage we can effect a similar elimination; Fig. 82 shows the same stage to the same scale and provided with the same inner proscenium, 2 ft. deep and set 1 ft. back from the proscenium line. Directly behind this hangs the 6-ft. proscenium border *A* belonging to the theatre.[1] The pros. opening is 16 ft. high. Notice, a sight-line through the top of the opening shows the height for the inner pros. side. This height must be such that the up-stage side of the piece cuts the sight-line (in this case 20 ft.)—otherwise we should have our non-masking triangle in evidence again. The pros. border is here hung to reach to the level of the pros. opening, though there is still a good foot of its depth left in reserve should we come to lower it to gain easier upper sight-lines.

If we now hang the first set border (*B*, also 6 ft. deep) at a level with the proscenium border, our border sight-line tells us it must be about 6 ft. up-stage from it.

We should now need a backcloth well over 24 ft. high to mask. Cloth heights usually come in multiples of 6 ft.—the width of the canvas material from which they are made (which 6-ft. width of canvas also governs the depth of borders). A 30-ft. cloth would, then, be necessary unless we use a second border. When we begin to place a second 6-ft. set border *C* at the same level as the other, our sight-lines show us it is to be situated at a distance of about 8 ft. back from the first set border, and we see that a border so placed would mask a backcloth as low as 19 ft. This is a foot over a standard height, but we may easily save a further 6-ft. width of canvas (most of which would be wasted) on our cloth by dropping the first border an inch or two and the rest to correspond. Then we shall mask with an 18-ft. cloth.

We noted that the height of the flats of the inner proscenium must be 20 ft. We must ask ourselves whether the

[1] It will be noted here that the pros. border is hung on the up-stage side of the inner pros., not as in Fig. 66, on the down-stage. This entails higher flats for the inner pros. sides but grants us easier upper sight-lines for the same height of opening. Were we to hang the border down-stage, we should, of course, have to drop it some three feet to gain as good a border sight-line, though we should be able to mask the sides with only 16-ft.-high flats.

arrangement we have made with the borders will allow our using wing flats lower than this 20 ft. in our set, for we do not readily accept the task of having to handle specially made scenery over regulation height (that is, over 18 ft.), if we can find a way of making normal full size stuff do. (The inner pros. flats may be 20 ft. because they are permanent.)

But to mask behind an opening as high as 16 ft. with 18-ft. flats involves a certain amount of restriction in their placing, they must be set at reasonably flat angles and each very close

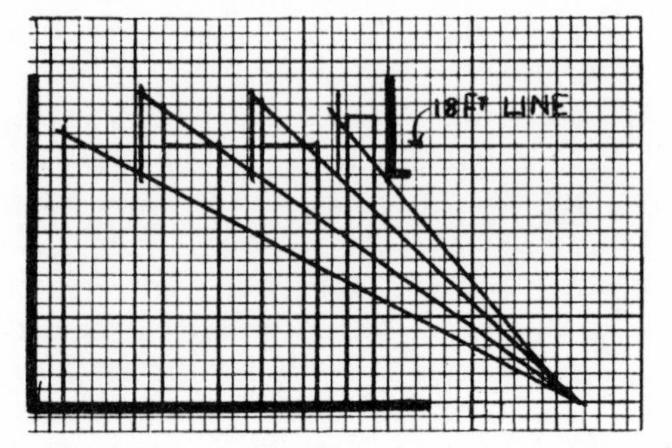

Fig. 83. Section showing the extension necessary to the top of 18-ft. wings.

behind its border. We had, however, already fixed the position and angle of our wings somewhat critically when we made our plan. We must be sure that in setting them up we avoid altering those planned angles in an attempt to get the wing tops to mask behind the borders; else we may achieve this only to discover we have shifted them to such positions that they now no longer mask the backcloth sides.

Upon the section in Fig. 83 we see that the 18-foot-line runs a little under the centre points of the borders, and we notice that the sight-lines through the border-edges cut that 18-foot-line so as to offer in no case much more than 2 feet of space that is masked behind each border at that level. Reference to the plan in Fig. 79 shows we cannot hope to splay our wings at so flat an angle that they only occupy 2 feet of stage depth. Even then the arrangement would only be satisfactory provided we set each wing so close to the border above as to touch it—allowing ourselves no freedom of placing, just as we could allow little freedom in angle.

What then is to be done in the circumstances? Correlation of Fig. 79 with Fig. 83 shows that the up-stage edges of the wings will come in the positions marked, from which it is immediately clear that we should be able to see over the top of the greater part of either wing.

We wish not to use a higher wing (for that would have to be specially made instead of coming from stock). We may not alter the angle of the wings nor move them down stage, for they would no longer mask the backcloth, which is already as wide as is convenient. We may not drop the borders, for our producer demands 16 feet of headspace. We will suppose there are no sets of lines available to take the borders farther up-stage—though any one of these moves would help to solve our problem.

We are thrown back upon a little-known but occasionally very useful emergency measure. Why not leave the flats as they are but profile the top of each? As soon as this step is suggested we turn to the section to note the necessary depth of this profile or extension. On the No. 2 flat 2 ft. 6 in. would suffice. On the No. 1 we must add a clear 3 feet to be safe.

Another consideration now arises, not, in this case, urgently, but sufficiently to allow our discussing it as a provision against a similar occasion more pronounced. It is unwise to add much weight to the upper edge of a flat. It upsets its balance (and a properly made flat is beautifully balanced for its job), and makes it top-heavy for the scene-shifter. Therefore if we allow topping-up at all we must reduce it to the very minimum.

There arises in the particular use of the system of sight-lines which solves this problem, a principle of considerable importance, and it is worth while turning aside for a moment to examine it in detail so as to precise it for use on other occasions.

Fig. 84 is a diagrammatic illustration of this principle. Let us suppose the line *A* represents a 6-ft. flat drawn to a scale of three squares to the foot, on the stage-left of a stage plan which is turned on its side for correlating and whose proscenium would consequently be to the reader's right hand of the diagram. This flat is a wing, set at an angle of 45 degrees. Above, at *B* is the representation of the top part of the wing projected on to a section and showing now only a virtual width of about thirteen squares. In front of this flat hangs a border represented in section at *D*, occasioning the sight-line *E*.

We may now see that the flat is short by the amount of nearly seven squares, that is to say, 2 ft. 4 in.

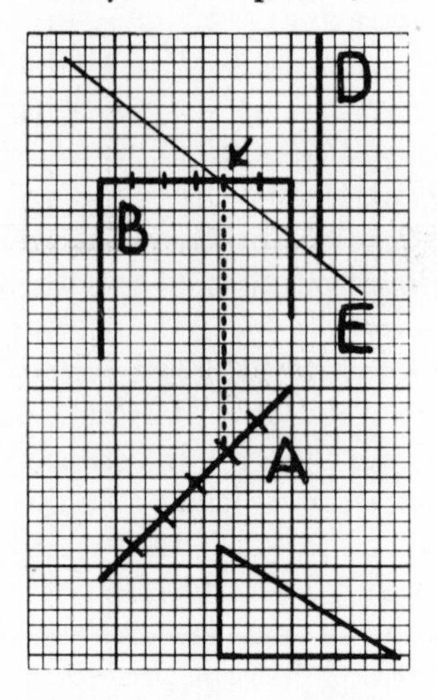

Fig. 84. The principle of sight-lines applied to diagonal surfaces. Scale: three squares to 1 ft.

But the sight-line shows that not all of the top of the flat is unmasked: at a point about eight squares from the side of the flat the top cuts the sight-line and is thereafter masked. So any extension need not pass beyond this point. But where is this point upon the flat?

We must not reduce those eight squares to feet by our scale, and suppose that gives the length of extension needed, for on a section only the virtual, and not the actual, width of a wing is represented. But we may easily obtain the exact measurement of this point by a reverse projection from section to plan. We note the position at which the wing-top cuts the sight-line, and carry a vertical line from there downwards till it cuts the plan of the wing. We then measure from the end of the wing on the plan up to this point, using the paper-strip-measure, and we discover at once that the amount of wing which needs extra masking is about eleven squares, say 3 ft. 9 in. (On this figure the lines of the wing top are ticked at intervals of a foot to aid measurement.)

Our extension-piece for the wing, then, needs to be 2 ft. 4 in. by 3 ft. 9 in.—or 4 ft. for safety, as it is always wise to add, in sight-line-measurements, an inch or two on the safe side, in case the piece be set on the stage not quite upright but slightly leaning back.

But a further point arises and allows a nicer estimate still by which we can halve the area, and so the weight, of the extension. For this extension-piece needs not to be a rectangle. Only part is needed to mask. What part?

If we carry up the ticks representing the foot-measurements on the plan to the section we can see that at the first foot the necessary height of the masking piece is reduced to just over five squares, or under 2 ft. And at the second-foot mark, to 1 ft. 3 in. or so, and so forth. To draw the length and height of the extension-piece and set off these heights from the base-line at the specific intervals gives a series of points which, connected, give the line and angle necessary for the top of the extension. At the bottom of Fig. 84 the piece is clearly shown as a right-angle triangle. It is here drawn in elevation and from it may be ascertained the exact shape of the piece which, when attached to the top, will mask, if the flat be set in the position and angle shown on the plan.

This angle of the top edge is of course equally given by connecting the two measured lines of side and base so as to form a triangle. The method of projecting at given intervals so as to obtain the line by connecting a set of resultant points was described, however, because it is by that means that similar calculations are made in circumstances where *curved* shapes have to be dealt with, either horizontally curved flats or vertically arched borders.

Perhaps, however, this digression has been long enough and the reader will gladly be excused the treatment of curves and sight-lines. (He has in fact sufficient indication in the foregoing to fit him completely for solving curve problems with no further help.)[1]

[1] This note may serve to point the way to any who are hesitant:

With curved scenery the system of sight-lines is as valuable as it is with normal stuff. Since, however, curved scenery is comparatively rare because of its expense, I do not feel justified in spending explanatory diagrams on the subject. Moreover, the principle involved is entirely covered by Fig. 84. One takes, for instance, a series of given points on the plan of an arch and transposes them into terms of height on the section, and by a combination of the evidence of the sight-lines through them one may plot out the exact area which, on any surface, is left unmasked by the arch form.

A certain amount of experience is necessary to think on two sheets of

To return, then, to our Fig. 83: the extension-pieces to the tops of a given group of wings will be lightest in weight if they are of triangular shape, each of a size to be ascertained by the above process.

There arises in connection with the above a point of technique about which some confusion may arise if it is not mentioned. It concerns the position of the border relative to the wing. It is very difficult to-day to answer the question: Should a border hang in front of a wing or behind it? It is none the less interesting to realize that there is a serious question here and to essay an answer, for it brings up an arrangement that once was of first importance.

Our old Fig. 62 had seemed to show that to-day the question has not only little importance but little meaning—the border hung between two wings and there it was. It was not so intimately related to any particular wing that one could say it was inherent it should hang before or behind that wing. The border is set with the specific intention of masking, and not of touching the back or front of a wing. Further we have seen that arrangements may occur to-day in which the num-

paper in this three-dimensional way. It will soon be found that the nearest-or-highest point (with regard to the stalls) of an arched, or diagonally-set, square-topped opening is a critical point through which one should always take care to draw the intersecting pair of sight-lines from the outermost seats on plan. The length shown between these two diverging lines as they strike the backing to that opening will always imply a corresponding straight edge at the top of the area left visible, though the portion of that area on either side may be curved at the top. It is interesting to note that a central arch masks-in an area of true arch form only if the backing is in direct flat contact with the opening; as it is moved away the area increases in width and height, but the top becomes a straight line, though the outer top corners retain their curve. Then, at a certain distance farther up-stage, these curved corners are so far divorced by the increasing line between them that they are pushed outside the sight-lines drawn through the side of the archway, and we are faced with the odd result that the area capable of being seen through the arch by the audience is a rectangular area.

Similarly may one examine the state of affairs existing when a curved —instead of an arched—border is used—such a border as, for instance, might be made to mask the railway of a curved traverse designed to follow the line of the front edge of a stage-revolve.

Such information is not commonly needed, but when it is required is almost impossible to gain by any other method than that of the sight-line system.

ber of pairs of wings is greater than the number of borders. Apart from this, it might be said, however, that as far as we have been able to relate a border with any specific pair of wings, we have rather suggested that the border hangs in front of them, in order to mask their tops, and the suggestion would certainly not have been untrue, but we must not leave it without an important qualification.

Concerning both these things there was formerly a difference: in the old system of scenery on the Continent each pair of wings had its specific border; and each border generally hung *directly behind* its own wings.

In England, up to about the middle of the nineteenth century, the procedure was different, since English wings were supported in a manner different from the Continental ones and had their top edges sliding in grooves. In order to mask these grooves the English borders then hung flat in front of the wing-tops. (Both in England and abroad the wings were at that time parallel with the footlights.)

During that century both methods of supporting wings were more or less revised and it became possible by a modification of the old machinery to set the English wings *in front* of their borders, like those abroad, and this system is still obtaining in some of the large traditional theatres.

In a Covent Garden pantomime, for instance, one may see wings in front of their borders. The advantages gained are (firstly) in height, and (secondly) in the more harmonious blending of wing to border. Let us see how this comes about.

The kind of scene where such an arrangement might be used is the typical old-style exterior, with wood-wings and tree-borders, or the large palatial interior. In this case the wings will be slightly different in principle from any we have discussed; they are likely to be *book-wings*, with the on-stage half set parallel (or nearly) with the proscenium line.

This arrangement relates the wings very closely with the old principle, and in one respect an identical disposition is attained, in that *the borders are in close and parallel contact with the wings* beneath them (or with part, at least, of those wings).

What is the advantage of this position? The answer is that

when the wings are parallel with, and touching, the borders a higher set becomes possible. That this point—not perhaps immediately evident—is true we may find by applying the principle mentioned in the discussion of Figs. 82 and 83, where we found that 'to mask behind an opening as high as 16 ft. with 18-ft. flats involves a certain amount of restriction in their placing, they must be set *at reasonably flat angles* and each very close behind its border'. We were then so concerned with economically masking the tops of the wings already set at a specific angle that we had no time to notice a possible application of the above if the wings had not to suffer such obligations as to their angle. This application we may now phrase as follows: *The flatter the angle of a wing and the closer it stands to its border, the higher that border may be lifted without unmasking*, and consequently, of course, the higher the set and the greater the impression of space one may create in comparison with the human figure on a sufficiently equipped stage.

Now we begin to see how it is that in little theatres the wings are best set at an angle—for so they mask the sides of the backcloth more economically—while in larger theatres they may still be found set parallel with the footlights, so giving higher sets. By the ingenious system of hingeing a wing up the centre and setting it with its two members at an angle—like the cover of an open book stood on end—the on-stage half of the wing may line up with the border and allow it to be lifted to its maximum elevation, while the off-stage half of the wing may be turned at the angle most effective for masking the cross sight-lines. The principle is similar to that of the 'flipper' explained in connection with Figs. 77, 78, and 79, at the beginning of this section, but now instead of a narrow hinged flipper, to turn parallel with the audience, we have the whole of maybe a 6-ft. flat with its profile attached firmly to the edge in the usual way; off-stage of this we have, as before, the body of another flat to turn to the required angle. And a double or *booked* 6-ft. flat (*i.e.* two 6-ft. flats hinged together) is capable of masking a very considerable area.

We now begin to see why the parallel part of such booked

wings is set *in front* of its border, and a curious attitude towards something analogous to the non-masking triangle now forces itself upon our attention.

Book-wings of this sort require borders which, besides being deep, are very long, and a certain sacrifice or modification of masking-principles is enforced, since, because the borders need now merely touch the top of the parallel half of the wings—or sink only a trifling amount below—it clearly follows they must leave unmasked the top of the next wing up-stage. But this wing, like the first, is touched at the top by a border and so, although it is not masked, we cannot see over it, for its border forms as it were a continuation upwards of the wing. But this happy arrangement does not apply to the oblique halves of the book-wings; these too are not masked but, set as they are at an angle, they part company with the border, and from the extreme opposite side front seats one may clearly see over and beyond their tops. This space is generally shadowy, and part at least of it is occupied by the end of the border going off as far as conditions allow into the wing-space. But frequently conditions do not allow this extension to be so great as to mask effectively all the space at the top of the wings, especially of those wings at the front of the stage. Here a glimpse of the stage walls or the fly-rail becomes possible. It is to hide this that the *aprons* are used. These are canvases hung from the fly-rails, or along the side of the stage, of such a size as to mask the view through above the down-stage wing-tops. Sometimes this small glimpse is reckoned of so little importance that nothing is done about it, but the scrupulous procedure is always to provide suitably painted aprons where necessary.

A possible alternative to aprons suggested by the sight-line system is the provision of the tops of the off-stage flats of the books with triangular extensions on the principle shown in Fig. 84.

Since the border is therefore so long, and since it hangs a little below the level of the wing top, it follows that any book-wing must generally be set in front of its border, and not behind, for then the border would foul the top of the angled, off-stage, half of the wing.

Finally, a last justification of the border hanging flat behind its parallel wing is that most of the light falling on the junction between wing and border comes in a downward direction from the batten above. Were the border hanging in front of the wing its edge might cast a shadow on the wing and betray the junction, but if the border is behind the wing, the wing-top can be profiled, and—lit as it usually is—the join becomes indistinguishable and the continuous suggestion of the arch is unbroken.

So unbroken is the suggestion that we have only mentally to strip the canvas off the on-stage half of the wing, discard the wooden framework, and sew the canvas to the border and we arrive at another technique of masking the sides of a stage, namely the cutcloth or *legged border* technique. And it is a pretty satisfactory technique for large stages with a high grid, and one often used in ballet. But the discerning reader will notice a residual element from this transition: the remaining half of the book-wing. In practice it must generally be included and in spite of the apparent simplicity of a set of cutcloths framing a backcloth, the purity of the style has generally to allow the inclusion of some at least of the displaced wings, to mask the cross sight-lines in the spaces between the legs of the cloths.

But such methods are rather those of special theatres and of types of set now not so popular; it is important to mention them and store in one's mind the several good points of the procedure that are suggestive for modern use, and then we may return to our main subject, which, before we found ourselves concerned with the top edges of flats, was a search towards a means of reducing the amount of pieces required to mask a stage.

Let us now proceed with the elimination of scenery. In Fig. 85 we represent the false proscenium with its ceiling-like top. The projection of the false pros. sides from the plan in Fig. 80 is shown in three dotted lines; the wider space representing the up-and-down-stage· flat, and the narrower the splayed flat.

The first point is that if this ceiling is the same height as the pros. arch and border (and we agreed not to reduce our set headroom), it will be necessary to erect a small 1-ft. deep return at the front edge of the ceiling to prevent glimpses over it from beneath the pros. border. Notice the flat ceiling is 4 ft. deep and covers both the flats of the side. Consultation of the plan would fix its length at 34 ft. A further point that may be useful on certain occasions is that, provided one extends the 1-ft. return at the front of the ceiling to 5 ft. in height, the pros. border may be dispensed with.

Turning now to the set borders we find a real difficulty: one 6-ft. border is not quite sufficient to mask an 18-ft. cloth

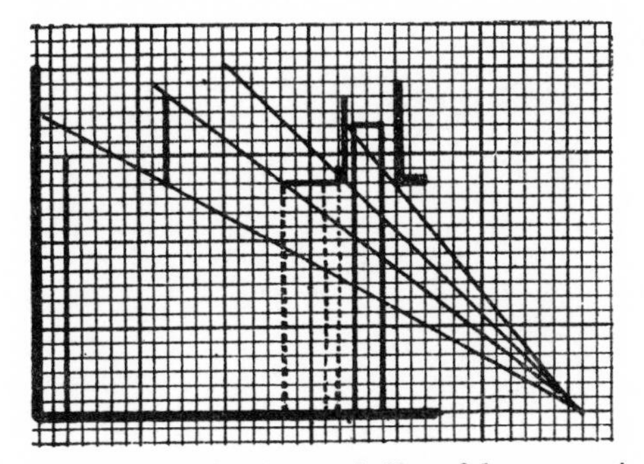

Fig. 85. Section showing a shallow false proscenium eliminating one border.

(and indeed an 18-ft. cloth is unusually low—the usual height would be 24 ft.). We have then to take one of four courses: heighten the cloth; drop the border a foot or so—bringing it down-stage in proportion to the drop; drop the ceiling of the false proscenium; or, lastly, drop, at the up-stage edge of the false pros. ceiling, a narrow return like that at the front but this time hanging down, not projecting up. (These returns to framed borders, or to ceilings, are often of the greatest assistance in solving problems of masking.) Of these courses, the second, the moving of the set border, is probably the most direct, provided we could stand the resultant fractional lessening of the height of the setting.

If, now, we plaster the back wall, we may dispense with the backcloth and use groundrows as detailed in the discussion of the plan.

Lastly, turning to Fig. 86 which corresponds with the plan in Fig. 81, we see the 6-ft. false proscenium in place, now set back 2 ft. from the inner pros., and so needing a higher front return than before, but enabling us, provided we can plaster our back wall to a height of 24 ft., to eliminate the border entirely. In this vertical dimension the curving forward of the top of the back wall to form the beginning of a cyclorama dome is not of so vital an importance as it was on the sides, though if we have, let us say, a stage with a low roof 21 ft. up,

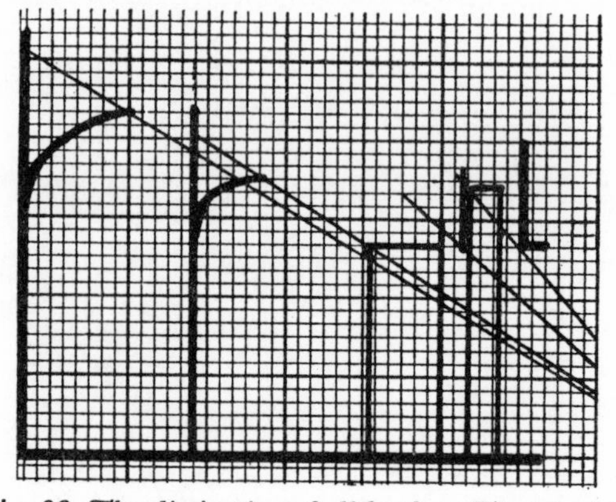

Fig. 86. The elimination of all borders. The principle extended to a 38-ft. deep stage.

we may still mask our back wall without lowering the false proscenium provided we curve the top of the wall forward to an extent of about 5 ft. 6 in., as shown in the figure.

I would like to add that though I have chosen a stage of very convenient size for the purposes of my discussion, the principles suggested may be readily adapted for larger stages. For instance, the stage here discussed is conveniently shallow: let us increase its depth and see if the system is still practicable. In Fig. 86 two back walls are shown to the stage, the farther is 38 ft. back from the proscenium line. Now there are only twelve stages in London (according to *Who's Who in the Theatre*) deeper than this—and some of those are specialized stages of abnormal depth—so it is a pretty fair test. If at such a depth we build a plastered wall, it has to be no more than

30 ft. high to mask if we allow ourselves the dropping of a 1-ft. return on our false pros. In nearly all full-size theatres there is sufficient headroom to make even this small concession quite unnecessary, but if we take the example of a stage whose roof is only 26 ft. above the stage—and no theatre in London save the Criterion represents its roof as lower than this (moreover, the Criterion stage is only 19 ft. 6 in. deep)—we may still achieve our elimination of the border without altering our quite reasonably sized false proscenium, by bringing forward the back-wall-top in a curve for a horizontal distance of 8 ft.

Truly a conclusion of importance and a witness of the assistance of the system of sight-lines to the thinking-out of stage shapes and scenery.

It is only fair to warn the reader in passing that there is a limit to the curving-forward of the extremities of a cyclorama. Excessively projecting arms at the sides cut off the deeper part of the stage from its wing-space and reduce the means of access for scenery in changes; and too deep a cove above completely cuts off those valuable up-stage sets of lines from the grid. A deep cyclorama so impresses its effect on a stage that, in the end, it restricts it to one type of setting and cuts out the box set and the full wing-and-cloth set—unless steps are taken to add quite remarkably elaborate mechanical systems of scene-change.

We may conclude this section by glancing again at the little stage we examined in Section 14, so as to notice the effect a false proscenium would have there.

Because of the tinyness of this stage we may combine the functions of the inner and the false prosceniums and build a mere 18-in.-deep arch to do duty for both. Its effect in economy is, however, remarkable.

This particular stage, when we left it, needed to mask: two wings a side, 5 ft. wide or three wings 3 ft. wide, one border 4 ft. deep and 25 ft. long, and a backcloth 17 ft. by 25 ft. Upon a box set composed of flats 13 ft. 6 in. high, a ceiling 9 ft. deep was needed.

Reference to the additional notes tells us that the back wall of the stage is plain brick. There is no difficulty in plastering this, but a serious difficulty arises in curving forward the ends of the wall, because of the door in the stage side-wall up near the corner, over which we cannot plaster. Let us, however, accept this check, in order to show to what extent we can simplify the working of a stage even without the full exercise of our possibilities, and by merely plastering the flat back wall and adding a shallow false proscenium. We accept the check

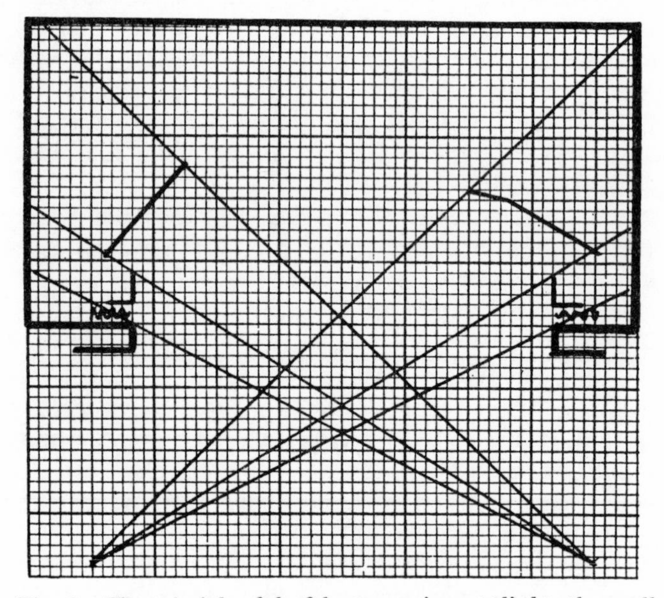

Fig. 87. The principle of the false proscenium applied to the small stage of Fig. 55. Scale: two squares to 1 foot.

the more readily because we see one more imperative still to be faced: before we plaster we must re-examine the problem of a passage across the stage from side to side. Our notes say that at present none exists. Then we must make one. There are two alternatives, either to make a passage below the stage, if the stage has, or can be provided with, a sunk storeroom beneath, or to leave the building and pass round the back, entering the stage from the opposite door. Even if some structural alteration is necessitated it may well be worth while in view of the immense value of the new arrangement.

(If no solution can be found in either of these two directions, then a canvas cyclorama would have to be erected, in which case our sight-lines would give us the most useful dimensions.)

We proceed on the supposition that the back wall is to be plastered. In Fig. 87 (scale, two squares to 1 ft.) you see represented on the plan a shallow false proscenium, no more than 1 ft. 6 in. deep. Notice that its returns do not reach the cross sight-line at their off-stage edge. This is not an oversight on the part of the designer, for he realizes that in the 1-foot space between proscenium and false proscenium, the bunched-up tabs will hang and effectually block any view through.

It is now clear that we need only one 6-ft. flat a side to mask (shown on the stage-right), though this is only just adequate and must not be set at any but a right-angle to the sight-line from the opposite corner seat. If we wish to display a profiled edge without suffering it to be foreshortened like the wing, we may use a 5-ft. wing with a 2-ft. flipper (shown on the stage-left). (Incidentally we have here, at last, the only solution to the problem on p. 135 of how an actor may pass round the down-stage corner of a wing on this stage to effect an entrance.) The scenery at the back of the stage consists of a groundrow, of what height we choose and of a length governed by the sight-lines and dependent on how far up-stage it is set.

Fig. 88 shows the sectional arrangement. We may note here, first, how the sight-line conditioned by the new false proscenium, provided we drop its top 9 in. below that of the real proscenium, now strikes the top of the back wall and eliminates the border, and then how a 14-ft. box set can be adequately masked with a 4-ft. ceiling.

It is, however, when the system of sight-lines enables us to make even greater improvements than these that it clearly shows of what great use it is in thinking about a stage. The very compactness of this stage contains a possibility which would scarcely ever suggest itself save on a scale section bearing its sight-lines. For we find that by nice adjustments we may make an arrangement for the lighting that is beyond the dreams of most stage electricians on less fortunate stages: we can put up a full box set, complete with ceiling, without cutting off the light from the sky batten. *We can actually light the back wall of a box set from the sky batten itself without moving that batten and without striking the ceiling.* On a small stage whose footlights and No. 1 batten are not very powerful and whose front-of-house lighting may be primitive, that possibility is highly desirable. Even on full stages a box set, whose ceiling cuts off so much of the top light, is a notoriously difficult problem for the electrician, for there is generally no lamp of

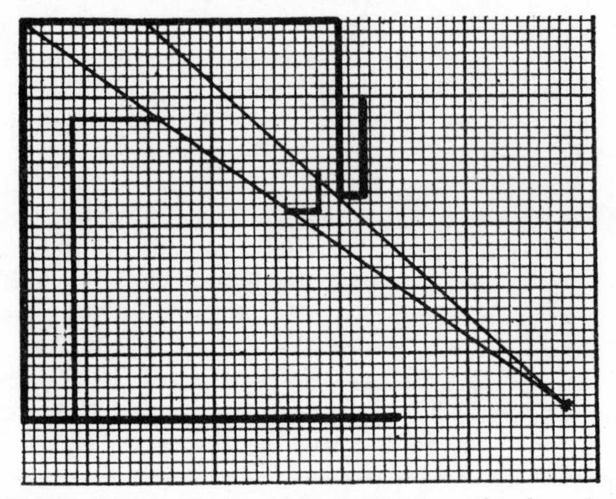

Fig. 88. Section showing a false proscenium cutting down depth of set ceiling.

much value with which he can illuminate the upper parts of the back wall of a box set.

In Fig. 89 the arrangement is shown. The sky batten is hung eight feet away from the back wall, and it is nicely adjusted in height so as to miss the false proscenium sight-line, and yet shine below the ceiling of a box set.

The sky batten is so tilted that none of its rays falls anywhere but on the back wall, and so, unless the actors go inordinately far up-stage, they cannot get their heads in its beams and throw shadows. It is the function of the proscenium—or No. 1—batten to light the actors and not the scenery. This batten is lodged just above the false proscenium and so tilted that its rays miss the back wall and so can throw no shadows on it. The footlights are tilted to light not only the actors well down-stage, under the false proscenium arch, but to illuminate that area—at least that part of it at face level—which is left between the lower rays of the sky batten and the upper rays of the proscenium batten.

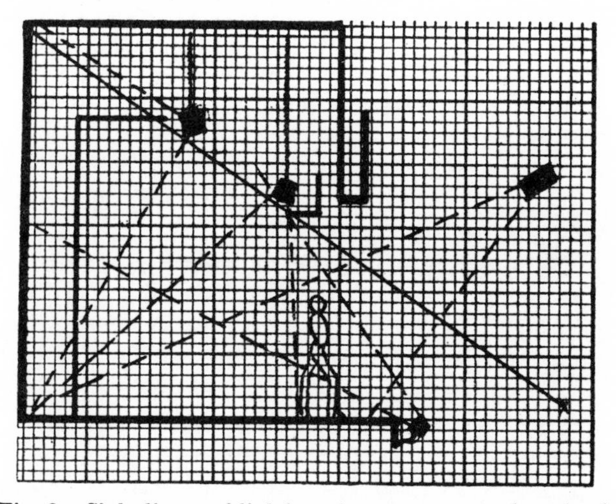

Fig. 89. Sight-lines and lighting. An arrangement where the sky batten may light the back wall of a box set.

Finally note that with a false proscenium, unless the space between it and the real proscenium is wide enough for another downward-directed batten of lights—and even then, if the stage has an apron, some form of front-of-house lighting is essential to pick up the faces of actors well down-stage. It is for this purpose that in Fig. 89 one of a group of focus lamps is indicated screwed to the side wall of the hall or to a beam across the roof.

But our concern is primarily with scenery and especially at the moment with sight-lines, and we may now make the following table:

The stage without plastered back wall or false proscenium needs:	The stage with plastered back wall and false proscenium needs:
4 wings 5 ft. 0 in. wide.	2 wings 6 ft. 0 in. wide.

1 border 4 ft. 0 in. × 25 ft. 0 in.	No border.
1 backcloth 25 ft. × 17 ft., i.e. area of 425 sq. ft.	1 groundrow, say 25 ft. × 3 ft., i.e. area of 75 sq. ft.
For depth of ceiling on a box set of 14-ft. flats: 8 ft. 0 in.	For depth of ceiling on a box set of 14-ft. flats: 4 ft. 0 in.
And the depth of the acting area would be 12 ft. 0 in.	And the depth of the acting area would be 14 ft. 0 in.

Were we able to curve our plaster back wall down the stage sides, we could, by careful arrangement, eliminate even the two side wings, but this stage is unfortunately so narrow that we may not do this comfortably.

Let us pause for a moment.

The system of sight-lines has at length led us to a landmark in modern theatre history. It has demonstrated that, with informed and careful planning, a very special state of affairs may be reached, and that, after our long and earnest study of the problems of masking which seemed to set an imperative condition upon all our work, a new principle may be evolved by which *the ideal stage masks itself*.

It is at this point that we break as it were from a tortuous side-road into a new open country which the foremost theatremen of the modern movement are to-day exploring.

For we are now thinking of a stage in a different way: no longer as a feckless box of tricks whose concealment is one of our chief duties, nor as a kind of peep-show in which the scenery must attain certain dimensions whether we need such profusion or no, nor as an unbeautiful barn, dim, shabby, and ancient, whose appearance was never conceived to be looked at, and where shadows and hanging ropes are the only candidates to any beauty. That was a place whose only saving graces were elaborate scenery, or the front curtain that clothed the unlovely skeleton.

Instead of all this, we see a stage that adds a grace to its own hall, a stage perfectly fit for contemplation without the slightest dressing, a stage that may be an architectural entity as integrally a portion of the building as the façade. And a stage upon which, when we go to give a show, we may set an atmosphere with a tiny, painted groundrow, or an elaborately built and patterned three-dimensional setpiece of self-contained beauty; with ten cubes and a sky, or with three ladders, two rostrums, a bridge, and a swag of trapezes; with a complex of parts and shapes, colours, shades, textures, of the greatest elaboration, or a little, delicate skeleton of a cottage; with an arrangement of the most detailed, subtly-chosen, significant, and complete realism, or with some light and a chair.

We have heard talk of a *permanent setting*, fit, with additions or modifications, for all scenes in a show, but we have now glimpsed the possibility of a *permanent stage*, fit—with or without additions and modifications slight as a shadow or complex as reality itself—for all the shows of our century.

But it was the purpose of this book to deal in detail neither with the designing of stages nor the designing of scenery. The design of stages is not for my pen, for it is intimately connected with the intricacies of building construction; and the design of scenery is so related to the crafts of scene-painting and carpentry that I prefer to treat it elsewhere in connection with these. Therefore our subject is now finished. Our purpose was to supply a preliminary or footnote to these two studies, and to do so with the somewhat ambitious intention of interesting equally the architect and the scene-designer—those two who, centuries ago, were one, and whose work, at least, is still brought into intimate relationship. Any elaboration of the preceding notes would have to be addressed specifically to one group or the other and could no longer be common to both. I prefer then to leave it as a method whose application must rest in the hands of its user.

One's appreciation of the sight-line system is accumulative. It is only as one begins to work on a plan with its help that one sees the immense scope of its aid. The further one goes, the better assistant it becomes.

APPENDICES

APPENDIX I

ELEMENTS OF STAGE LIGHTING TECHNIQUE USEFUL IN THE PRACTICE OF THE SIGHT-LINE SYSTEM

Concerning the lighting of stages, it is helpful to realize that there may be two approaches so different in effect that they involve two different principles.

We may name the two principles 'Straight Lighting' and 'Theatrical Lighting'. Straight lighting is easily understood: it involves simply the illuminating of the stage evenly so that all the things upon it can be equally well seen. Its function is to illuminate the stage purely in order that the audience may see clearly all there is to see, but beyond this straight lighting does not aspire.

The practical equipment of this form was elaborated to suit the wing-and-border type of set. As Fig. 3 suggested, early in the book, scenery in this style may be likened to a series of arches, one behind another, with a backcloth to close the vista and a proscenium arch to frame it. To light such a system of scenery so that everything shall be clearly seen, an arrangement of lights closely repeating the forms of the scenery is needed. Each border is lit up by a horizontal row of lights hanging behind the previous border, and each wing is lit up by a vertical row of lights hanging upon the back of the wing in front. Since wings and borders may not only be changed but replaced in different positions for different scenes, these lights must also be variable in position. The border lights are called *battens* and further distinguished by the name of the border they have to light, as *proscenium batten* lighting the pros. border, *No. 2 batten* lighting the first set border, followed by *No. 3*, *No. 4*, and so on according to the size of the stage, up to the *back batten* or *sky batten*, lighting the back-scene. These *battens of lights* are hung from the flies and are therefore easily altered in the vertical direction, but cannot be moved up or down-stage without considerable difficulty, involving lowering out the lines, disconnecting the whole batten, and carrying it bodily to its new position and attaching it to new lines. The vertical rows of wing-lights, called *strips*, are far less cumbersome affairs and are provided with a large hook at the top by which they may be attached to the top toggle-rail of a flat. These strips may be easily unhooked in a change, leaned against the side, and hooked again in any desired position on the backs of a new set of wings. Only the first pair, or *proscenium strips*, are ever likely to be found fixed in position, though in the eighteenth century even the wing strips were permanently fixed in their place to special vertical columns of wood behind each wing-position.

To this system, providing light for the two sets of sides and the tops of our row of arches, we may add the *ground length*, which resembles a strip save that it is laid on the floor of the stage behind a groundrow to light the next groundrow behind, or the foot of the backcloth. A permanent length built in at the front of the stage forms the footlights.

Imagine, now, such a complete system turned full on, and lighting the traditional form of exterior scene. And in this mind's-eye picture, imagine one of the border battens switched off. Immediately the border it lit grows dark and out of tone with the others. A simple result, completely what one would expect, but one giving rise to a long trail of drudgery and compromise since it occasions the rule: *every border involves a batten of lights behind it.* And though a border is a comparatively cheap article and a most valuable aid to masking, a batten of lamps is not cheap. It follows that in many stages there are not sufficient battens for certain effects. And there arises that very frequent situation when, upon a small stage, we find a back batten to light the backcloth, and a pros. batten to light the front border, but nothing at all to light the intervening border or borders, the argument being: 'Two battens give adequate light for seeing the stage, so why have more?' 'But what about your No. 2 border'? 'Oh, blow the No. 2 border! We're not going to the expense of another batten of lamps just to light a border.' Yet, with the traditional-type sets used on this particular stage, a second border may be indispensable.

Another difficulty arises with this system of lighting: visualize the arrangement again—a number of horizontal battens across the top of the stage, and a number of vertical rows on either side. Now suppose we strike our wing-and-border set and put up a box set. The result is, of course, absurd. Every single batten of lights is cut off by the horizontal set-ceiling, save perhaps the pros. batten; and upon what are we now to hang our side strips? Briefly, there is nothing to light our set save one batten of lamps, the footlights, and occasionally the proscenium strip. All the rest of the more or less expensive installation of lamps is useless.

Clearly a need is open for another system of stage lighting than the 'straight' system. Let us leave the box set in the shadows and turn to consider this other system.

Our approach is now from an entirely different point of view. The motive is not to illuminate evenly everything on the stage—indeed for a scene to be 'lit too evenly' may, in this new scheme, become a serious fault, and the contributory factor to a 'lifeless' set—but instead (to go to the farthest extreme) to imagine the stage for a moment as completely dark, and then throw a single beam of light upon just that thing that most matters to us in all the scene—whether that thing be an object or an action. Thereupon, the question has to be asked, 'Is that sufficient light?' At one end of the scale and for one type of scene the answer will be 'Yes', and the lighting of the scene will then have been achieved; at the other end, it will be, 'No: add another light there', and 'Another here', until in broad effect this stage will seem to be as brightly lit as the old one, but now with an arrangement of lights every one of which is in strength, colour, and direction used not with the motive of illuminating everything so that all shall be equally seen, but with the motive of *lighting* the important points so that the assembled lights both illuminate *what is desired*, and in their totality make an effect that is well composed and contributory to the atmosphere of the scene—that is *theatrical lighting*.

If we now turn to the practical equipment for this form we find a difference from that for straight lighting in every point. And though in common practice a judicious selection from, and mixture cf, the equipment of the two styles may be most practical (certainly for ordinary box sets), an examination of the second system in its purest form will be the most use.

In its purest form, then, 'theatrical' lighting employs as its unit, not a row of lamps sharing a batten, but a single high-power lamp in its own lantern, capable of direction at will, and, reduced to barest statement, the system of lighting a scene is now to build your set and place as many individual lamps as you like and in whatever places you find give the best effect. Theoretically there are no limitations, save the obvious ones, and the price of success in lighting is merely a process of trial and error. (The weary length of most modern lighting rehearsals witnesses the latter point.) The trouble with the system is that its very freedom encourages too many people to begin a lighting rehearsal with no previously prepared plot. A lighting plot should be as fully prepared for a lighting rehearsal as a property plot for a dress rehearsal. And no better aid to the working out of this plot can be found than the plans and sections of the sight-line system.

But to use the system to best advantage a knowledge of essential lighting technicalities must be present. A statement of the present technical equipment so far as general and skeleton needs go on a typical, modern stage might run much as follows:

Footlights (Fig. 90, 4). These, more than any other lights, have kept their old form, and little improvement in basic principle has taken place. The revolutionary attitude has been not to cure but to kill, and it has recommended their complete abolition.

But they have their uses. Among the chief of these is (paradoxically enough) the lighting of the top of the back wall of a typical box set, for which there is no other means. By lighting, I mean in this case not brilliantly illuminating—for we have no wish ordinarily to illuminate brightly the ceiling of a room—but adding a relief to a shaded area. And indeed the chief use of footlights to-day lies in just this function (and it is one that I would not willingly lose) of stealing-in a controlled amount of extra glow upon a previously set scheme of light that needed yet a finishing touch. It is decidedly an auxiliary function.

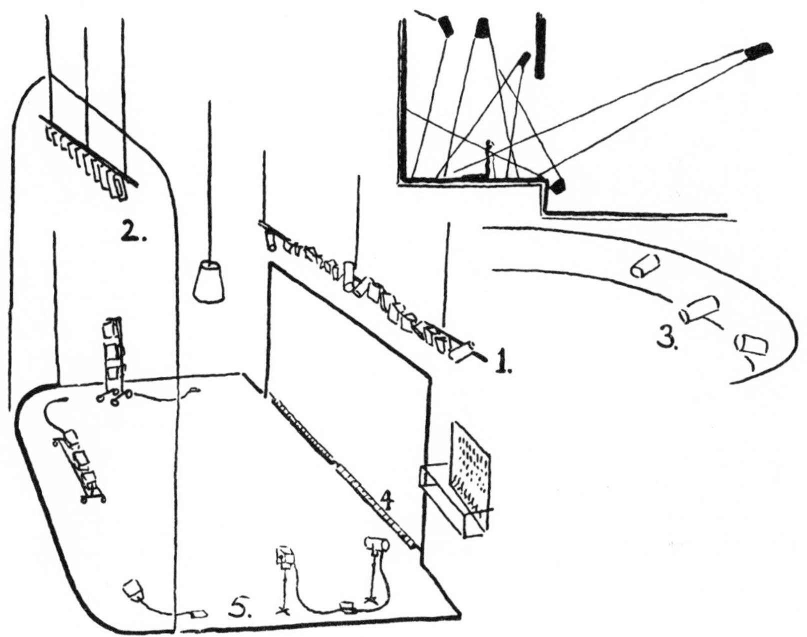

Fig. 90. A diagram of essential points of stage lighting.

Should we elect to have them, we may always instal them upon a system which allows their revolving into the stage, or sinking, or being covered with a trap-door, so as to leave the unbroken stage floor when they are not needed.

However that may be, one primary point about the placing of footlights is important to any modern stage installation: the lamps must not be slightly above the stage (as in the old straight system) but sunk in a trough. The depth of the sink should be such that the up-stage side of the trough prevents direct rays of light from the footlights to the lower part of the backcloth, or the back wall in the case of a box set. This lower part (up to about seven feet above the stage) should be in shadow as far as the footlights are concerned. An even higher area should be left in shadow on a cyclorama or sky. This precaution is taken so that the actor who walks up-stage sinks, as it were, into a lake of shadow as he moves, and when at length he approaches close to the back he is completely submerged and hence the footlights can cast no shadow of him upon the sky.

The footlight batten should be of the compartment type, that is, with each lamp in its own box and with each box capable of taking its slide containing any coloured gelatine. The number of lamps depends, of course, on the width of the proscenium opening, generally they are placed at about 7 in. centres. They are best wired in parallel on three circuits. On larger stages it is useful to divide the footlights in half, operating each half separately, each with its three circuits. This allows the lighting of the two halves of the stage in different colours and the altering of the colour of either half independently of that of the other; as for instance, the two halves steel colour, then the creeping up of a warm colour on one half of the stage simultaneously with the burning up of the fire in a stage fireplace.

But with the footlights, similarities with the 'straight' system cease. The remaining lamps on the stage are treated as separate units, there are no more 'battens'. The lanterns containing these lamps are, moreover, divided into two classes, the open 'flood' lantern, which consists of five sides of a box open on the sixth; and the 'spot' lantern, generally cylindrical and always with a lens at one end, the other end being closed. The spot, of course, throws a controlled beam of light through the lens, making a circular pool with a more or less sharply defined edge. The flood splashes out its light in a wide angle with little definition of the edge of its field. The purpose of the flood is to illuminate a general area, that of the spot is to pick out with light a detail, a figure, or a group. Owing to the concentration of its rays the spot is generally more powerful than the flood over a small area, and this gives the sense of *relief* in lighting which is a feature of the system in this way:

A number of floods may be clamped to a steel tube and hung and used very much as was the old batten of the straight system. Indeed, stage parlance will give it the same name, and call it 'No. 1 batten' or whatever it may be. But now interspersed with these floods—this general illuminant—will be a number of spots, clamped to the same steel tube and intended for the specific extra-lighting of given spots on the stage, and these will be carefully angled and adjusted at the lighting rehearsal and will then remain fixed and must not be knocked or jolted out of position. These extra-lights give that touch of emphasis to needful points ensuring that what is therein is especially defined, though the area around may be dimmer or even considerably darker, and their contribution by means of lights and shadows to theatrical effect may become considerable.

Top lights (Fig. 90, 1). To turn in detail now to the placing of these lamps above the stage we find, as was just suggested, that a steel tube carrying a whole battery of them (mixed floods and spots, either 250 or 500 watts each) takes the place of the old pros. batten. A less expensive and more traditional batten may be made up of lengths of compartment batten, like the footlights, wired similarly in three circuits, and of course now confining itself to floodlight, the spots being in another position.

Front lighting (Fig. 90, 3). It is the special nature of the controlled beam of the spot that allows of this new other position, for it makes possible for the first time true front-of-house lighting (nick-named 'F.O.H. lighting'), that is to say, spot lanterns or, a more proper term, focus lanterns, may be situated in any part of the auditorium and throw their beam on the stage from a distance. (A flood may not be used in this way because its unrestricted beams would light up the front of the proscenium and auditorium as well as the stage.) This ability to throw from the front as well as from above means that one may avoid the heavy face shadows that top-lighting alone can cause, and which footlights are necessary to relieve when no F.O.H. lighting is obtainable.

Sometimes these F.O.H. spots are grouped together in a batten just outside and above the proscenium opening, then the general effect is much the same as with the first-described, mixed spot-and-flood pros. batten, save that the spotlights are now farther from the stage, and so fall upon the players at a slightly more favourable angle.

One especially important point concerning the position and training of an F.O.H. spot is made clear in the sight-line section, and it is this: the angle of the beam with regard to the stage should not be too acute. One sometimes finds, especially in a small theatre, that a point of fixture may present itself in the structure of the building that seems admirable at first sight. When, however, a test sketch is made on the scale section it may be found that from this position the spot is almost useless, since to light the actors' faces it must be tilted up to strike the back scenery. To avoid the back scenery the beam must be so depressed that it lights only the legs and bodies of the actors and not their heads. In the small section at the top corner of Fig. 90, the position of the F.O.H. spot illustrates something of this drawback. To light the face of an actor standing in the position shown, the spot must be tilted upward till its beam cannot avoid the scenery. In an extreme example the actor, even when he moves right to the front of the stage, cannot get his head low enough to be in the beam without stooping. The remedy is *either* to lift the lantern bodily upwards and tilt it so that its rays fall more obtusely on the stage, *or* to retain it at its present height but bring it nearer to the proscenium, when it can again be tilted more directly downward.

It is important, in this matter, to decide whether the true function of the spot is to supplant footlights and illuminate the faces of actors down-stage only, or whether it is to act as a relief light to pick out a figure at any position in the acting-area; in the latter case it should be higher or nearer than in the former. The reason for keeping a lantern lower in the former case, when it is primarily to replace footlights, is to avoid the top-lighting effect to the faces which makes them less distinct to watch. It may be added that the spot is far too useful to be limited to down-stage use and, in practice, it should always be placed so as to be capable of relief lighting.

Having touched on footlights, top lights and front lights, there remain two fundamental points still to be outlined: back lighting (after which we must return to top lighting for a moment) and side lighting.

Back lighting (Fig. 90, 2). In the modern system back lighting, that is the lighting of the backcloth or of the cyclorama, may well involve the heaviest battery of lights in the theatre. Harold Ridge recommends that 'the backcloth will need about the same power (in watts) as the whole of the acting area, and something more'.[1] The batten itself is most likely to be another steel tube or set of tubes on which a row or a series of banks of cyclorama lanterns are clamped. These lanterns are floods, or modifications of the flood type, and are marked by a wide angle of throw. There are, it will be seen, only two battens now above the stage, the sky batten and the pros. batten. Occasionally a No. 2, or even a No. 3, batten is needed, in which case it is usually of the simple compartment type and is essentially for auxiliary lighting, but generally some one or other of the principles recommended in this book will have been employed to mask the stage without the use of borders, and the modern stage is likely to need reinforcement of its pros. batten and sky batten only when a deepish false proscenium is used, whose ceiling and rising front-piece prevent the light from the pros. batten going far up-stage, and even then, only when the F.O.H. lighting is inadequate to cover this up-stage area. In such a situation a second batten similar in all respects to the mixed flood and spot batten may be hung above the up-stage edge of the false pros. ceiling; so that the stage is divided into two areas as to lighting, the first in front and under the false pros., cared for by the pros. batten, and the second up-stage of the false pros. and cared for by the second batten.

Occasionally an alternative means, only slightly different in the main, will be used for lighting the middle depth of a stage—that is the suspension over it of one or more big acting-area- or arena-floods such as are used in circuses.

[1] *Stage Lighting* (2nd ed., Heffer, 1930), p. 75.

Side lighting (Fig. 90, 5). Side lighting now is almost always by means of standard flood lamps, that is floods on stands (generally singly, but occasionally in vertical groups of three or so, on wheeled trucks). These side floods are placed at need and can be raised or lowered within limits by extending the telescopic column of the stand, and they are fed from leads running to plugs under small trapdoors in the sides of the stage floor, called dips.

Briefly to sum up the main lighting requirements of a stage, as far at least as concerns the planning of that stage and the sight-line system, is not difficult; the sub-divisions and electrical details of the installation would go into far greater detail. The main points are these (see Fig. 90, in which floods are distinguishable from spots by the square shape of the former and the cylindrical shape of the latter):

Above and behind the pros. opening should be a batten (1), most simply a compartment batten, more flexibly a composite batten of separate floods: to these can be added with advantage some spot lanterns. On a small stage the length of the compartment batten is governed by the width of the opening (than which it should be a couple of feet or so shorter) and the lamps will be 100 watts each, wired in three circuits and, on slightly larger stages, in two independent halves. On a large stage, if the steel tube principle is adopted, as many lamps as required for an occasion can be clamped on. Their wattage will be either 250 or 500 each. Each then should be on its own circuit, preferably with its own dimmer in series. Turning to the section of the stage, the sight-line system requires the batten to be an ascertainable height above the opening to mask, and this will affect the throw of the beams up-stage past the ceiling of the false pros. if there be one: the higher the batten the less it can peep under the false pros. ceiling and light the upper stage.

(2) Upon the question of whether or no there is a false pros. depends the position and hence, to a certain extent, the number and strength of the lamps in the sky batten. If it is a cyclorama stage, they must be above the false pros. sight-line. The

sight-line section shows further that the more down-stage the sky batten is, the lower it may come without being seen, and consequently the more nearly it may send its rays directly at the surface of the cyclorama: and it is a rule that the more obliquely the rays fall on an object, the less brightly they light it, as well we know in comparing the oblique winter sunlight with the more direct beams of summer. The system shows further that, in a stage specially and carefully designed for the purpose, the sky batten may be eliminated and all the lamps concentrated in a regular arsenal of banks above and behind the proscenium opening. Such a stage would of course be one where flies were little used and the scene was changed by a revolving or sliding stage. There are several patterns of cyclorama lantern; that in the figure is cylindrical in shape with the flood of light coming through an opening in the side of the cylinder. It must not be confused with a spot where the light comes through a lens in the end of the cylinder.

(3) The F.O.H. lighting, consisting exclusively of spots, may number anything from a couple to a score or more of lanterns, the more distant being 1,000 watts or over, distributed over the auditorium in the most desirable places for their effects. That is, either on a beam across the hall, or in a specially built bridge, or from a box, or from the front of the circle or gallery, or from the back of the house, or from a dome in the roof above the stalls. Such lamps are very rarely set to allow their light to fall on the scenery.

(4) The lamps of the footlights need rarely be more than 60 watts each, save on very large stages. The whole apparatus should disappear into its trough when not needed. The wiring should be in three circuits, and on large stages the two halves should be wired separately. The rays should not strike the lower portion of the back scenery.

(5) Side lights are purely a matter of individual arrangement: the only matter that affects the lay-out is that sufficient dips or pockets in the stage floor at the side should be made to feed them. Generally this means two near the back, one near the front, and one half-way up, on either side of the stage; on

larger stages the number of pockets is not increased, but within each provision is made for two or three plugs instead of one. In this connection, in a group of extras, it might be remarked that a system of plugs either side on the level of the fly-floor (or on a bridge or gallery specially built for the purpose) will allow diagonal side lighting from above, by means of spots or floods, either on their own stands or clamped to the rail of the gallery. Such upper, side lighting is little used in this country, but the possibility of its development should not be overlooked.

Further provision must be made in stages using orthodox scenery of the wing-and-border or cutcloth description for auxiliary battens, generally of the simple compartment type, and in all stages a point or two from which to feed a central acting-area flood or group of floods is useful.

Lastly, the position of the switchboard is of vital importance. The electrician must have a view of the stage. His three possible positions are in a small gallery above the prompt or O.P. corner; under the stage, which he sees in a mirror placed in the orchestra (or he himself may see it direct from a kind of continental prompt-box in the footlights, with his switchboard set sloping like a desk before him); or, thirdly, he may be at the back of the auditorium.

Very generally it may be said that there are three things to be lit—the acting-area, the back scenery or cyclorama, and the side scenery. All the lighting except that of the sky batten is concentrated exclusively on the acting area and the players; the sky or back has its own lighting (the sky batten), which should never strike the actors; while the sides are left with only reflected light, except for a special occasion.

APPENDIX 2

HOW TO MASK THE TOP OF A CRAMPED, LOW-ROOFED STAGE, CLOSE TO THE SPECTATORS, WITHOUT RESORTING TO MANY BORDERS, WHICH INCUR EITHER COMPLICATED OR INADEQUATE LIGHTING

Since I have chosen to deal in this book with the system of sight-lines alone, believing it to be sufficient for one volume, I have said little about the modifications of setting that it brings within reach. One of the possibilities, however, I feel I may well point out here.

I can epitomize the situation to which it relates by anticipating the following criticism:

'Your counsel as regards masking is a counsel of perfection but there are cases in which such counsel is impossible to follow. In the village hall, when it is a hut or schoolroom, the front seats are often only four or five feet from the front curtain; and to mask the top of the stage, without reducing the height of the set to five or six feet, one must use four or five borders. We have seen them so used—and the small amount of light power available distributed pathetically between them. On the other hand we have seen them not used and have looked (but without too much horror) at the beams in the roof between the too-few borders: then the lighting for the actors was better. Had you at least referred to this problem, though we realize we can expect no solution, you had made a fairer presentation of your system.'

Of course there is a solution! The only attitude permissible to any stage-manager or designer is that *that is no problem in the shaping and placing of scenery which cannot be solved by direct study and examination under the guidance of the sight-line system*, and his adamant creed must be: there are no legitimate circumstances in the world where failure to mask is excusable.

Let us consider the above in the light of the contents of this book. Our more or less imaginary speaker (for he is not entirely imaginary) presupposes a stage of abominably difficult dimensions. Let us specify them and not dilute their difficulty. Let us suppose a front-spectator's eye-point only three feet away from the stage. Let us further imagine what is profoundly obnoxious in the circumstances—a stage as high as three feet above the auditorium floor. Let us put the hall at 14 ft. high to the ridge, and have it roofed with a pitch roof of such an angle that the side curtains of our set may only go up nine feet from the stage before they foul the sloping roof. In front of this we may allow a proscenium opening only eight feet high, which means we are forced to borders of very minimum depth or they will touch the actors' heads. To add to these difficulties let us suppose a stage unexpectedly deep for these cramped, front dimensions, namely 17 ft. Then let us suppose as a last touch that the front-row seats are to be occupied by children whose eyes, as they sit, will be no higher than stage level.

I believe these to form a fair example of abominable dimensions.

Upon stating our problem in sectional terms we find that if we include the full depth of the stage but permit ourselves to lower the set to within 18 in. of a 6-ft. actor's head —that is, 6 in. below the proscenium top—we need *ten borders, each 1 ft. 6 in. wide, to mask an 8 ft. 6 in. high backcloth!* (Fig. 91).

I should like to say in passing that for the difficulty of a pitch roof, the solution of shaped or arched borders is no solution at all, for reasons to be discerned in what was said concerning the shape of the backing to an arched opening in the note to p. 178, namely that the upper cross sight-line penetrates as deeply as before in its course, diagonal in two planes, through the crown of the arch and so reveals the dropped top of the far end of the next border just as before. The only value of a cut-arch border (and it must have the usual straight top) is in lifting the height of a set in effect, and it involves an increase in the height of the hung scenery in proportion.

Now apply the system that has been the subject of the book to the section of this stage and you will see that by a little carpentry and one audacious innovation we may reduce the number of borders to three and still mask as efficiently as before.

But that must not content us, for we shall not thereby have completely solved the problem raised by our critic, who wisely observes upon the difficulties of lighting when there are

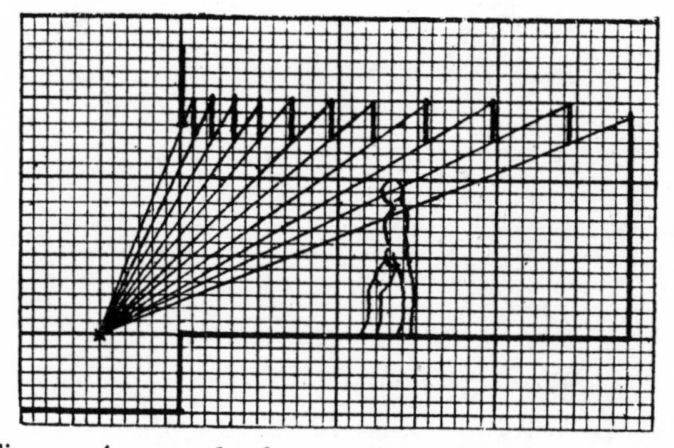

Fig. 91. An example of most unfavourable stage conditions demanding ten 1 ft. 6 in. borders.

many borders. Let us play fair with him and offer him a situation where he need use no more lights than are in any case necessary.

We are on the point of tabling one of those structural recommendations that are always shaping themselves out of the application of the constructive sight-line system to a badly-formed stage.

Three borders demands four battens of lights. Can we reduce the number of borders to two? By a structural alteration to the stage floor (of the utmost benefit incidentally to our shows and the comfort of our spectators) we can.

But can we reduce the borders to one and so involve only the minimum two rows of lights? By a further shift we can do even this.

Now we are at the end of our legitimate resources. There can be found no method of arranging the parts (short of deepening the false proscenium unwarrantably) which would allow the masking of our 8 ft. 6 in. backcloth without using a border at all. Even were we to build this extremely deep false pros. we should still be in difficulty with our lights. And we should realize we have reached an irreducible minimum.

Let us consider the practicalities.

If we examine Fig. 92 we shall see that by building a simple false pros. 2 ft. 6 in. deep, with a rising return to the

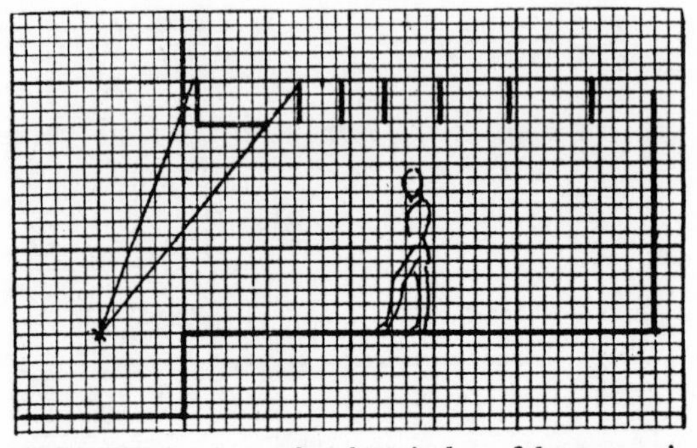

Fig. 92. The borders reduced to six by a false proscenium 1 ft. 6 in. deep.

top of 1 ft. 6 in. (as shown) we may immediately eliminate four of the ten borders.

Now for the others—and here our innovation will come in: consideration of the sight-lines and border-lines in Fig. 91 may suggest to the reader the situation we faced early in the book when we were discussing the masking powers of a row of parallel wings on plan. The border-lines here are like the wing-lines on the plan, and the upper sight-lines on the section resemble the cross sight-lines. And the requirement is exactly similar—namely to reduce the number of pieces needed to mask. With the wings it was simple: we set them obliquely. An exactly similar solution is at hand for the section; though it occurs to so few to hang a border anyhow but straight that it needed the cold clarity and lucidity of sight-line reasoning to suggest it.

Fig. 93 indicates the new position. The means of effecting the oblique hang of a curtain border are simple:—a batten is attached along the lower edge of the border and the batten is *brailed back*. In practice a brailed curtain generally has a certain amount of belly to it and this, together with an admission of its curtain-nature by the setting of the lower batten not at the edge but a little higher, gives a section to the border representable as in the No. 3 border in this figure. The brailing back may be effected by snap-hooking to a screw-eye, set some feet in from the end of the new batten, a line whose other end is similarly attached to the side-batten of the set at

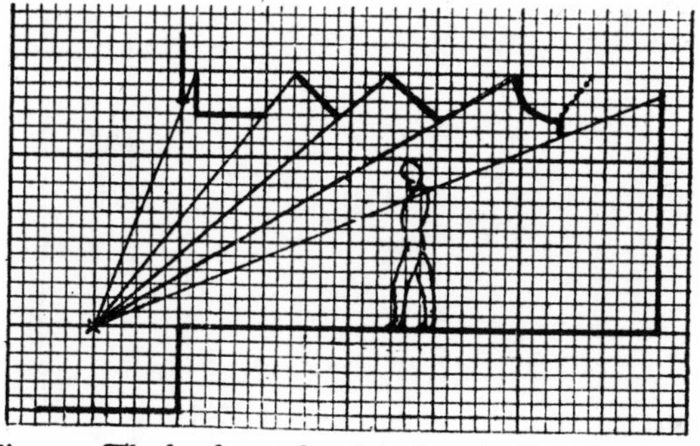

Fig. 93. The borders reduced to three by 'brailing back'.

a point somewhat up-stage of the crossing of the border-top batten. The line is adjusted to give the required obliquity to the border.

In fit-ups which have to be adjusted to suit various stage-measurements, one end of this brailing-line may be doubled back on itself after passing through the screw-eye and attached to a runner on the principle of a tent-rope.

In Fig. 95 there is shown the immense relief we obtain if we lower the stage a foot—a relief to be shared gratefully by the necks of the front spectators—and upon the supposition that such a stage will only be found in a short hall, we may make this structural alteration with no misgivings. Should the hall be so long that we materially deprive the back spectators of part of their view of the stage, it will still pay to lower the stage and lift up instead the back rows of seats.

The relief now offered enables us to hang deeper borders without coming any nearer our players' heads, and deeper borders means fewer of them—in fact we may, as is shown, reduce them to two. A sketch diagram of such an arrangement showing the appearance of the brailed borders is given in Fig. 94.

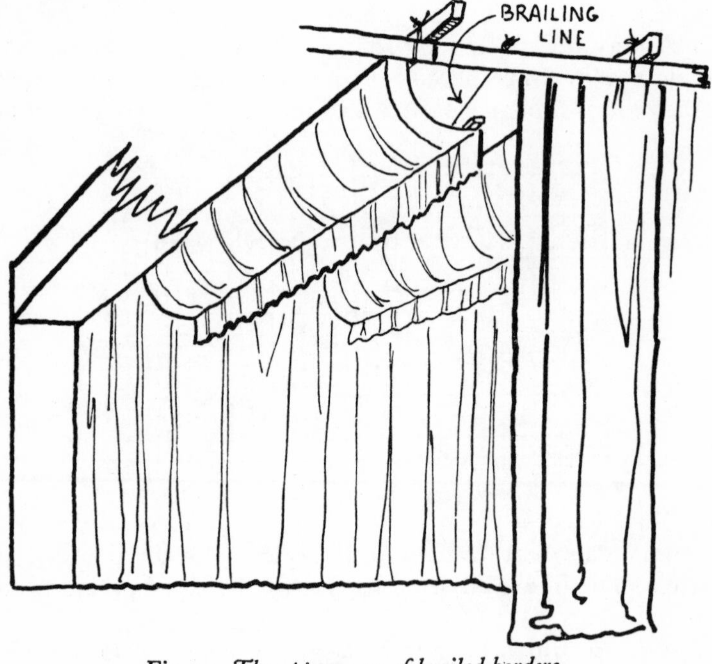

Fig. 94. The appearance of brailed borders.

The arrangement of the borders is always closely interdependent with the arrangement of the lights. In Fig. 95 the typical light arrangement would be the usual 'proscenium batten' above the false pros. and the usual 'sky batten' behind the last border, but that still leaves the No. 2 border in darkness, and though the tilt of the borders allows the light from the pros. batten to light the stage area adequately, yet we must add a low power No. 2 batten between the borders to illuminate the No. 2 border in key with the first and to help to light the faces of actors up-stage where the light from the pros. batten is cut off by the No. 1 border; but this auxiliary batten must be so arranged as to avoid casting shadows of the actors on the sky, as it might if it were too near the lower edge of the No. 1 border, and directed too far up-stage—and if the light from the sky batten were not sufficiently strong to kill such shadows.

As with almost all false pros. arrangements, front-of-house spots are necessary for lighting actors right down-stage.

It is the slight clumsiness of this auxiliary batten that still forces us to seek a better solution—one in which there is only

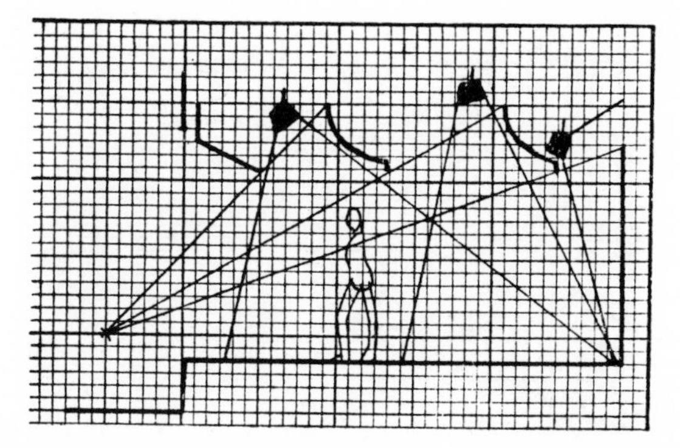

Fig. 95. The borders reduced to two by increasing their depth and reducing the height of the stage.

one masking element in the whole top of the set and with which consequently there are needed only two battens, the pros. batten in front and the sky batten behind.

To find such a solution we must turn to a somewhat different principle, in fact to an extension of that alluded to briefly on p. 183. We must combine the ceiling and the border.

Fig. 96 shows the method. We have in effect a 7 ft. ceiling over the centre of the set, with, at the down-stage edge, a vertically-rising return 2 ft. high, and at the up-stage a short 9 in. dropped return. (Or we might dispense with the latter and allow the ceiling to hang slightly obliquely, its up-stage edge being 9 in. below the level of the down-stage edge. This incidentally would add a little to the effect of space on the stage, by endowing it with a slight suggestion of perspective.) Such a ceiling begins admittedly to point to another realm than that of pure curtains, for no curtain can be true to its nature and yet assume the position of a ceiling—its material must, at the least, be stretched tight on a frame and so offer a different surface from the presumably folded surface of all its vertical fellows. However, the practical value of the arrangement is sufficient to press us to a little ingenuity to render it decoratively consistent.

It is with the somewhat over-simplified lighting problem that we shall have to spend most care on this deep stage, for,

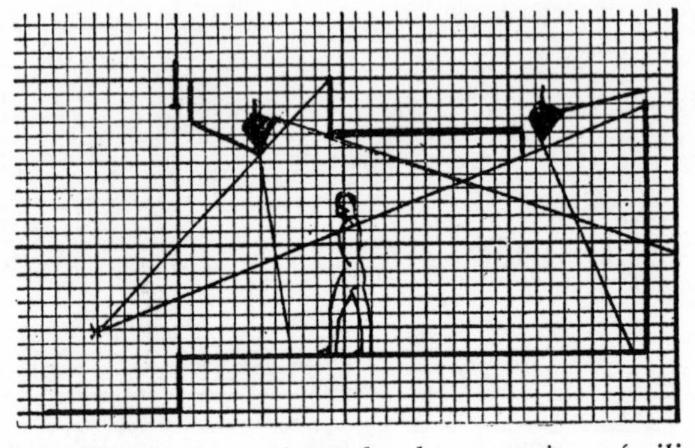

Fig. 96. The upper masking reduced to one unit—a 'ceiling-border'.

now that we have discarded our No. 2 batten, we have to lower the pros. batten and direct it more sharply up-stage in order to light the whole area, and we must have an increasingly high power in the sky batten to kill certain shadows that begin now to be inevitable upon the sky.

(Through all the preceding I have been presuming an arrangement of lights which would be effective even if the back curtains were drawn aside and a sky used behind as discussed in *Stage-Setting*.)

But in stressing the danger points of this most extreme solution, it is only fair to remind readers that the conditions we set in the stage dimensions are correspondingly extreme and that no forcing of any technique gives opportunity for its best achievement.

We have offered our problem to the scrutiny of sight-lines and even in face of such difficulty they have not failed us; although they have warned us how we are pressing our tools to the limits of reason and can expect no result that is free from considerable limitations.

Suffice if I have shown that even in circumstances as hard as these an ingenious and informed stage-manager or designer need never condone faulty masking.

APPENDIX 3

ON THE CONSTRUCTION OF A SIGHT-LINE GAUGE AND MODEL STAGE

If a designer wishes to possess a model stage in which to set up and test his model scenes, one of the most disserviceable forms for his purpose is a realistic model of an actual theatre. Expecially is a model of this sort a nuisance if he is making settings of various types for various stages.

The following is my own attempt to provide myself with something intended, not to look like a miniature theatre, but to supply (1) a frame possessing just those essential features of a stage which affect scenery and sight-lines, (2) to provide a means of hanging such things as borders (always a difficulty in models), and (3), most important, to supply each feature *in variable form* so that it can be set approximately in the same relative position as on any actual specific stage for which a design is made. Lastly, (4) the whole must be something to take up very little room when not wanted or when packed for carriage to interviews and conferences.

Fig. 97 shows the appearance of the model. Its dimensions are of considerable importance. They must allow the adequate scale representation of a very wide range of stage sizes. The dimensions I finally decided were:

Proscenium opening, 1 ft. high by 2 ft. wide; this at the scale of one inch to the foot gives an opening equivalent to 12 ft. high by 24 ft. wide, a typical Little Theatre size, which may be reduced by a system of pros. wings and border to a minimum of 6 ft. high by 12 ft. wide, than which one can scarcely wish to go smaller (if one should—say for a puppet stage—then one can increase the scale). On the other hand the same pros. opening can, by using the scale of half an inch to a foot, do duty for a 24 ft. by 48 ft. pros. arch. (Only the Dominion and Coliseum Theatres have wider openings.[1] True, several theatres have, in fact, openings higher than 24 ft. but very rarely is the extra height used, the top being masked-in with a pelmet or border.) These measurements

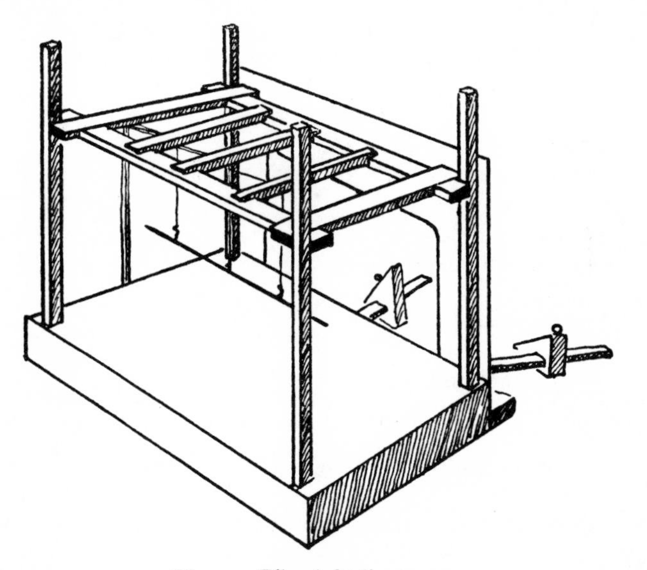

Fig. 97. The sight-line gauge.

can be reduced on the model by the sliding in of the pros. wings and border.

The width of the stage floor is 3 ft.—equivalent to 36 ft. or 72 ft. according to the scale used—and the stage depth 24 ft. or 48 ft. There are five stages in London deeper than 48 ft.—the Adelphi, 49 ft.; the Coliseum, 92 ft.; Covent Garden, 74 ft.; the St. James', 53 ft.; the Scala, 54 ft.—were one working for any of these, additions to the stage floor space are very easily made.

The grid from which pieces may be hung is capable of a height of 64 ft. by simple adjustment, or of a height of 74 ft. by the addition of certain extension pieces. (The highest two

[1] All actual stage dimensions in this appendix are quoted from *Who's Who in the Theatre, 1936.*

London grids are 72 ft., at Covent Garden and at Drury Lane.)

Upon these dimensions the construction of the model follows in this way: a sheet of ply, 5 ft. by 4 ft. by ¼ in., and the following pieces of wood are needed:

3 pieces 3 in. × 1 in. × 2 ft. (ends and gauge base)
1 piece 3 in. × 1 in. × 1 ft. (gauge heads)
2 pieces 2 in. × 1 in. × 3 ft.
2 pieces 2 in. × 1 in. × 2 ft. } (grid)
3 pieces 1 in. × 1 in. × 2 ft.
3 pieces 1 in. × 1 in. × 3 ft. (grid columns)

also:

2 pairs pin hinges
staples
7 screw-eyes
nails
1-in. panel pins
2 small butt hinges
screws
2 right-angled screw hooks
stair-rods
strong cardboard for wings 1 ft. 0 in. × 2 ft. 6 in.

The ply is marked out as in Fig. 98 (carefully noting, however, that all timber is given in round measurements as regards thickness; an eighth of an inch or so will be taken off in the planing, hence all ply that is cut to match a thickness of timber will be a fraction under the full measure.)

For the floor of the stage, which also becomes the box-container of all the loose parts when the model is folded up, one of the 3 ft. by 2 ft. pieces of ply (*A* in Fig. 98) is taken, and along either end is nailed a piece of 3 in. by 1 in. timber on edge, each piece cut so as to be short of the two feet at either end by exactly the thickness of the ply. The two long sides are now ready to be added in ply. For these, the single original sheet does not allow our cutting two strips 3 ft. by 3 in. without encroaching on a larger piece that will be wanted for other parts, and there are two courses open, either to cut the two strips from other spare pieces of ply, or if economy restricts us to the original sheet, to join short lengths *B* to *C* and *D* to *E*, battening out either join with a plate cut from the spare portion, *X*. Before the sides are nailed in place, a square

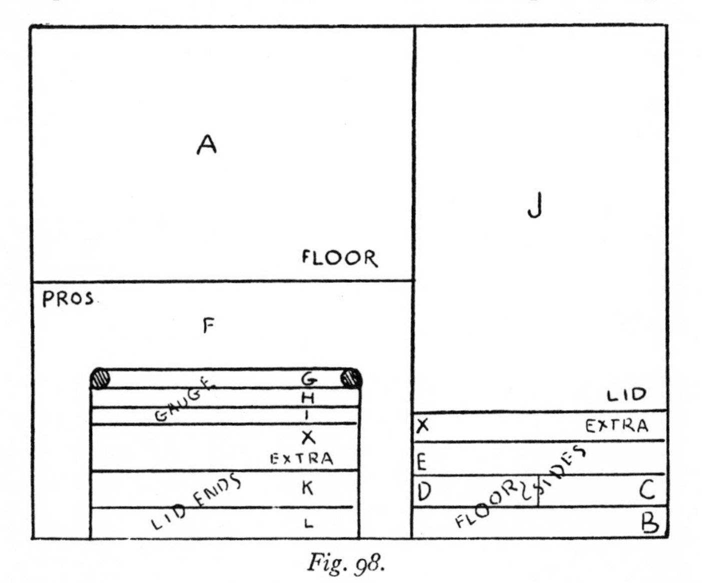

Fig. 98.

hole must be cut at each corner of the stage floor to take the 1 in. by 1 in. corner posts. These holes are cut as near to the edges of the base as the adjacent supporting end and side will allow, so that the foot of the post, when put through the hole, will nest snugly against these. The sides are then added to the stage floor so as to come under the top and outside the ends, see Fig. 99. The ply is nailed to the timber with ordinary wire nails, but when ply is fixed to the thickness of another sheet of ply, fine panel pins should be used and driven carefully and straightly home.

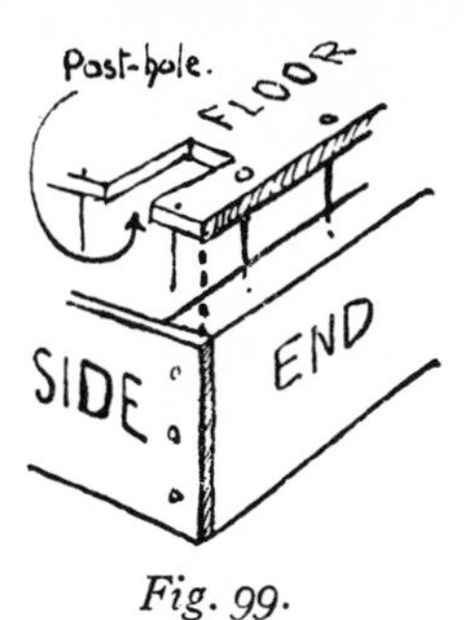

Fig. 99.

The proscenium is next made (*F*, Fig. 98), drilling two one-inch holes at the top corners of what is to be the opening, in order to allow a key-hole saw to make the first cuts of the line along the top of the opening. The cuts up the sides are simply sawn in the usual way. The piece cut out will be needed later. The pros. arch is now hinged to the floor (Fig. 100).

The four corner posts may now be dropped into their holes. If they fit too loosely a strip of ply (cut from either

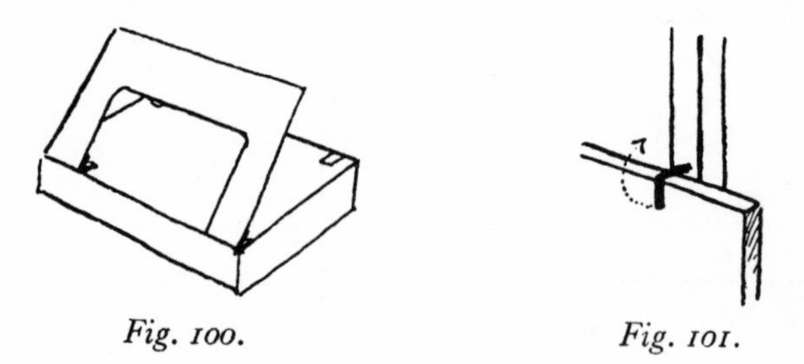

Fig. 100. *Fig. 101.*

spare piece *X*) may be nailed inside the end-piece underneath the stage to form a channel to keep the post upright. Generally this is only necessary, however, with the two up-stage posts, for the two down-stage are fixed to the pros. by means of angle-hooks, screwed into the upright and turned over the ply proscenium after the fashion of a turn-button (Fig. 101).

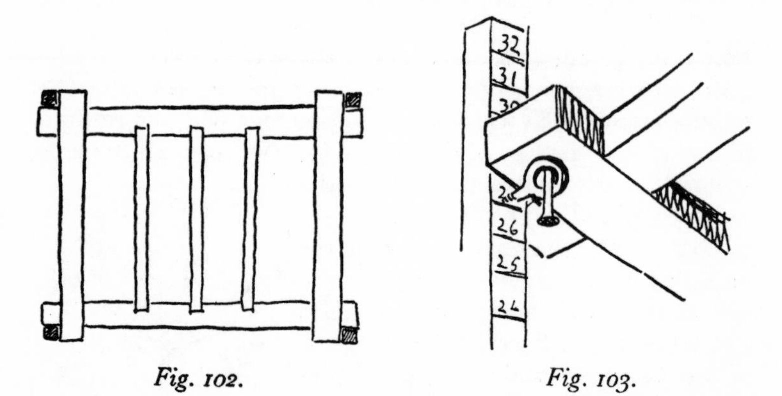

Fig. 102. *Fig. 103.*

The 'grid' is now made in the form of a frame of 2 in. by 1 in. wood assembled with halve joints, and with the battens crossing at the corners (Fig. 102). This frame is made of such a size as just to fit into the base-box under the stage floor for packing. The overlap of the corners is such as will allow the whole to rise or fall between the four corner posts, indicated by shading in the diagram. The frame is maintained at its required height by means of screw eyes inserted in the posts, with which projecting nails on the under side of the frame are made to engage (Fig. 103). In this figure it is to be noted that the corner posts are graduated in inches, starting from the stage floor and going up. The screw eyes may then be put in to support the grid at any desired height.

The suspending function of the grid is represented by three other strips of 1 in. by 1 in., halved at the ends to drop in and fit tightly between the two longer sides of the frame (Fig. 102). These represent: one the line of centre pulleys, the others the pulleys of the short and long lines respectively. The two outer pieces can be set with regard to the centre piece, in whatever position corresponds with the distance between the pulleys in any given theatre. For tiny theatres with only two lines in a set, one of the pieces is omitted. On the under side of each piece, and also on the under side of one or other of the two short sides of the frame (most usually that on the stage left) a row of wire staples is fixed as close together as possible (Fig. 104). These stand for the pulleys of the grid, and those on the side of the frame for the head blocks that return the lines down to the stage.

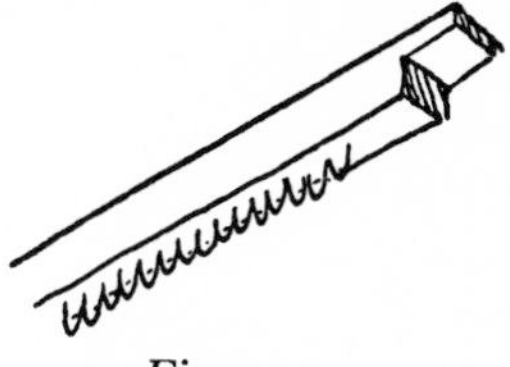

Fig. 104.

Lastly we have to consider a characteristic feature of the model which alone justifies its inclusion in a book on the sight-line system. This feature we may call 'the sight-line gauge'. Its purpose is to enable us to place with regard to our model all the vital points from which sight-lines are taken, and place each of these in the exact scale relationship that its original bears in any theatre you may have to work for. The apparatus is simple (Fig. 105). To a piece of 3 in. by 1 in. wood, as long as the pros. opening, three one-inch-wide strips of ply are screwed (cut from the spare piece we took out of the pros. opening, Fig. 18, *G*, *H*, and *I*), one in the centre and one at either end, so as to point out into the auditorium and pivot on their inner ends. The piece is now alined with the stage, laying it on the table against the stage front (to which it may be attached with a loose-pin hinge). Next the proscenium line is carefully ruled on the stage floor in pencil; there will be the space of the thickness of the ply between it and the stage front. Next rule in the centre line of the stage. Now arrange the centre ply strip in the sight-line gauge to line up with the centre line and begin carefully to graduate the strip in inches measuring from the proscenium line.

We now turn to the sliding gauge-pieces themselves. There are three, all cut out of 3 in. by 1 in. Two are right-angled triangles of base 3 in. and height 2 in., and the other is equilateral, 6 in. high and 3 in. wide. Each is pierced at the height of an inch above its base by a rectangular hole of such a size

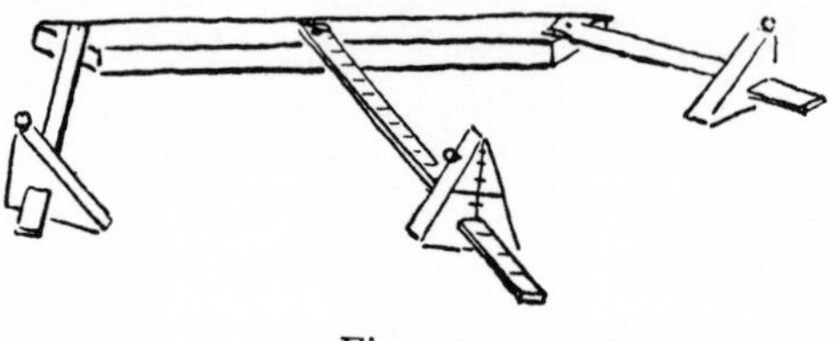

Fig. 105.

as to take the strip of ply and to allow the triangle to slide to and fro upon it. A screw-eye is fixed into the apex of each right-angled triangle and those pieces are slipped on their respective ply strips. They are to represent the position of the outermost seats of a theatre. They can be slid to and from the stage and swung inwards and outwards to produce any desired position. The third piece for the centre strip is treated a little differently. A line is ruled across it at a level with the stage floor, and a vertical line is ruled down the triangle from top to bottom. This latter line is graduated in inches and half-inches up and down from the stage-level line. The screw-eye is in this case to be put into the edge of the triangle at whatever level corresponds with the nearest spectator's eye-level. The triangle is now slid, by the graduations on the plywood arm, to its proper distance from the stage, and the gauge is now set.

Notice that the level of the screw-eyes upon the side gauges is relatively unimportant, their function is to settle the cross sight-line, but the level on the centre gauge is vital, for it is situate *not necessarily at a point corresponding with the centre-front spectator*, but at a point corresponding with the *nearest* spectator. That is, at the virtual centre of the stalls. The relative height above the stage of this spectator is important, for upon his position are the upper sight-lines based.

For use and for demonstrations a stout white thread may be tied to each screw-eye and led through the pros. opening to the stage. Keep the thread taut and it will demonstrate the sight-line occasioned by any piece of scenery whose edge it is made to touch, and show exactly the demarcation between the masked and unmasked areas beyond. On occasion the thread may be dispensed with, and by closing an eye one may peer through a screw-eye and so arrive at some idea of what amount of the set may be expected to be seen from any given seat.

It is useful to graduate the whole of the stage floor into 864 inch squares, numbering the down-stage row out from the centre line on either side. Also the sides of the back of the pros. arch should be marked off in inches and numbered upwards. Then three strips of stout cardboard, one 30 in. by 6 in. and two 15 in. by 6 in., can be set, like pros. wings and border, to give exactly the right proscenium opening, the larger piece being drawing-pinned along the top of the opening at the back, and the two shorter wings with their top edges slipped between border and pros. so as to slide and stay at any given place. These are placed to adapt the opening to that of any given theatre.

Much can be done in the way of temporary additions to reproduce special theatre conditions—a rough cardboard forestage, or an extension to side or back, and it is most illuminating, when gauging a small stage with the abominable pitch roof, to pin on the back of the proscenium lengths of red tape (or to mark in chalk) exactly reproducing the outline of that roof, then you may watch that no piece of scenery ever projects beyond that limit. In a similar way may odd shapes of stage floor be marked out on the base.

The grid is simply rigged by passing three stout threads through those staples corresponding to their pulley-positions for every set of lines on the stage. Each set is led through its proper staple in the row on the side batten of the grid-frame itself and then down to the stage. The tying-off of these sets of lines is something of a problem, and rather than evolve a complicated system of cleats I found that I was quite happy to give each set a single turn round a drawing-pin pressed well home into the side of the stage base, but pressed home slightly askew, so that only one side of the head touched the wood.

Now we come to the only item which presented me with any difficulty in the obtaining. Because of the slightness and lightness of the lines, some weight is needed to keep them

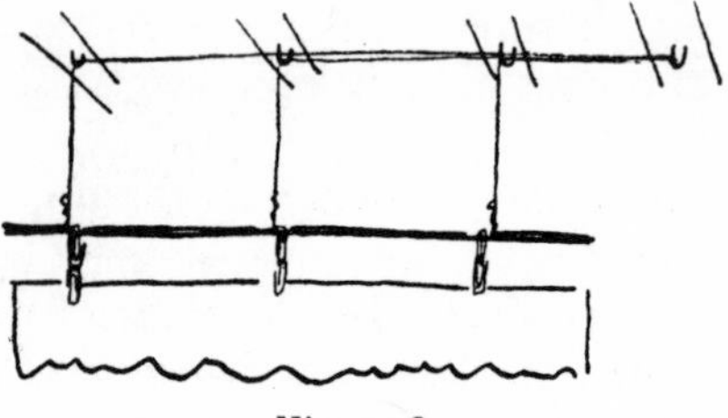

Fig. 106.

taut. This is in theory easy to arrange by imitating the principle of the fly-bar, used in counterweight systems, where the stage ends of the lines are not attached to the scenery at all but to a steel tube, called a fly-bar, to which bar the scenery is attached. If to metal rods, between 25 and 30 in. long, we attach each set of three lines we should have an effectually working reproduction of the flying system of a theatre. But I found the metal rods difficult to obtain; the stoutest wire (at any rate, the stoutest easily obtainable) is a little too light to work effectively, meccano rods are too short, and about the nearest thing, failing having a set specially made, is the brass stair-rod.

Fig. 106 shows a single set of lines, with a border attached to the fly-bar. By far the least troublesome method of attachment, and one that allows slight adjustment, analogous to 'deading', is a pair of linked wire paper clips at three points on the bar, as the figure shows.

For packing, the sight-line gauge is detached from the stage, the grid and posts are dismantled, the pros. folded back, and the floor turned upside down; the gauge-heads are slid off their arms and the parts may then all be packed in the base and will leave room for a store of model scenery as well.

The last touch to the construction is added by making a lid for the box. To the piece *J* (Fig. 98) the ends *K* and *L* are nailed, this time the pins must pass through the ends and into the thickness of the lid. We are left to seek the sides of the lid. These our original sheet will not supply: we must cut them off another piece or use strips of stout millboard, in which case it is good to glue linen strips all round and up each corner.

When the lid is placed on, a pair of portmanteau-straps with a carrying handle may be passed round and the whole carried like a suit-case.

APPENDIX 4

CONCERNING A TABLE FOR STAGE MEASUREMENTS

I have had several occasions to quote, with appreciation, from the long table of stage-dimensions of London theatres published in *Who's Who in the Theatre*. That the data is of great use to the profession and a valuable feature of the book no one will doubt who has used it. But we have now reluctantly to criticize the table. All setting-design (which is the contractor's and the artist's affair), and all placing of the elements of a setting (which is—among others'—the stage-manager's and master-carpenter's affair), is dependent on sight-lines. For none of the fifty-six theatres in this table is sufficient data given to draw a single sight-line. For any precise work it is useless.

Overleaf will be found the sort of table which, when filled up for any theatre, would give the designer, stage-manager, or carpenter absolutely complete data to work out any of his dimension problems or masking problems—and even such of his working problems as are connected with the measurements of his stage—according to the system outlined in this book. (It is not to be forgotten that, as pointed out, certain subsidiary data may be added in special cases.) Were the table from which I have quoted reshaped on these lines, not only would it offer an immense aid to the puzzling-out of all planning problems related to scenery on those stages, but would offer for the first time in history a means of ascertaining and comparing with exactitude the whole sight-line desiderata of the theatres of London.

To the stage-managers of to-day I would suggest that they might adopt the system I have outlined in this book as a standard; and the table would afford them means of doing so. It is, in fact, only the slightest extension—if any at all—of the method they use to-day, but it is perhaps arranged in a more definite form than before, and will enable a more standardized approach to the problems of the development of the stage and the setting, and therefore, it is to be hoped, would make for a clearer and quicker progress.

It would entail a certain expense of labour and time for a single person to complete the table for any great number of theatres, but if individual stage-managers would fill it up for their own theatre or theatres they would have as complete a record as possible of their own working conditions.

MEASUREMENT TABLE

Name of Theatre					
1. Back to Pros. L.					
2. Pros. L. to V.C.					
3. V.C. to outermost stall / box					
4. Outermost stall / box to Pros. C.					
5. Pros. C. to Pros. L.					
6. Width of Pros.					
7. Height of Pros.					
8. Diff. in eye-level					

ACCESSORIES

9. Height of highest Seat					
10. Dist. of highest Seat					
11. Wing-space					
12. Height of grid					
13. Between Fly-rails					
14. Height of fly-floor					
15. Sets of lines					
16. Setting-line length					
17. Set. L. to Pros. L.					
18. Cyclorama					
19. Forestage					
20. Stage rake					

INDEX